D1728673

Negotiating Racial Politics in the Family

Egodocuments and History Series

Edited by

Arianne Baggerman (*Erasmus University Rotterdam
and University of Amsterdam*)
Rudolf Dekker (*Center for the Study of Egodocuments
and History, Amsterdam*)
Michael Mascuch (*University of California, Berkeley*)

Advisory Board

James Amelang (*Universidad Autónoma Madrid*)
Peter Burke (*Emmanuel College Cambridge*)
Philippe Lejeune(*Emeritus, Université de Paris-Nord*)
Claudia Ulbrich (*Freie Universität Berlin*)

VOLUME 11

The titles published in this series are listed at *brill.com/egdo*

Negotiating Racial Politics in the Family

*Transnational Histories touched by
National Socialism and Apartheid*

By

Barbara Henkes

BRILL

LEIDEN | BOSTON

Cover illustration: Close-up of ALESSANDRO MENDINI's *POLTRONA DI PROUST*, 1978.
'Reality is comprised of "an endless collection of memoires and fragments"' (A. Mendini). Photo: B. Henkes.

Chapter 6, 'I never set out to Wage War Against my Family'
Cinematic Explorations of Whiteness, is a revised version of Barbara Henkes (2013) Negotiating the '(Ab)
normality' of (Anti-)Apartheid: Transnational Relations within a Dutch-South African Family, South
African Historical Journal, 65:4, 526-554, DOI: 10.1080/02582473.2013.858763. © South African Historical
Journal reprinted by permission of Taylor & Francis Ltd., http://www.tandfonline.com on behalf of South
African Historical Journal.

The Library of Congress Cataloging-in-Publication Data is available online at http://catalog.loc.gov
LC record available at http://lccn.loc.gov/2020008963

Typeface for the Latin, Greek, and Cyrillic scripts: "Brill". See and download: brill.com/brill-typeface.

ISSN 1873-653X
ISBN 978-90-04-39966-2 (hardback)
ISBN 978-90-04-40160-0 (e-book)

Copyright 2020 by Barbara Henkes, Koninklijke Brill NV, Leiden, The Netherlands.
Koninklijke Brill NV incorporates the imprints Brill, Brill Hes & De Graaf, Brill Nijhoff, Brill Rodopi,
Brill Sense, Hotei Publishing, mentis Verlag, Verlag Ferdinand Schöningh and Wilhelm Fink Verlag.
All rights reserved. No part of this publication may be reproduced, translated, stored in a retrieval system,
or transmitted in any form or by any means, electronic, mechanical, photocopying, recording or otherwise,
without prior written permission from the publisher.
Authorization to photocopy items for internal or personal use is granted by Koninklijke Brill NV provided
that the appropriate fees are paid directly to The Copyright Clearance Center, 222 Rosewood Drive, Suite
910, Danvers, MA 01923, USA. Fees are subject to change.

This book is printed on acid-free paper and produced in a sustainable manner.

Printed by Printforce, the Netherlands

Contents

Acknowledgements

The close-up of Alessandro Mendini's *Poltrona Di Proust* (1978) on the cover of this book shows the upholstery pattern of the artist's huge chair. Mendini wanted to emphasize that reality is comprised of 'an endless collection of memoires and fragments'. It struck me as a fitting motto for this book, in which I want to merge various memories and fragments of life stories into a meaningful whole.

After the publication of *Heimat in Holland. Duitse dienstmeisjes 1920–1950* (1995) about the way National Socialism affected the life stories of German-Dutch women in the Netherlands, I continued my research into national and political identifications by looking at the political entanglements of folklore studies (*Uit liefde voor het volk. Volkskundigen op zoek naar de Nederlandse identiteit 1918–1948* (2005). The transnational research by Dutch, Flemish, and German scholars for a ('greater') Dutch or Germanic identity after the First World War took me once again into the realm of National Socialism.

After so many years of these painful histories and sometimes nasty historiographical debates, I wanted to get away from National Socialism and what in my eyes was an unproductive distinction between perpetrators, victims and so-called bystanders. I decided to focus on Dutch migrants settling in postwar South Africa. This choice, however, shows once again my abiding interest in the various policies of inclusion and exclusion by national governments and the dynamic subject positions implying acceptance, legitimation, denial, resistance, and often a combination of these in the face of violent repression. This time I focussed on Dutch migrants' postcolonial gazes, their loyalties and responsibilities at the intersection of Dutch and South African political and social networks.

In *Negotiating Racial Politics in the Family* I bring together the continuing use and meaning of egodocuments and oral history for all of my research, as well as the different geopolitical spaces and times that have informed my work. The 'kick-off' for this book was an invitation by Rudolf Dekker to talk about the significance of egodocuments in my research at the Auto/Biography Seminar of the Huizinga Institute, the Dutch national Research Institute and Graduate School of Cultural History. Afterwards Dekker suggested turning my presentation into a book for his *Egodocuments and History Series* with Brill Publishers. Crucial for the reworking of earlier publications in combination with new work was my introduction to the concepts of 'touching tales' and 'multidirectional memory'. This helped me to connect the histories of racial inclusion and exclusion in different times and spaces. Besides, the notion of the 'implicated subject' supported my exploration of the various subject positions taken by the protagonists during National Socialism and Apartheid.

I would like here to acknowledge the importance of interdisciplinary networks and their coordinators, such as the aforementioned *Auto/Biography Seminar*, the network *Unhinging the National Framework* coordinated by Babs Boter, and the Oral History Group of the Huizinga Institute, initiated by Selma Leydesdorff. And not to forget the inspiring meetings over the years of the now defunct history workshop *Andere Tijden* (Other Times). These regular gatherings remain a welcome addition to the feedback students give me in my courses at the University of Groningen, and the exchanges with colleagues during national and international conferences or symposia. Many more exchanges have contributed to the making of this book, not least my encounters with the main protagonists of this book and their relatives in the Netherlands, Germany and South Africa. They gave me access to private documents and shared their personal memories, for which I cannot thank them enough. 'Doing family' in this book also means 'doing history', and vice versa.

Although friends or colleagues are not generally referred to as 'family', there are parallels, for example when an ad-hoc group of valued historians gathered around my dining table to comment on earlier stages of my drafts Mieke Aerts, Martijn Eickhoff, Remco Ensel, Marijke Huisman, Vincent Kuitenbrouwer and Susan Legêne all read the first draft of the Introduction and a chapter each. Thanks to their input these have since been radically changed. Tanny Dobbelaar later organized a meeting with Leonieke Vermeer and Fleur van der Bij to help me get to grips with the overall argument of the book. In addition to the anonymous referees with their constructive comments, Mieke Aerts and Martijn Eickhoff once more offered critical support in the final phase. Richard Johnson and Timothy Ashplant provided my English translations with both stylistic and substantive comments, so that Ineke Smit could finally dot the i's and cross the t's. Any remaining errors are of course my own responsibility. Finally, I want to thank Victor van Bentem for transcribing the handwritten letters that formed the basic source material for chapters four and five, and Sidney Groeneveld for his indispensable technical and moral support.

This book is dedicated to Erwin Karel (1956-2019), my sparring partner from the start of my intellectual trajectory.

Figures

Introduction

'Henkes speaking'.
'Hello! This is another Henkes calling, Barbara Henkes, the daughter of Hendrik Jan, so to speak'.
'I know who you are'.

I was no stranger to him, it seemed; yet he was a stranger to me. As far as I could remember we had not met before. Anyway, Freek was happy to receive me at his home. 'Oh yeah, you are the eccentric one', he responded, amused, when I told him that I would arrive by train as I had no car. I asked him what tram or bus I could take from the station to his house? No way: he was going to pick me up and I was welcome to stay overnight with him and his wife if I wanted to. 'How do I recognize you?' I asked. 'I'm driving a beige Volvo', he informed me. 'I am afraid that I haven't got a clue about car brands, but I myself wear a leather jacket and have got short blond hair'. That was enough to find each other.

I was well informed: Freek was indeed the guardian of thirteen cardboard boxes with the remnants of the Henkes archive, a legacy of his uncle Wim, who had died childless in the 1980s. He described the content as 'a big mess'. During Wim's funeral there had been a burglary in his house. The neatly ordered papers were scattered all over the floor, and after a quick rescue operation Freek had stacked the boxes with papers in his own loft. Uncle Wim had been a controversial descendant of the Henkes family. He was the 'bad' mayor-in-wartime, collaborating with the Nazis, which caused the rest of the Henkes family great embarrassment. In combination with the large number of cats with which he shared his postwar life, his name evoked a piteous image. Uncle Wim was a 'loser', but a loser who had taken care of the remaining archives of the Henkes Distillery.

And that's why on a sunny day in August we were sitting in a heavenly garden, talking about uncle Wim's National Socialist engagement, that – according to his nephew – 'had absolutely nothing to do with politics and even less with antisemitism'. Uncle Wim's best friend was Jewish, my second cousin stressed. In all sincerity Freek was using a well-known trope by which people proved their innocence after National Socialist repression was overcome: the one Jewish friend deployed as a witness for the defence of an active participant in the Nazi regime. While we were talking, a half-remembered story was triggered from the back of my mind. My father had once told me about two young cousins who were harassed after the occupation because of their father's Nazi

© BARBARA HENKES, 2020 | DOI:10.1163/9789004401600_002

sympathies. Were these Freek and his elder brother? In that case it was not only his uncle Wim, but also his own father who had been active in the Nazi party. When I asked Freek about this controversial issue, the answer was affirmative, although he could not remember that he himself had suffered any harassment. Freek seemed okay with sharing this sensitive issue with me in the company of his wife, to whom he had been married for more than forty years. His father, who had held a leading position in the Nazi voluntary *Arbeitsdienst* (Labour Service) during the occupation, was interned for two years after the Allies had liberated the Netherlands.[1] Freek, together with his mother and brother, had also been interned for a certain period. After their release, when his destitute mother asked my grandfather for support, she was shown the door, Freek remembers – without noticeable resentment. He had learned how National Socialism and the political-moral controversies it implied had driven the Henkes family apart.

It was precisely these relatives, excluded or even expelled from the family, who had saved the archives of the family business from the garbage container. Like his uncle Wim, Freek had planned for years to make an inventory of all the documents he kept in the attic. Was it a form of 'reparation' to the rest of the Henkes family? In any case, it was a way to recapture a place in the family annals. Perhaps a similar motive drove Freek to use his first savings to buy shares in the Henkes Distillery. The shares offered him access to shareholder meetings, where Henkes relatives had to accept his presence. In the meantime, Freek was also involved in processing his historical research into a Henkes family tree. 'Do you know that there are Jews in our family too?', he asked me.

Our meeting was part of my exploration of the intriguing phenomenon described as 'family': a phenomenon that is not limited to close relatives, but indeed is part of a much larger cultural and political field where family ties and kinship networks are forged or lost.[2] This brought me to the leading question for this book: how did relatives within multinational kinship networks deal with racial repression during National Socialism in Europe and Apartheid in South Africa? The book takes us on an odyssey through several family

---

1 National Archives, The Hague: *Centraal Archief voor de Bijzondere Rechtspleging* (Central Archive of Special Jurisdiction) with files on specific members of the Henkes family.
2 Barbara Henkes, 'De tweede schuld, of over de last familie te zijn. Nationaalsocialisme en de overdracht van historische ervaringen binnen familieverband' (The second guilt, or about the burden of being family. National Socialism and the Transfer of Historical Experiences within the Family), in: N.D.J. Barnouw, e.a. (red.), *Tiende Jaarboek van het Nederlands Instituut voor Oorlogsdocumentatie*. (Amsterdam: NIOD/Walburg Pers, 1999) 89–113, and a series of columns entitled 'Familiegoed' in the *Historisch Nieuwsblad* (1998-2000).

histories in which the tension between personal and political loyalties and responsibilities in times of violent exclusion is the central issue, against the backdrop of the transnational dynamics of the twentieth century.

Migration extends family ties to other countries and makes the people involved part of a transnational kinship network. If these nations come into conflict with each other, it has its effects on the dynamics within these networks. That was the case when German migrants in the Netherlands were confronted with the occupation of their country of residence by Nazi Germany. Also, when Dutch migrants left for South Africa after the war, the politics of Apartheid had repercussions for exchanges with their relatives in Netherlands. *Negotiating Racial Politics in the Family* follows this dynamic process along two lines. The first line takes us across the German-Dutch border: How did German newcomers and their kin in Germany and the Netherlands relate to National Socialist policies – and what consequences did this have for their identifications with Germanness and Dutchness? The second line takes us in another direction under quite different circumstances. This time we follow Dutch migrants who left their country of origin and moved to South Africa during Apartheid. Their Dutch-South African histories give insight into the variable identification processes with both nations, in relation to their handling of racial inequality.

By bringing together family histories that are scarred by National Socialism and Apartheid, I want to challenge us to think about the entanglement of twentieth-century forms of racial inclusion and exclusion in Europe and the former European colonies. 'Touching tales' is the concept used by the literary scholar Leslie Alderson for this narrative strategy: 'touching' in the sense of emotionally charged tales of insecurity, loss, fear, defense, shame, and guilt – but also, importantly, 'touching' in the sense of bordering on each other, of interconnectedness in complex as well as pivotal ways.[3] The versatile literary scholar Michael Rothberg also explores connections between different tales about painful pasts with his concept of 'multidirectional memories'.[4] He demonstrates how the Holocaust has enabled the articulation of other histories of

---

3 'Touching Tales' is a concept that Liesbeth Minnaerts brought to my attention in reference to the work of the literary scholar Leslie A. Adelson on *The Turkish Turn in German Literature* (New York: Palgrave Macmillan, 2005) Adelson uses the term to explore how, in literature, the history of labour migration and that of the Shoah – two traditionally 'discrete' histories – 'touch', and echo affects and meaning in relation to each other.

4 Michael Rothberg, *Multidirectional Memory: Remembering the Holocaust in the Age of Decolonization.* (Stanford: Stanford University Press, 2009). He shows himself indebted to Hannah Arendt's seminal work *The Origins of Totalitarianism* and her introduction of the 'boomerang effect' linking European imperialism and Nazi genocide (Cleveland: The World Publishing Company, 1958 (2nd enlarged edition).

victimization while at the same time being declared 'unique' among human-perpetrated horrors.[5] Besides, he shows how public memory of the Holocaust emerged thanks in part to postwar events that may seem to have little to do with it. My presentation of transnational family histories belonging to different times and circumstances is informed by Adelson's and Rothberg's approaches. I intend to pay attention to the ways histories touch in many directions and in complex ways, rather than writing a comparative history.

Nevertheless, the work of historians who studied the Nazi and Apartheid regimes in comparison to each other is also important for this book.[6] After all, crucial differences, similarities and transfers between the two regimes contributed to the shape of these family histories and the memories involved. Notably, there are continuities regarding the pursuit of a racially and culturally unambiguous 'folk community' (*Volksgemeinschaft/volksgemeenskap*) that fitted the ideal image of the nation.[7] People who were expected to tarnish the purity of that community had to be excluded, forced to move, or in the last resort killed. Other people were needed to strengthen the national community, either through expansion of national borders or through an active population and hence immigration policy. This book looks at the significance of these political commitments for the narratives about the migrants' departure and establishment in the new country of destination – and for their loyalties to their country of origin and the relatives they left behind.

There is no simple answer to the question of how migrants and their relatives in both countries negotiated the tensions caused by their personal and political loyalties and responsibilities in times of racial exclusion and oppression. For this reason the question must be approached from different angles, with the help of unique material such as private correspondences, travel reports, memoirs and film footage – and always in combination with personal memories of the emigrated family members, their relatives who stayed behind or their next of kin. The answers from these sources offer a lens through which

---

5   The systematic mass murder of Jews by the Nazis is referred to as both the 'Holocaust' and the 'Shoah'. The term 'Holocaust' has become commonplace with a wide audience – certainly after the TV series of the same name. Holocaust is derived from the ancient Greek word ὁλόκαυστον (holokauston) which literally means burnt offering. Although I think the term Shoah (the Hebrew for destruction) is more appropriate, both terms will be used in this book.

6   For instance, the work of the historian George M. Fredrickson, who investigated the pursuit of 'racial purity' in the 20th century by – what he called – 'overt racist regimes' in the South of the United States, Nazi Germany and Apartheid South Africa. See e.g. his *Racism: A Short History* (Princeton: Princeton University Press; Revised edition 2015).

7   Arendt, *The Origins*, 223 and 232.

changing constructions of national identities and the acceptance or rejection of a nationalistic policy on racial grounds can be observed in everyday life.

Family and Nation as Imagined Communities

The family, extended into a kinship network, is for many the first group of people for whom they develop feelings of loyalty and responsibility.[8] From there, or in opposition to it, identifications are established with individuals, groups or communities such as school, church, sports club or colleagues at work. The sociologist Helen Fein aptly called it 'the universe of obligation', that is, 'that circle of persons toward whom obligations are owed, to whom the rules apply and whose injuries call for expiation of the community'.[9] Coming back to the inner circle of the family: I use the notion of kinship network to emphasize the flexible nature of personal ties, also between family members. Family is not a delimited entity, linked by blood ties or family trees, but rather an activity. Relatives, although sharing a history, must make an effort to create and maintain a bond between them – or to break it. We *are* not, or do not *have* family, but we *do* family: we ourselves bring a family, as a community, to life. This approach to family as a construction is at odds with how 'family' in daily life is often used to indicate a self-evident unity. However, the people we count as family and the meaning we attach to family is – as with an intimate circle of friends – subject to change, even though some ties are perceived as more solid than others.

In a study with the significant title *A World of their Own Making,* the historian John R. Gillis stresses how modern Western society is not only organized around family, but that family also determines our self-image and therefore our evaluation of social responsibilities.[10] To understand these evaluations in the process of 'doing family', Gillis makes a distinction between the family 'we live with' (we encounter in daily life) and the family 'we live by' (we imagine to be part of). The former is often more complicated and therefore less

---

8   Abram de Swaan, 'Widening Circles of Identification: Emotional Concerns in Sociogenetic Perspective' in: *Theory, Culture & Society,* 1995: 12(2), 25–39.

9   Helen Fein, *Accounting for Genocide: National Responses and Jewish Victimization during the Holocaust* (1979; repr., Chicago, 1984), 33, referred to by Remco Ensel and Evelien Gans, 'The Dutch Bystander as Non-Jew and Implicated Subject', in: Christina Morina and Krijn Thijs (eds.), *Probing the Limits of Categorization: The Bystander in Holocaust History* (New York/Oxford: Berghahn, 2018) 107–127, at 116.

10   John R. Gillis, *A World of their Own Making. Myth, Ritual and the Quest for Family Values* (Cambridge: Harvard University Press, 1997).

stable than the latter, although they are interdepent. They jointly determine
the power of family ties. The common idea of 'the family' is a cohabiting community with children who grow up in harmony under one roof with their father and mother, and who in due course form a family themselves, and so on.
Ideally, there should be a close mutual bond within that community: a safe
space that offers protection against unrest or violence from outside. It is well
known that this representation of things rarely corresponds to the lived reality.
Apart from the violence that can manifest itself within the domestic sphere,
families are subject to permanent changes and tensions: they can be extended
with foster, adoptive, or stepparents and stepchildren, and can be reduced by
divorce, quarrels, departures or death. The family is in an unstable balance
that requires the necessary commitment to hold it steady and can easily be
toppled.

Family is constructed, maintained and strengthened in many ways, for instance by shared family housing and holidays, or later in life by remembering
shared experiences through stories and pictures, by the transfer of favorite re-
cipies from grandmother's cookbook, by creating family trees depicting a mutual connection between the living and the dead, or by visits to the cemetery
and other rituals that create continuity and offer support within the kinship
network. It is especially for relatives who are far removed through migration
that keeping the family alive requires a lot of work – 'kinkeeping', as the maintaining of family ties is called.[11] What is more, kinkeeping is facilitated, and
acquires meaning, through imagination. This imagining (the 'family we live
by') is decisive for the way relatives interact and for the extent to which they
can endure, tolerate and support each other in politically turbulent times. In
what follows we will see how this process of kinkeeping is accompanied by
what the historian Richard Johnson calls 'safe' stories: cheerful accounts, informative gossip or colourful anecdotes with which people confirm their position
in relation to others within and outside the community. These are stories that
help them to avoid potential conflicts. Yet a close reading, against the grain of
such 'safe' stories, shows that their 'risky' counterparts are never far away.[12]
After all, the reassurance that safe stories are expected to provide is based on

---

11   See e.g. Margaret S. Leach and Dawn O. Braithwaite, 'A Binding Tie. Supportive com-
        munication of family kinkeepers', *Journal of applied communication research* 24 (1996)
        200–216.
12   Richard Johnson, 'Two Ways to Remember. Exploring Memory as Identity', *Nothing bloody
        stands still. Annual Magazine of the European Network for Cultural and Media Studies* 1
        (1991) 26–30.

the assumption of a lasting loyalty, while everyday life entails ever-changing views and relationships; ambiguities are always everywhere.

John Gillis's approach to family as a construction is in line with Benedict Anderson's approach to the nation as an 'imagined community'.[13] With his research into the binding power of the imagination as regards nation-building, Anderson also emphasizes the reality of the imaginary: the genuine sense of responsibility for a national community and the undeniable identification with compatriots whom we do not know and have never met. Both 'the nation' and 'the family' are constructed around a boundary that divides the world into 'ours' and 'theirs'. The 'own' world is often built on myths about a shared origin, a common culture and future.[14] And both the nation and family are important landmarks when people are negotiating different identifications and responsibilities. These negotiations are not easy, and they are especially difficult for migrants who experience increasing political tensions or even war within their transnational configurations.

Race and Narratives of Whiteness

With his book *Dark Continent,* on Europe in the twentieth century, Mark Mazower refers to the European label for the African continent.[15] 'Look at ourselves', the British historian seems to indicate with his book title. After all, Europe was then the scene of large-scale violence, while European colonial powers also sowed death and destruction outside of Europe. A crucial factor that enabled the massacres on the European continent and beyond was the distinction between groups of people based on race, also known as the 'global colour line'.[16] Once nation-building and imperialism became inextricably linked in

---

13   Benedict Anderson, *Imagined communities. Reflections on the Origin and Spread of Nationalism*, Revised Edition (London/New York: Verso, 2006). See also John R. Gillis (ed.), *Commemorations. The Politics of National Identity.* (Princeton: Princeton University Press, 1996).

14   See also Nira Yuval-Davis, *Politics of Belonging: Intersectional Contestations* (London: Sage, 2011) 84–85.

15   Mark Mazower, *Dark Continent. Europe's Twentieth Century* (London/New York: Penguin books, 1998).

16   The Afro-American historian W.E.B. DuBois declared in 1900 that the problem of the 20th century would be the 'problem of the color line', referred to by Marilyn Lake and Henry Reynolds, *Drawing the Global Colour Line. White Men's Countries and the International Challenge of Racial Equality.* (Cambridge: Cambridge University Press, 2008) 1.

the last decades of the nineteenth century, race became a central category in policy making and its execution. People's self-image was also determined by it, that is to say our everyday experiences of who we are (and are not). But race was – and is – a variable concept, sometimes linked to language, to specific skills or cultures, sometimes to genealogical or physical characteristics. Just like family or nation, race is not an unchanging, 'natural', given category, although recognizability through external characteristics plays an undeniable role. Race *is* not; we *do* race.[17] Since the Middle Ages, inequality between different population groups in terms of race has been legitimized with an appeal to Biblical narratives and the order of God's given creation. In addition, at the end of the nineteenth century scientific racism developed, when Charles Darwin's earlier observations on a natural selection for survival in living nature ('the survival of the fittest') were picked up and applied to the human species: a new biological doctrine, eugenics, flourished.[18]

The link between physical 'race' characteristics, intelligence and other psychological or (anti)social characteristics paved the way for far-reaching population policy measures. From then onwards, 'race' became part of political discourse. Immigration restrictions, for example, were designed to prevent the arrival of people of a 'lesser kind' from affecting the body of the national community, resulting in a 'sick nation'.[19] Such restrictions could also target groups of nationals who worked and lived in the country for many generations. As soon as they were classified as 'racial inferior' and 'out of place', German Jews since 1933 were confronted with increasing measures to isolate them from the rest of the national community. Badges in the form of a yellow star and stamps with a J on official documents that – as a Brand of Cain – identified them and restricted their access to public spaces. Jews were subjected to forced group removals to closed areas (ghettos) in order to block contact with the people defined as 'proper' nationals. This does not alter the fact that different 'contact zones', both hidden and visible, were inevitable; these are important to identify social areas where actors from different 'racial' backgrounds did meet, collide and wrestle with each other, in a context of profound asymmetric power

---

17   Hazel Rose Markus and Paula M.L. Moya (eds.), *Doing Race: 21 Essays for the 21st Century*. (New York: W.W. Norton & Company, 2010).

18   Philippa Levine and Alison Bashford, 'Introduction: Eugenics and the Modern World', in: Alison Bashford and Philippa Levine (eds.), *The Oxford Handbook of the History of Eugenics*, Vol. 36, Iss. 2, 1979.

19   Liesbet Nys, Henk de Das, Jo Tollebeek & Wils (red.), *De zieke natie. Over de medicalisering van de samenleving 1860-1914* (Groningen: Historische Uitgeverij, 2002).

relations.[20] For Blacks in South Africa it was not only the colour of their skin, but also their *dompas* that identified them as 'out of place' as soon as they were in prosperous White areas and not in one of the the the alleged impoverished 'homelands' (*thuislande*) or Bantustans that were assigned to them by the government since the 1950s.[21] Still, their presence as cheap labourers in White areas was needed and therefore had to be controlled. Legal bans on interracial sexual intercourse and 'mixed' marriages were among the first steps in the pursuit of a 'purebred', monoracial, White national community.

'Race' in its many manifestations was often mixed up with national or regional elements – as in Europe between the so-called Slavic and Germanic peoples. It was always used to indicate an essential distinction in relation to 'the character of the people', 'the national culture' and the 'level of civilization', both in Europe and in the areas where Europeans had established themselves in so-called White settler societies.[22] Although the South African War (1899– 1902), also known as the Anglo-Boer War brought about a distinction in terms of the British and the Afrikaner 'race' in the first decades of the twentieth century,[23] this racial distinction between European settlers soon faded in the light of the colonial sun. There they were transformed into one White, European or Caucasian breed, in contrast to the indigenous population and migrants from elsewhere who were typified and marginalized as Asian, Indian,

---

20 'Contact zones' is a concept introduced by the literary scholar Mary Louise Pratt, in her *Imperial Eyes: Travel Writing and Transculturation* (2nd edition, London/New York: Routledge, 2008),7–8 in relation to intercultural texts, exploring the possibilities and perils of writing. In the realm of history writing the concept of 'contact zones' also proves useful for the exploration of oral and written accounts of past interaction on the intersections of national and racial or 'transcultural' divides.

21 British colonial administrations in the 19th century, and subsequent South African governments, established 'reserves' in poor and uncultivated territories with the intention of segregating Black South Africans from White settlers. The National Party built on this policy, introducing the so-called homelands or Bantustans as a means to exclude Blacks from South African citizenship and voting rights (the 'great' Apartheid), in order to reshape South African society such that Whites would be the demographic majority.

22 See also Saul Dubow, *Scientific racism in modern South Africa* (Cambridge/New York: Cambridge University Press, 1995); Kenan Malik, *The Meaning of Race. Race, History and Culture in Western Society* (London: Macmillan, 1996).

23 The 1921 South African census report refered to 'the two great European races' on which South Africa was built: the British and the Afrikaner. Sally Peberdy, *Selecting immigrants. National Identity and South Africa's Immigration Policies, 1910-2008*. (Johannesburg: Wits University Press, 2009) 74.

Coloured or Black (Negroid) breeds. Racism thus became more than a theory about human difference; it was also about establishing a racial order.[24]

For the main characters portrayed in this book, race was a category that was difficult to ignore in their lives. This also applies to myself as the author of this book in a time of fierce debates about resurgent antisemitism and the legacy of the violent colonial past in the twenty-first century. There is the presence of what – following the example of the literary theorist Edward Said – we can call the 'cultural archive'. Said described this archive as a repository of specific knowledge, (body) language, images and 'structures of feeling', which often un-wittingly define the way in which unequal social relationships are articulated, in this case 'a deep structure of inequality in thought and affect based on race'.[25] The cultural archive is expressed in a 'colonial gaze', as Mary Louise Pratt calls it: a way of looking and interpreting that is closely linked to the natu-ralness of a superior, European, colonial power.[26] Also the 'master narrative of Whiteness', introduced by Melissa Steyn when referring to the tangle of tales which give meaning to the world around us in terms of racial inequality and White supremacy, can be seen as resulting from this cultural archive.[27] The danger of concepts such as 'master narrative' or 'cultural archive' is the lack of specificity and acknowledgement of historical change. It should be stressed that the cultural archive and the master narrative of Whiteness are not imme-diately tangible, nor omnipresent – that is precisely why it is important to examine their concrete operation in everyday life. Therefore, we need to re-search the ever-changing meaning of 'race'.

In this study the focus will be on attitudes and practices associated with race, within kinship networks and across national borders. Two geopolitical developments during the twentieth century take centre stage: Part 1 is about

---

24   Saul Dubow, *A Commonwealth of Knowledge: Science, Sensibility and White South Africa 1820–2000* (Oxford: Oxford University Press, 2006) 2.

25   Edward Said in *Culture and Imperialism*. London: Vintage, 1993). The notion of 'cultural archive' has recently been re-introduced in debates on the impact of 'race' in Dutch soci-ety by Gloria Wekker in her *White Innocence. Paradoxes of Colonialism and Race* (Dur-ham/London, Duke University Press, 2016) 2.

26   Pratt, *Imperial Eyes*.

27   Melissa Steyn, *Whiteness Just Isn't What it Used to be. White Identity in a changing SA.* (New York: State University of New York, 2001). Steyn's book leans strongly on the work of Jan Neederveen Pieterse, *White on Black. Images of Africa and Blacks in Western Popular Cul-ture* (Yale: Yale University Press, 1995). The working of this *master narrative* in all the lay-ers and spaces of the global society was addressed before by Franz Fanon, in his oeuvre and more specific in his seminal work *Black Skin, White Masks* (London: Pluto Press, 1986; originally *Peau Noire, Masques Blancs*. Paris: Editions du Seuil, 1952).

negotiating the impact of National Socialism within German-Dutch families, and Part 2 looks at the impact of Apartheid in Dutch-South African kinship networks. Each chapter offers a case study on the way in which political practices that reduce people to a single racial group – either Jewish, Aryan, White, Asian, Brown or Black – become part of interactions within kinship networks. Did lovers and family members manage to ignore the politics of racial inclusion and exclusion? And if that failed: what kind of negotiations took place if there were fundamental differences of opinion within their kinship network about the desirability or unacceptability of such a policy? The developments within the six kinship networks examined here show how changing constructions of 'race', 'culture', 'people' and 'nation' influenced the positions of the main protagonists, and how they got themselves entangled in situations that go beyond their agency as individual subjects within a dynamic transnational community.

A First Acquaintance

The basis for the first chapter was a selection of the correspondence between Irmgard Brester-Gebensleben in the Netherlands and her relatives in Nazi Germany published earlier, supplemented by the unpublished diaries of Irmgard's brother Eberhard and some war-time memories of her daughter Hedda Kalshoven-Brester. The history of the Brester-Gebensleben family shows how they cherished their close relationship within the kinship network, despite the politics of National Socialism that divided the family in the Netherlands and Germany. There is also a second storyline about the dilemmas Irmgard's brother Eberhard faced as a convinced member of Hitler's *Nationalsozialist-ische Deutsche Arbeiterpartei* (NSDAP). His negotiations on the crossroads of personal and political loyalties were not limited to dealing with his beloved sister and her family in the occupied Netherlands, but also extended to his German sweetheart who had a Jewish grandmother.

Chapter 2 tells the story of Marie Seyler, who, like Irmgard Gebensleben, emigrated from Germany to the Netherlands during the interwar period. She, too, acquired Dutch nationality before the outbreak of the Second World War through her marriage to a Dutchman. Both women shared an aversion to the antisemitic polities of the Nazis. However, while the German-Dutch Irmgard Brester-Gebensleben combined her dislike of those political practices with an unconditional loyalty to her National Socialist relatives, this was different for the German-Dutch Rie Ton-Seyler. Her written memoirs and life stories show little bonding with her family members in Germany; rather, they are dominated by her ambivalent bond with her country of origin. Shame about the atrocities committed by her National Socialist compatriots is expressed at the same time as a longing for the lost land and the 'good' Germans, as they live on in literary classics. It is not her relatives or friends, but books – especially Jewish world literature – that offer her a transnational 'home', in which she can live as a Dutch woman of German origin since the Shoah.

Young birds on the heath and stars in the infinite universe figure as metaphors of innocence and freedom in the letters that Lukas Plaut wrote to his wife from the Havelte labour camp in Drenthe. He too had the German nationality when he moved to the Netherlands in 1933 under the pressure of antisemitic measures. Central to Chapter 3 is the history of the Plaut-Witte family. In this case the meaning of 'race', 'family' and 'nation' – and thus also of Germanness and Dutchness – was primarily determined by the distinction between Jewish and non-Jewish (or 'Aryan' in the terms of that time). Lukas Plaut's letters from the camp, which was designed for Jews who were married to non-Jewish wives, show how he and Stien were determined to maintain their marital and family life despite their forced separation and all other antisemitic threats. Thanks to these and other letters carefully preserved by his widow Stien Plaut-Witte, the voices of Lukas Plaut and his relatives in China and the United States are integrated into a dramatic narrative, which is further based on Stien Plaut-White's memory work.

In the first Part of this book the histories are centred around German migrants who, already in the lead up to the German occupation, distanced themselves from the political aspirations of Hitler's Germany. There certainly also were German migrants in the Netherlands who, in the course of the 1930s, identified with the 'New Order' in their country of origin and welcomed the German occupation of the Netherlands. When German newcomers had joined local organisations such as the Nationalistic-oriented German Evangelical Church (*Deutsch Evangelische Gemeinden*), the German gymnastics and rowing clubs or choral societies, it was difficult to unravel the feelings of cultural and social affiliation with the *Heimat* from political agreement with National Socialism as it was promoted by the German Ministry of Foreign Affairs in these cultural and religious German communities abroad.[28] The appeal to feelings of loyalty to their country of origin in that environment often had the desired

---

28   Barbara Henkes, 'Gedeeld Duits-zijn aan de Maas. Gevestigd Deutschtum en Duitse nieuwkomers in de jaren 1900-1940' (Shared Germanness on the Maas. Settled *Deutschtum* and German Newcomers in the Years 1900-1940) in: P. van der Laar and others, red., *Vier eeuwen migratie, bestemming Rotterdam*. (Rotterdam: MondiTaal Publishing, 1998) 218-139.

effect. The enthusiasm of relatives in Nazi Germany, after their wounded national pride and their confidence in the future had been restored by Hitler's politics, contributed to this national and political identification, even more so when German nationals were given a heightened sense of racial superiority.[29] These feelings could also be prompted and reinforced by meetings with Dutch people who were inspired by their neighbours' National Socialism. The many Dutch people who became National Socialist show that neither national origin, nor the country where one lives, determine political choices.

Nevertheless, for most German migrants, especially after the invasion of the Netherlands in May 1940, their settling in the neighbouring country promoted a critical attitude towards the expansionist and racist policies of Nazi Germany. In the presentation of the German-Dutch kinship networks and histories in the first Part of this book, the emphasis is on the *condemnation* of the repressive Nazi regime by migrants of German origin in the Netherlands. This is reflected in the nature of their narratives: impending doom, imminent loss and resistance form the ground tone, sometimes reinforced by the contrast with the enthusiastic support for the Third Reich their relatives expressed from the other side of the border. The narrative form of a tragedy was also promoted by anti-German sentiments in postwar Netherlands and the feelings of guilt and shame towards the victims and survivors of the Holocaust.

The second Part of the book has a different tone, as the emphasis is on a self-evident, even cheerful *acceptance* of the repressive Apartheid regime by migrants of Dutch origin in South Africa. In these family histories, the dramatic consequences of racial Apartheid politics in South Africa are held at a distance. Yet the tales in both parts touch each other. The shocked reaction of the Dutch media to the victory of the South African National Party in May 1948 shows how a direct link was made between the pro-German attitude of the South African Nationalists during the Second World War and their programme of far-reaching racist politics of Apartheid.[30] But soon the initial indignation about the undisputed racial exclusion gave way to a renewed rapprochement between the two countries. The support of the South African Apartheid regime

---

29   See e.g. the statement of the German colonial ruler Carl Peters (1856-1918), who was responsible for mass murder in South West Africa in the beginning of the 20th century. He openly admitted that he 'was fed up with being counted among the pariahs and wanted to belong to a master race', in: Paul Ritter, *Colonien im deutschen Schrifttum*, 1936, Preface, quoted by Ahrend, *The Origins*, 189.

30   Bart de Graaff, 'De Nederlandse publieke opinie over apartheid 1948-1963: van begrip tot verwerping' (Dutch public opinion on Apartheid 1948-1963: From understanding to rejection), *International Spectator 39* (november 1985) 679–685.

for the Dutch recolonization war in Indonesia contributed to this positive turn, as well as the desire to promote Dutch postwar emigration to South Africa.[31]

From the end of the 1940s, Dutch policy makers aimed at combating post-war unemployment, housing shortages and the predicted overpopulation by stimulating emigration.[32] An added stimulus for many who wanted to leave the Netherlands was fear of a Third World War, as the antagonism between the capitalist West and the communist East (with Europe in the middle) hardened to a Cold War. Canada, Australia, the United States, South Africa and New Zealand were then obvious destinations.[33] For centuries the Dutch had left for these White settler societies that were the result of European – including Dutch – colonization. Their access to these countries was promoted by a policy, which gave priority to immigrants from European descent at the expense of migrants from other parts of the world and the indigenous populations.[34] However, these selective entry policies went unnoticed by most Dutch migrants, who were determined to make 'the best' of their new life by adapting to the habits and customs of the receiving society.

Organisations involved in the promotion of Dutch emigration propagated South Africa as a destination of choice for the Dutch. Emigration to that country was framed in terms of *stamverwantschap*, which has been translated with

---

31   Between 1948-1960, some 30,500 Dutch citizens emigrated to South Africa, according to the inventory of Peberdy, *Selecting Migrants*, appendix 2. See also: Barbara Henkes ' Shifting identifications in Dutch-South African migration policies (1910-1961)', *South African Historical Journal*, Vol. 68, nr. 4, Dec. 2016, 641–669.

32   B.P. Hofstede, *Twarted Exodus. Post-War Overseas Migration from the Netherlands* (The Hague: Martinus Nijhoff, 1964) is a classic on post-war Dutch emigration. For a brief overview of the postwar Dutch emigration policy see also Marijke van Faassen, "Min of meer misbaar. Naoorlogse emigratie vanuit Nederland: achtergronden en organisatie, particuliere motieven en overheidsprikkels, 1946-1967', in: Saskia Poldervaart e.a., *Van hot naar her. Nederlandse migratie vroeger, nu en morgen.* (Amsterdam, Stichting beheer IISG, 2001) 50–67.

33   Most Dutch emigrants went to Canada (more than 40 percent) and Australia (a small 30 percent); followed by the United States (more than 10 percent) and South Africa (over 9 percent) as destinations. New Zealand and South America also offered new opportunities.

34   Not all Europeans were equally welcome. For example, the government in South Africa made it difficult for the few survivors of the Holocaust to enter the country. Henkes, 'Shifting', 647–651. See also Barbara Henkes, 'De Britten, de Zwarten en de Joden in twintigste eeuws Zuid-Afrika', in: Remco Ensel (red.), *Sjacheren met stereotypen. Essays over "de Jood"als sjabloon* (Amsterdam: Het menasseh Ben Israel Instituut, Studies No. XII, 2016) 85–89.

the naturalising vocabulary of 'kinship ties'.[35] This family-related terminology suggests that Dutch migrants, due to their Dutchness, would automatically affiliate themselves with 'the' South African society. That is to say, with the White, Afrikaans-speaking part of the South African population. Through the notion of *stamverwantschap*, which had emerged at a time of escalating nationalism in the late nineteenth century,[36] an appeal was made to a shared cultural and geneological (biological) origin. *Stamverwantschap* was traced back to the colonial presence of the Netherlands in South Africa. The similarities between both 'mother' tongues (Dutch and Afrikaans), between geographical and family names in the two countries, between the Dutch and Afrikaner Protestant churches, and not least between racial features such as skin colour and hair structure, called for feelings of recognition and affection, in which – as Benedict Anderson mentions – 'there is always an element of fond imagining'.[37]

Although the passionate identification with the heroic fight of the Boers against the almighty Brits did decline after the Boer surrender in 1902, the idea of *stamverwantschap* as an organic bond between the Dutch and Afrikaners remained alive – and manifests itself even to this day.[38] Once more we can see how tales from different places and moments in time can touch and involve multidirectional memories. A revival of *stamverwantschap* as a topos in postwar emigration discourse went along with the expectation that Dutch migrants in South Africa would identify themselves primarily with White Afrikanerdom. As such it would facilitate an effortless integration within the 'stamverwante' Afrikaner community in South Africa. For years the fact that this integration of Dutch immigrants was aimed at reinforcing the White, Afrikaner part of the

---

35   Barbara Henkes, *Stamverwantschap* and the Imagination of a White, Transnational Community'. The 1952 Celebrations of the Jan van Riebeecks Tercentanary in the Netherlands and South Africa', in Gemma Blok, Vincent Kuitenbrouwer and Claire Weeda, eds., *Imagining Communities. Historical Reflections on the Process of Community Formation*. Amsterdam: Amsterdam University Press, 2018), 173–195; 'Turbulent Kinship: the Dutch and South Africa', in: Martine Gosselink, Maria Holtrop, Robert Ross (eds.), *Good Hope? South Africa and the Netherlands from 1600*. (Amsterdam/Nijmegen: Rijksmuseum Amsterdam/ Uitgeverij Vantilt, 2017) 279–291.

36   Martin Bossenbroek, *Holland op zijn breedst. Indië en Zuid-Afrika in de Nederlandse cultuur omstreeks 1900* (Amsterdam 1996); Maarten Kuitenbrouwer, *The Netherlands and the rise of modern imperialism: colonies and foreign policy, 1870-1902* (Oxford: Oxford University Press, 1992); Henk te Velde, *Gemeenschapszin en plichtsbesef. Liberalisme en Nationalisme in Nederland, 1870-1918* (Den Haag: SdU, 1992).

37   Anderson, *Imagined communities*, 154.

38   'Stamverwantschap' is a favorite theme of the populist politician Martin Bosma of the Dutch *Partij voor de Vrijheid* (PVV) when it comes to the necessary support for a White Afrikaner culture in present South Africa now that it has lost its dominant position.

South African nation was not a point of discussion. Only a few newcomers were able to take a critical look at racial inequality from the frame of reference available to them in these years. If it did come to that point, leaving South Africa became almost inevitable.[39]

In the correspondence between family members in the Netherlands and South Africa, references to inequality and exclusion on a racial basis could be read between the lines, and was easily ignored. However, it has been stressed before by the social scientist Eviatar Zerubavel, that 'ignoring', like 'noticing' are not just personal acts, since they are always embedded in particular social communities in specific political contexts.[40] Only after 1960 – when the violent death of 69 peaceful demonstrators became internationally known as 'the Sharpeville massacre' – did Apartheid policy give rise to more and sharper protests in the Netherlands and other countries. The growing Civil Rights Movement in the United States, which placed racial discrimination prominently on the international agenda, also contributed to a widely supported criticism of Apartheid.[41] These national and transnational protests against Apartheid became a stumbling block for Dutch-South African relationships.

Matters had not reached that point yet when the correspondence between the Dutch Pim Valk and his South African penfriend Lena Dusseljee started in 1946. Their letters form the basis of a romantic narrative in Chapter 4. The two adolescents had never met in person when they sent their first letter to each other. From that moment on, they formed an epistolary bond through which stories about faith, the nation, family and friends of the one became part of the experiences of the other. With their writing and in their letters, they created a space 'for Whites only' in which their images of the Netherlands and South Africa became intertwined. The 'stamverwante' image of South Africa as a former colony of the Netherlands contributed greatly to Pim's actual emigration to South Africa, his marriage to Lena and his orientation on the White, Protestant church and Afrikaner people. In addition to this early correspondence, Mr. Valk in South Africa and his relatives in the Netherlands gave me access to their memoirs, photo albums and letters that he sent them. Together with our conversations, it was possible to assess the extent to which, more than ten years after the end of Apartheid, he had been able to revise his view of South

---

39   This was documented in an interview with the Reverend J.A. Don, who returned to the Netherlands with his wife and their three children: 'It's almost too late for South Africa. Powerless return because apartheid ruined his job', in the regional daily newspaper *Rijn en Gouwe*, May 17, 1961.

40   Eviatar Zerubavel, *The Elephant in the Room. Silence and Denial in Everyday Life*. (Oxford: Oxford Press, 2006) 20.

41   Håkan Thörn, *Anti-Apartheid and the Emergence of a Global Civil Society* (New York en Oxford: Palgrave Macmillan, 2006).

Africa as a primarily White nation – whether or not in relation to the changing views in the Netherlands.

On the same ship that brought Pim Valk to South Africa, in 1952, there was the Dutch couple Beusekom-Scheffer with their one-year old baby. After more than three years, the family (enlarged by two more children) would return to the Netherlands. Thanks to the unpublished letters from Wendela Beusekom to her parents in Amsterdam, we can in Chapter 5 follow the scope of a master narrative of Whiteness developing from the moment she was introduced to the African continent and South African society. Her letters show the importance she had learned to attach to 'good taste' as expressed in clothing, cooking, home decoration and other material manifestations of a specific cultural and racialised embeddedness in her assessment of the people around her. Wendela's alignments were determined by the responsibilities she experienced as a young, European wife and mother who had to serve the welfare of her White husband and children. In retrospect, Mrs. Beusekom tries to negotiate a space in which she remains loyal to her life and friends in South Africa, while realizing that she needs to distance herself from the racial order she and her family once had enjoyed.

The final chapter presents the history of the Huisman-Grotenhuis family in Pretoria (now Tshwane city) and their relatives in the Netherlands. Their negotiations concentrate on the 1980s, when a cousin from Amsterdam planned to make a documentary about his family in South Africa. The emigrated members of the Grotenhuis family and those who stayed in the Netherlands were in regular contact, which offered the young film maker access to the everyday life of his uncle and aunt and their four adult children. His stay in Pretoria resulted in an unfinished 'family film', which shows how the political discourse of Apartheid was picked up in various ways by the individual family members in South Africa. In the years that followed, the film maker became actively involved in the *Anti-Apartheidbeweging Nederland* (AABN), which resulted in several critical documentaries about the violent repression by the Apartheid regime. The raw and processed film material, together with the film maker's memory work and conversations with relatives in the Netherlands and South Africa, demonstrate how they tried – and still try – to negotiate their different experiences and views on Apartheid within the Dutch-South African kinship network.

With the selection of these six intimate histories, the study of the complex intersections of migration with national, religious, racial and cultural identifications focuses on the position of the 'privileged' protagonists. It concerns the experiences and memories of those who were not categorized as Jews by a virulent antisemitic regime (although Stien Plaut-Witte got to know that experience from the inside), nor those who were seen as Blacks or Coloureds in (post) colonial societies. Even without their supporting a racist regime, they were part of a system of consistent exclusion, inequality and repression under National Socialism or Apartheid. In that sense they acted as 'implicated subjects', as Michael Rothburg so aptly points out, when he analyses how we all 'are entwined with and folded into ("implicated in") histories and situations that surpass our agency as individual subjects'.[42] The concept of implication helps to avoid the rhetoric of blame that is neither intellectually nor morally sufficient, and it invites us to think about the ways we are enmeshed in histories and actualities beyond our apparent and immediate reach. Many of us help produce history through impersonal participation rather than direct perpetration or resistance. Thanks to the central position and articulated voices of Gentiles and Whites in this book, it is possible to explore how the 'race' category has coloured and still colours all our lives.

Shifts in Time and Tongue

In this book, negotiating inclusion and exclusion on grounds of nationality and race is examined within the context of transnational family histories. The cross-border kinship networks formed the breeding ground for the unique historical sources on which this book is based. At the same time the networks also offered access to these sources, which are not (yet) to be found in institutionalized archives. Private correspondences, dairies, travelogues, autobiographies, memoirs, snapshots and film recordings bring us closer to the agency of our historical subjects, their self-perception and their perception of others around them in a period of undeniable racist repression. These egodocuments present us with the outcomes of different responsibilities and loyalties and the limits of agency as individual subjects, all the more so in times of racial exclusion.

In addition, oral history, the recalling of personal memories half a century later, adds an extra time dimension. That retrospective gaze from the present can help to re-evaluate the meaning of past observations as they were put on paper at the time. It allows us to revisit past experiences from a different perspective and determine if and how the positions of the historical actors have changed. This approach allows us to recognise the complexity of subject positions and their negotiating different loyalties and responsibilities which

---

42   Michael Rothberg, 'Trauma Theory, Implicated Subjects, and the Question of Israel/Palestine', https://profession.mla.org/trauma-theory-implicated-subjects-and-the-question-of-israel-palestine/. See also Rothberg's *The Implicated Subject. Beyond Victims and Perpetrators* (Stanford: Stanford University Press, 1919).

were entangled in various cultural, social and political settings. It shows how 'the personal' in multiple moments and in many ways could be or could become 'political'.[43] Both life-writing, photographing and filming in the past, as well as the act of remembering (memory work) in the present, are performative acts: they are activities that may represent what has happened and at the same time are constitutive of the meaning of what happened.[44] Researchers are part of the reality they study, which is particularly true for oral historians, who meet their interlocutors and ask them to move back in time.[45] Whether it is about recalling personal memories in the present, or preserved letters, diaries, photos and films from the past, the nature of the information is always, consciously or unconsciously, geared to the expectations of the addressee: the imaginary viewer, reader or listener at that very moment. It is therefore better to understand egodocuments, including the outcome of our memory work, not just as 'a sincere act of self-expression but as a many-voices act of self-presentation whose self varies according to the intended audience'.[46]

The process of remembering is characterized by the tension between what is revealed and what is being withheld or forgotten. In the interview situation, the past is kept at bay by appealing to 'the time of then'; at the same time that 'the time of then' is made part of the present by talking about it in 'the time of now'.[47] Shifts in time during the conversation – which are indeed

---

43   By subjecting the feminist slogan 'The personal is political' to a critical revaluation at an early stage, Mieke Aerts showed how its significance, as well as the political commitment, varies. It may refer to shared personal experience, which can help to gain political insight and *political mobilisation* – or it may refer to the pursuit of changing *the style of politics* by taking these shared experiences as a starting point. Aerts connects those differences with a plea for approaching societal relationships as an ongoing struggle in which equality, differences and inequalities should be seen as different articulations of historical power relations. Mieke Aerts, 'Het persoonlijke is politiek. Een poging tot herdenken' in: *Te Elfder Ure 39: Dilemma's van het feminisme*, 1986: 78–107, at 105.

44   W.G. Ruberg, *Conventional Correspondence. Epistolary Culture of the Dutch elite, 1770-1850.* (Leiden: Brill, 2011) 4; Lynn Abrams, *Oral History Theory* (New York: Routledge, 2010) 130–152; Jay Winter, 'The performance of the past: memory, history, identity, in: Karin Tilmans, Frank van Vree en Jay Winter (eds.), *Performing the Past. Memory, History and Identity in modern Europe.* (Amsterdam: Amsterdam University Press, 2010) 11–23.

45   See e.g. Allesandro Portelli, 'Living Voices: The Oral History Interview as Dialogue and Experience', *The Oral History Review* 45: 2 (Summer/Fall 2018), 239–248.

46   Margaret R. Higonnet, *Nurses at the front: writing the wounds of the Great War.* Boston 2001, Introduction VII-XXXVIII, at XXIX, referred to by Mieke Aerts, 'De brieven Tan-Schepers – een unieke collectie, maar waarom precies?': http://brieven-tan-schepers.nl/index.php/artikelen/item/703-de-brieven-tan-schepers-een-unieke-collectie-maar-waarom-precies.

47   See e.g. Berber Bevernage en Chris Lorenz (eds.), *Breaking Up Time: Negotiating the Borders between Present and Future* (Vandenhoeck & Ruprecht in 2013.

performances – are often expressed by alternating languages, accents or vocabularies. This is when racist vocabulary suddenly may pop up from the remembered past despite the present taboos. The permeability of the past and present is also noticeable when the present and past tenses alternate in the life stories. This tango between the past and present is manifest in the process of remembering, as it is in history writing. Historians, too, are constantly moving between the present and the past, trying to place the past at a distance and at the same time bringing it closer to the present. In order to position the information of the protagonists in the 'proper' time, I have made a distinction in the ways I introduce them. When I refer to letters or other egodocuments from the past, I mention first names, sometimes followed by birth name or successive surname – if desired with a pseudonym. If the narrative is situated in recent times, when the protagonists recall their past experiences, I have chosen to use Mrs. or Mr., even if we called each other by our first names.

Language is not neutral or indifferent. In addition to the actual meaning of the chosen words, the emotional value is equally important. Besides, language is alive and changes: words fall into oblivion or move to the sphere of taboos, while new words and meanings come to life. Words behave like chameleons: their meaning changes depending on the context in which they are brought forward. Therefore, it is relevant not only to approach the words and phrases as data carriers, but to pay attention to the connotations – the emotional values of specific words and the nature of the narrative. After all, that is what determines the meaning of the story.

The sensitivity of language to political discourse has been signaled before by the Jewish-German philologist Viktor Klemperer. In a linguistic notebook he recorded the rise and development of what he called the *LTI, Lingua Tertii Imperii*, the language of the Third Reich.[48] He took notes of what struck him when reading the newspaper or listening to the radio and casual conversations in the street. In this way he showed, like no other, how words and the use of certain phrases – such as superlatives and metaphors – have the power to reduce people to an inferior category, how language can strip them from their humanity and identify them as the enemy within society. Language provides us with a rich set of instruments with which we can transfer our emotions and indicate how we want to see ourselves in relation to others.[49] For this reason I

---

48   Victor Klemperer, *LTI – Lingua Tertii Imperii; Notizbuch eines Philologen*. (Berlin: Aufbau, 1946).

49   See also Judith Buttler, *Excutable Speech: a Politics of the Performative* (New York: Routledge, 1997; National Museum of World Cultures (red.), *Words matter: An Unfinished Guide to Word Choices in the Cultural Sector. Work in progress* (2018). https://issuu.com/tropenmuseum/docs/wordsmatter_english, retrieved 8 June 2019.

want to briefly consider my use of some words, capital letters and punctuation marks at the start of this book.

As indicated earlier, family, nation and race may be self-evident, even natural categories at first sight. With quotation marks I want to articulate the constructed – and therefore variable – nature of these categories, as is the case with notions such as 'the people' (*Volksgemeenschap*) or the untranslatable *stamverwantschap*. However, I do not always do this consistently, as I want to prevent the text from taking the form of a series of words held in place with clothes pegs. The designation of individuals in terms of nationality, race, or, for example, religion may have tangible, sometimes dramatic, consequences, and poses problems for every writer when it comes to formulations. While I do not want to pin down the subjects in our histories to their labels as Jewish, Germanic, African, European, German, Dutch, White, Black or Coloured, I do want to indicate how those designations may determine their opportunities and can be sources of oppression and empowerment. To emphasize this, I use capitals when the labelling refers to race or nationality. While no one fits such categories singularly or univocally, some are with a particular ambiguity positioned within 'pure' racial or national cateogies. Indeed, there is a whole other vocabulary in racially elaborated societies like Apartheid South Africa for people who do not fit the unambiguous categories: the so-called 'half-breeds', 'mixed married' couples, or '*kafferboeties*' (White brothers of the Blacks).[50]

The central position of egodocuments created at the time means that racist terms and oppositions, like those between the Aryan and Semitic or the Black and White 'races', are part of this book. Since the 1970s the term 'Black' has been advocated as one category in opposition to 'White', partly to stress the similar position and promote a political unity to people of African and South Asian heritage and other 'people of colour' against common racist oppressions. This White-Black dichotomy may, however, become equally problematic not only because it enhances simple oppositions, but also because the differences and the dynamics within these categories, which result from the intersection of different axes of distinction, such as gender, class, and religion, may be lost sight of.[51] Although in this book terms like Black or Jew are used at times as an indication for all categories not covered by the label White or Aryan, respectively Gentile, there are inevitably histories in which these categories overlap.

---

50   Literally: brothers of the kaffers. It is an Afrikaans swear word for Whites in South Africa who befriended Africans. See also Chap. 5.

51   Such a dynamic has been impressively problematized on stage and in literature, e.g. Athol Fugard's *Blood Knot* (1961, revised 1986) and in Zoë Wicomb, *Playing in the Light. A Novel* (New York: The New Press, 2008).

I will introduce the story of a 'mixed-blooded in the second degree' in Nazi Germany, just as I will refer to the so-called 'Coloureds' (*bruin mense* in Afrikaans) and Asians or Indians, in South Africa. Every time such categories are used, we need to be alive to their effects and the power of the 'imagined communities' these categories produce. I hope that I have managed to find a way to use these categories and at the same time keep them at bay.

PART 1

National Socialism Across the German-Dutch Border

∵

CHAPTER 1

'Will My Own Brother have to Fight Against us Now?'

Safe and Risky Stories in a German-Dutch Family

After a long train journey from Brunswick in Germany, the thirteen-year-old Irmgard Gebensleben arrived in 1920 at Utrecht Central Station in the Netherlands.[1] Awaiting her were Mr. and Mrs. Brester-Wurfbain, who took her to their family home in the Willem Barentzstraat. Her temporary 'foster parents' shared the house with their two sons Carel (1897) and August (1900), who both studied at Utrecht University.[2] 'At home there was a hot meal with soup, meat, vegetables and stewed fruit', Irmgard wrote enthusiastically to her parents in Germany. With amazement she noted the Dutch eating and drinking habits: 'In the morning at half past eight you get bread and coffee, at one o'clock once more coffee with bread and at half past six there is a warm meal. In between, they drink tea nonstop'. She herself got milk instead of tea: 'Mr. Brester says that for the first weeks I have to drink a litre of milk every day, later even more'.[3]

Irmgard was one of the many thousands of children from Germany, Austria and Hungary who in the years after the First World War exchanged their impoverished country for the Netherlands, which had remained neutral during the war years. Dutch organisations took the initiative for so-called 'children's transports' to offer children the opportunity to get some more flesh on their bones and colour in their cheeks.[4] This worked well for Irmgard, under the care

---

1   This chapter is a re-working of my contribution 'Letter-Writing and the Construction of a transnational Family: A Private Correspondence between the Netherlands and Germany, 1920-1949 ', in: Marijke Huisman et al. (eds.), *Life Writing Matters in Europe* (Heidelberg Universitätsverlag Winter, 2012) 177–192.

2   Hedda E. Kalshoven-Brester, *Op zoek naar de Bresters*. (Bergen: a self-edited genealogy, 2002) 89, 91.

3   Irmgard Gebensleben, 13. June 1920, quoted by Hedda Kalshoven-Brester (red.), *Ik denk zoveel aan jullie. Een briefwisseling tussen Nederland en Duitsland 1920-1949* (Amsterdam: Uitgeverij Contact, 1991) 49. To indicate when I quote from the selected letters published in *Ik denk zoveel*, reference to the pages in the book are added. The original letters, written in Gothic German, the diaries and their transcripts are now available at the NIOD Institute for War, Holocaust and Genocide Studies: 906 Brester-Gebensleben, E.I.

4   Already during the First World War organisations were established to allow children from war zones to recuperate in the Netherlands, such as the *Nederlandsche Centrale voor Vacantiekinderen*. In 1919, permission was given for 560 children per month to come. Barbara Henkes, *Heimat in Holland. Duitse dienstmeisjes 1920-1950* (Amsterdam: Babylon-De Geus, 1995) 31.

© BARBARA HENKES, 2020 | DOI:10.1163/9789004401600_003

FIGURE 1.1
Irmgard Gebensleben, 1922.

of the Brester family: within two weeks she wrote to her parents that she had already become 'very fat', thanks to 'the tastiest things' that she was treated to, on top of the bananas and oranges.[5] After a month Irmgard returned to her family in Germany, but the contact with the Bresters in the Netherlands was maintained. Nine years later, in 1929, she married the younger son August Brester and so exchanged her German for a Dutch citizenship. She and August had four children.

Although Irmgard effortlessly linked her German origin to her Dutch nationality, this combination of Germanness and Dutchness became problematic with the rise of National Socialism, and especially after the German invasion in May 1940. Like many other German immigrants, she met with distrust from her Dutch compatriots.[6] Things did not get any better after her younger brother Eberhard (1910) visited Irmgard and her family in Amersfoort in German *Wehrmacht* uniform. Dealing with her dear relatives and friends who sympathized with the Nazi regime went together with unavoidable dilemmas and confrontations. How they negotiated these tensions can be traced in what remains of the many letters Irmgard and her relatives in Germany exchanged with each other.

This private correspondence of over two thousand letters, preserved in a crate in the attic, was discovered by Irmgard's eldest daughter Hedda Kalshoven-Brester. In 1991 Hedda published a selection and translation from this collection, entitled *'Ik denk zoveel aan jullie. Een briefwisseling tussen Nederland en Duitsland 1920-1949'* (*translated as Between Two Homelands: letters across the Borders of Nazi Germany*).[7] The published letters and notebook fragments, in

---

5   Irmgard Gebensleben, 21 June 1920, quoted in Kalshoven-Brester, *Ik denk zoveel*, 50.
6   Barbara Henkes, 'Changing images of German maids during the inter-war period in the Netherlands: from trusted help to traitor in the nest'. In Raphael Samuel and Paul Thompson, eds., *The Myths We Live By* (London/New York: Routledge: 1990) 225–238.
7   In the book, Kalshoven-Brester occasionally supplemented the translated correspondence between Germany and the Netherlands by letters between family members in Germany and

FIGURE 1.2   The Bresters in Utrecht, 1922.

combination with the diaries of Eberhard Gebensleben, give a fascinating insight into the way in which notions of 'family' and 'nation' shape our lives, lend
each other meaning and can either strengthen or collide with each other in
times of political tension and repression.

Although Irmgard's relatives in Nazi Germany supported a hated political
order, mutual contact was maintained. However, that did not happen by itself:
an effort had to be made to tolerate divergent national and political orientations and to retain a sense of belonging together. This effort was enacted by
letter writing. The writers were 'kinkeepers': they maintained family ties and
gave them meaning.[8] The exchange of letters played an important role in perpetuating the transnational kinship network. Its symbolic function was at least
as important as, and perhaps even more important than, the transfer of information. A letter in a characteristic handwriting on recognizable letter paper,
folded in an envelope with a distinctive stamp delivered by a postman, can be

---

notes from the Irmgard's diary. The English edition of the book, entitled *Between two Homelands: Letters across the Borders of Nazi Germany* (Chicago: University of Illinois Press, 2014)
was first translated from Dutch into German by Hester Velmans and later from German into
English by Peter Fritzsche. Unless otherwise stated all translations from the Dutch are my own.
8   Leach and Braithwaite, 'A Binding Tie'. See also the introduction to this book.

experienced as the extension of someone's hand that bridges the distance. Or, in the words of the historian David Gerber: 'the personal letter is simultaneously a poor substitute for and an important embodiment of those from whom we are separated'.[9]

Viewing the transnational correspondence between relatives as a form of kinkeeping puts it in line with gender expectations, namely that it was especially the women in the kinship networks that took on this task.[10] This was initially the case with the Gebensleben family. After Irmgard settled in the Netherlands, the correspondence between Germany and the Netherlands was mainly maintained by her mother Elisabeth Gebensleben-von Alten (1883) and Irmgard herself, with a single contribution from her grandmother, father, brother, and husband. After the death of her mother in December 1937, almost two years after the death of Irmgard's father, grandmother Minna von Alten-Rausch (1859) ensured that the correspondence was continued. After she, too, died in December 1940, Irmgard's only brother Eberhard realized: 'From now on, I am primarily the one who must ensure that you continue to receive greetings and letters from Germany'.[11]

A correspondence not only stems from a sense of belonging but at the same time also evokes that feeling. This dual function is further strengthened when relatives move to different countries, and it becomes even more important as soon as these countries enter into conflict with each other, as did the Netherlands and Germany after the outbreak of the Second World War. Letters show how several relatives on both sides of the national and political divide put pen to paper to reach each other. It also shows how restless and 'cut off' they felt when that regular stream of letters stopped, such as during the German invasion in the May days of 1940 or later, when the field post to and from Eberhard had become 'a kind of lottery'.[12]

Political Controversies

In her introduction to the selected letters, Irmgard's daughter Hedda Kalshoven-Brester describes how she started to think about some of the events she remembered from the past. 'I saw my mother's white face again on the morning

---

9   David A. Gerber, *Authors of Their lives. The Personal Correspondence of British Immigrant to North America in the Nineteenth Century.* (New York: New York University Press. 2006) 2.

10   Tamara K. Hareven, *Families, History, and Social Change. Life-Course and Cross-Cultural Perspectives.* (Boulder: Westview Press, 1999).

11   Eberhard Gebensleben, 5 Dec. 1940, quoted in Kalshoven-Brester, *Ik denk zoveel*, 311.

12   Eberhard Gebensleben, 12 Mar. 1944, quoted in: Kalshoven-Brester, *Ik denk zoveel*, 356.

of May 10, 1940, when she said, "Will my own brother have to fight against us now?" Hedda continues with the memory of the evacuation from their home-town of Amersfoort, where her father stayed behind because of his work in the local hospital. When her mother was asked by local police officers where she was born, 'she muttered: "My husband .... in Arnhem" and we were allowed to drive on'. From that moment on, Germanness, so familiar to the Brester-Gebensleben family, suddenly gained a new, threatening meaning. There were inconsistencies that daughter Hedda only became aware of years later: for ex-ample, when she greeted her German Uncle Eberhard in his grey-green uni-form of those despised 'Krauts' (*Moffen*) with undiminished enthusiasm. And when the message came of Eberhard's death at the front, it was not only his sister Irmgard but also her children that burst into tears. The Jewish boy in hid-ing, who stayed with them for nine months, also had to cry when he saw them so sad.[13]

When making selections from the overwhelming number of letters, Hedda Kalshoven-Brester was guided by a clear question: what repercussions did at-titudes to National Socialism have on the correspondence? When she indicates that she left out stories about 'maidservants, disagreements within the family and love affairs',[14] she acknowledges the inevitable dilemmas involved in the publication of letter collections: a well-considered choice is often necessary for accessibility, but selection detracts from the insight that the complete series of letters can offer into the complex world of letter writers' feelings and thoughts.[15] That does not alter the fact that her selection gives a sharp picture of the dis-may on the German side of the family after the collapse of the German Empire after 1918: the material needs due to the dramatic inflation in the early 1920s and the economic crisis after 1929, the fear of rising Bolshevism, the growing enthusiasm for National Socialism during the interwar period, and finally the disillusion after the collapse of the Third Reich. On the Dutch side, Hitler's rise to power and his political movement were monitored with a combination of hope for the best and fear of the worst. After the relief about the Munich Agreement 1938 and the horror of the outbreak of the war in September 1939, cautious messages followed about life in the occupied Netherlands and con-cerns about the German activities at the front and Allied bombing. Of course, not a word was written about the involvement of Irmgard's husband in the doctors' resistance.

---

13   Kalshoven-Brester, *Ik denk zoveel,* 11–24. See also Peter Fritsche, 'Preface', in Kalshoven, *Between two Homelands*, ix-xix, at xix.
14   Kalshoven-Brester, *Ik denk zoveel*, 20.
15   Gerber, *Authors of Their* lives, 54–55.

In vivid colours, the letters paint the consequences of the political changes and measures for German everyday life. In addition, they show how different national and political discourses in Germany and the Netherlands evolved in opposite directions over the interwar years. Irmgard had been brought up at a time that most men, driven by nationalist enthusiasm, plunged themselves into the First World War, often encouraged and waved goodbye by their wives, sisters and children when they left for the front. After the defeat there was political chaos. In 1919 her father signed up voluntarily to the *Bürgerwehr* (militia) to protect *Braunschweig* (Brunswick) from the dreaded 'Red Terror'.[16] After her stay in the Netherlands, Irmgard joined the political orientation of her parents and became a member of the *Bismarckjugend*, the youth group of the *Deutschnationale Volkspartei*, DNVP (German National People's Party).[17] Following their nationalist engagement, her parents, brother, grandmother and other family members increasingly identified with emerging National Socialism. Their regularly expressed admiration for the 'willingness to sacrifice', 'burning patriotism', 'strict discipline' of the Nazis, and for their leader who had brought about 'national revival', resulted in their membership in 1933 of the *Nationalsozialistische Deutsche Arbeiterpartei*, NSDAP (National-Socialist German Workers' Party).[18]

From 1929, Irmgard lived in the Netherlands as a newly-wed doctor's wife in a liberal environment with a strong aversion to militarism and militant nationalism.[19] That did not prevent her 'German heart' – as she called it in a letter to her mother – from leaping up in August 1931 at the sight of the Graf Zeppelin, which flew 'quietly and majestically' over their house as 'a symbol of German energy and power that will prevail despite the serious condition of the

---

16   Kalshoven-Brester, *Ik denk zoveel*, 30. The *Bürgerwehr* was a local force of civilians who could be mobilised in emergencies to strengthen the regular police forces or army.

17   Fritzsche, 'Preface', xii. The DNVP (1918-1933) was the major conservative and nationalist party in Weimar Germany. It was an alliance of nationalists, reactionary monarchists, *völkisch* and antisemitic elements supported by the Pan-German League. After 1929, the DNVP co-operated with the Nazis, forming coalition governments in some states and finally supporting Hitler's appointment as Chancellor (*Reichskanzler*) in January 1933. The party quickly lost influence and eventually dissolved itself in June 1933, giving way to the Nazis' single-party dictatorship.

18   Karl Gebensleben, 28 Apr. 1933 to his wife Elisabeth during their visit to the Netherlands, quoted in Kalshoven-Brester, *Ik denk zoveel*, 165.

19   Kalshoven-Brester, *Ik denk zoveel*, 11. See also references to this philosophy of life in letters from her (then) foster father Jan Brester written in 1920, 1922, 1924 and 1927, quoted in Kalshoven-Brester, *Ik denk zoveel*, 53–54, 59, 66.

FIGURE 1.3   Eberhard and his mother Elisabeth Gebensleben-von Alten in
Brunswick, Christmas 1934.

moment'.[20] Initially, the increasing enthusiasm of her family in Brunswick for
National Socialism was followed charitably, but soon Irmgard expressed her
growing reservations. On 11 March 1933 she wrote to her mother: 'From a distance one sees everything much more objectively and calmly, one judges much
more soberly than when one is right in the middle of the events. One thing I
hope is that Hitler will pursue his goals by peaceful means, and that everything
he does is primarily for Germany's sake, but also for all the people who are now
suffering from the crisis everywhere. His actions against the communists are
greeted with cheers over here, as long as they do not lead to dictatorship'.
Searching for possible clues, she connected with the existing fear and revulsion towards communism among her relatives and their politically kindred

20   Irmgard Brester-Gebensleben, 18 Aug. 1931, quoted in Kalshoven-Brester, *Ik denk zoveel*,
        102.

FIGURE 1.4 Nameplate of Dr. Werner Liebenthal, notary and solicitor. The plate hung outside
his office on Martin Lutherstrasse in Berlin. In 1933, following the Law for the
Restoration of the Professional Civil Service, the plate was painted black by the
Nazis, who boycotted Jewish-owned offices.

spirits, while adding that the German boycott of Dutch goods only increased
the tension between the two peoples (*volkeren*).[21]

Less than a month later – shortly after the Nazi boycott of Jewish businesses
(*Judenboykott*), which also applied to Jewish doctors and lawyers – an unequivocal condemnation of 'the horrific Jewish persecution' followed, with the addition that this 'evokes an enormous antipathy against Germany everywhere
abroad!'[22] Irmgard substantiated her horror by referring to the Jewish son-in-
law of a well-known acquaintance, a lawyer in Berlin. Two 'SA men' had been
posted in front of his door to block clients' access to his practice. 'Isn't that a
shame? What can he do? He is simply driven out of his home country! [...] Of
course you cannot call this "atrocities", but what is it then? You can't pretend
that those facts don't exist, even though the Nazi press is trying to deny them
in every way possible'.[23]

Around the time she sent this letter, her brother Eberhard enlisted in the
same SA (*Sturmabteilung*), also called Storm Troopers (*Sturmtruppen*) or
Brownshirts (*Braunhemden*), a Nazi paramilitary force founded by Hitler in
1921 to protect party meetings and to intimidate political opponents and

21   Irmgard Brester-Gebensleben, 11 Mar. 1933, quoted in: Kalshoven-Brester, *Ik denk zoveel*,
      147–148.
22   Irmgard Brester-Gebensleben, 3 and 12 Apr. 1933, quoted in: Kalshoven-Brester, *Ik denk
      zoveel*, 160 and 164. For direct consequences of this *Judenboykott* see also Chap. 3, n. 5.
23   Irmgard Brester-Gebensleben, 3 Apr. 1933, quoted in: Kalshoven-Brester, *Ik denk zoveel*,
      160.

FIGURE 1.5   Elisabeth Gebensleben with her children and grandchildren
in Brunswick, August 1937.

Jews.[24] It was not the first time that Irmgard expressed her disgust of the antisemitic acts of the Nazis.[25] Her writing signals that there was a limit to what
she could tolerate in praise of National Socialism and antisemitic propaganda.
Then, as if shocked by her own disapproval of her parents' accommodating
attitude, she quickly switches to a different theme that could bring them closer
again: 'For now I stop writing about politics, as one could go on for hours. I was
very happy with your long letter. So, our holiday plans are well received by
you?' The replacement of a pointless political confrontation by an evocation of
domestic intimacy – in this case their being together in Brunswick during the
summer holiday of 1933 – became a proven formula in the correspondence of
the following years.

24   In Jan. 1933, the SA already included 400,000 men and had become a force in itself. Its
power was broken in June 1934 by Hitler and the SS.

25   See Irmgard Brester-Gebensleben, 18 Mar. 1933, quoted in Kalshoven-Brester, *Ik denk
zoveel*, 154.

As the divergent political discourses became more pronounced in the Netherlands and Germany, the commitment of the Gebensleben relatives to bridging or avoiding those differences grew. They sent each other magazines and newspaper clippings in the hope of bringing the addressees round to their own point of view.[26] When that failed, they searched diligently for 'safe' stories, which could prevent controversial themes from popping up within the family, or for other ways to preserve their mutual affection.[27] Thus, Irmgard tried to steer her mother's jubilant, if not exalted, verbiage about National Socialism in a different direction by encouraging her to pay a visit to the Netherlands. In the company of her grandchildren, surrounded by 'picturesque flower carts full of daffodils and tulips', Mrs. Gebensleben-von Alten could relax. During the mutual visits, the grandchildren were an important bond: they were the centre of attention and they ensured that political disagreements could be held at bay.

In this period, the correspondence is increasingly characterised by 'codes of compromise': tacit agreements that are indispensable to create moments of intimacy when substantial differences threaten to drive the letter writers apart.[28] In April 1933, after Irmgard had so plainly put down her horror at the Nazi persecution of the Jews, she was confronted with her mother's antisemitic statements in response: 'The Jews want to rule, they do not want to serve'.[29] Subsequently, she left her criticism of antisemitic policies out of her letters. Instead, she looked for any positive developments in Nazi Germany that she could share with her parents: 'I totally agree with the plans to create a new modern motorway between Germany and Holland!', she wrote in October 1933.[30] Apart from the admiration that the modernization of the German road network evoked abroad,[31] the motorways also made the physical distance to

---

26   Irmgard regularly received magazines and newspaper clippings from her parents and grandmother. In addition, from 1929 she had a subscription to the conservative *Braunschweiger Landeszeitung*. See Kalshoven-Brester, *Ik denk zoveel*, 76, 114, 133, 137. After Feb. 1933 the paper was no longer mentioned. A letter from Eberhard Gebensleben, Berlin 18 Jan. 1940 reveals that he often bought ' a Dutch newspaper ', 274.

27   Johnson, ' Two Ways to Remember'. See also the introduction to this book.

28   Michelle Perrot, 'Het familieleven', in Michelle Perrot, (ed.) *Geschiedenis van het persoonlijk leven, deel 4. Van de Franse Revolutie tot de Eerste Wereldoorlog* (Amsterdam: Agon, 1989), 163–167, at 163.

29   Elisabeth Gebensleben-von Alten, 6 Apr. 1933, quoted in Kalshoven-Brester, *Ik denk zoveel*, 162.

30   Irmgard Brester-Gebensleben, 7 Oct. 1933, quoted in Kalshoven-Brester, *Ik denk zoveel*, 179.

31   Lisa Pine, *Hitler's "National Community". Society and Culture in Nazi Germany* (London: Hodder Arnold, 2007) 209, referring to E. Schutz and E. Gruber, *Mythos Autobanen. Bau und Inzenierung der 'Strassen des Führers' 1933-1941* (Berlin: Ch. Links, 1996).

her family in Brunswick shorter, or at least faster to bridge. For their part, Mr. and Mrs. Gebensleben, after their praise of the New Order, repeatedly emphasized their affection for 'the Dutch', as Irmgard and her family were called.[32] The question is whether this expression of transnational affection would be enough to let them ignore the growing political-moral divide.

A German-Dutch Royal Family

Relatives in both countries tried to bridge the gap by ignoring their contrasting views of National Socialism and look for elements with which they could jointly identify. The alliance between the Dutch Crown Princess Juliana and the German Prince Bernhard von Lippe Biesterfeld in January 1937 contained almost all the ingredients needed for this. First of all, a German and a Dutchwoman had found each other; just as Irmgard and August and many other German-Dutch couples and their mutual families had come together, so had the royal couple. Once again, this marriage showed that 'love' could cross national borders. Moreover, since it was a connection between two royal houses, it was also a sign of German-Dutch rapprochement in a time of rising political tensions between the two nations.

Crown Princess Juliana symbolized the Dutch nation. And even though under National Socialism the German dynasties no longer counted, many people saw Prince Bernhard as a representative of the German nation. The hopeful expectations for a stable German-Dutch future evoked by the royal unification resounded in the words with which the Queen's Commissioner in the province of Groningen introduced the festivities in honour of the marriage: 'Could we see this wedding as a prelude to better times, as an indication of the arrival of that peace, tranquillity and prosperity that we so eagerly await in the harsh cold of international tension, of turmoil and poverty?'[33] Because of this royal alliance, the formal relationships between the two nation states were transposed into the human dimension of 'family' with its usual rituals of an engagement, a marriage and joy around the birth of the first baby and subsequent children.

---

32   See e.g. Elisabeth Gebensleben – von Alten, 12 May 1933 and Karl Gebensleben, 25 May 1933, quoted in Kalshoven-Brester, *Ik denk zoveel*, 168 en 172.

33   [J.B. Visser], *Officieel programma voor de festiviteiten ter gelegenheid van het huwelijk van Hare Koninklijke Hoogheid prinses Juliana en Zijne Doorluchtige Hoogheid Prins Bernhard op 7 januari 1937, gedurende de feestweek 4–9 januari 1937 te Groningen* (n.p., n.d. [Groningen, 1937]). (Official programme for the festivities on the occasion of the marriage of Her Royal Highness Princess Juliana and His Inventive Highness Prince Bernhard on 7 Jan. 1937).

FIGURE 1.6   August Brester and Irmgard Gebensleben on their
              wedding day, Utrecht 1929.

That transposition is well illustrated by responses from the relatives in Germany to the engagement. Elisabeth wrote on 10 September 1936: 'Now, if you had still been here when Eberhard and I heard about Princess Juliana's engagement with a German prince on the radio, we would certainly have opened a bottle! I was really overjoyed by the news, surely you, too, Immeken?'. A few months later, in January 1937, the relatives in Brunswick passionately shared the joy around the wedding festivities, and after the birth of 'the heir to the throne in the House of Orange' the family in Holland was congratulated. 'May a good star watch over the little princess, her family, and the whole country, including you!' wrote Aunt Bertha from Leipzig, while Irmgard's grandmother, in line with the Germanic ideal of beauty, gushed about the 'blue eyes' and 'blonde hair' of this new born 'fellow compatriot of your children'.[34] Memories of the heyday of the German Empire will have played a part in the minds of

----

34   Irmgard's cousin Bertha, 1 Feb. 1938 and grandmother Minna von Alten, 2 Feb. 1938, quoted in: Kalshoven-Brester, *Ik denk zoveel*, 238.

those who rejoiced in this regal union, besides the fairy-tale fantasies evoked by a royal wedding complete with sparkling jewels, decorated uniforms, soft satin robes and a real 'Golden Coach'.[35] Around this royal alliance, family and nation became intertwined into a shared site of identification for family members in the Netherlands and Germany.

Yet, not everyone in Germany was happy with Bernhard's marriage to the future Dutch head of state. Hitler and his Minister of Propaganda Joseph Goebbels in particular had major problems with the views of both Prince Bernhard and the Dutch government. In the journals of Joseph Goebbels, Bernhard is characterized as 'cowardly and characterless' because he distanced himself far too easily from his Germanness.[36] Initially, he had stated that he did not appreciate 'foreign national anthems' being played during the gala party two nights before the wedding, referring to the 'Germany song' (*Deutschland über alles*), which had meanwhile been extended with the first verse of the National Socialist 'Horst Wessel' song. Soon Bernhard and Queen Wilhelmina reconsidered this decision and the controversial anthem was indeed played, but followed by the English national anthem in honour of the British guests.[37] Nevertheless, in the eyes of the Nazi authorities the German prince had sided with the Dutch government, which from the outset had tried to shift the accent from Bernhard's German citizenship to his royal descent.

Also, in the official Memorial Book (*Gedenkboek*) on the occasion of the wedding the emphasis was on Bernhard's family ancestry, with an extensive genealogy that connected the two royal families.[38] It is noteworthy that in the case of Bernhard and Juliana's marital commitment there was a deviation from

---

35   'We have shared the experience of your wedding festivities as thoroughly as possible, especially the Golden Coach made a big impression on us', Minna von Alten-Rauch, 14 Jan. 1937, in: Kalshoven-Brester, *Ik denk zoveel*, 225.

36   Elke Fröhlich (ed.), *Tagebücher von Joseph Goebbels. Sämtliche Fragmente I, Aufzeichnungen 1923-1941* Iii. (Munich: De Gruyter, 2000), 309 (31 Dec. 1936) and 314 (3 Jan. 1937).

37   This reconsideration came about after the Nazi authorities threatened to forbid German wedding guests to leave the country. The addition of the English national anthem was a compromise on the part of the Dutch government. Albert van der Schoot, 'Waarom klonk het Horst Wessellied? Op de gala-avond van Juliana en Bernhard', *Historisch Nieuwsblad* 5/2019. For more information on Bernhard's controversial attitude regarding the Nazi regime, see Annejet van der Zijl, *Bernhard. Een verborgen geschiedenis*. (Amsterdam: Querido, 2010) and Gerard Aalders, *Prins Bernhard 1911-2014. Niets was wat het leek*. (Amsterdam: Boom, 2014).

38   W.G. de Bas, ed., *Gedenkboek Oranje-Nassau-Mecklenburg Lippe-Biesterfeld. Uitgegeven ter gelegenheid van het huwelijk van H.K.H. prinses Juliana met Z.D.H. prins Bernhard* (Amsterdam 1937), in particular the contributions of the historian J. Sturgeon and the legal scholar B.C. de Savornin-Lohman.

the gendered principles on which membership of a national community was based. The rule was that in the case of two different nationalities the woman had to take on her husband's nationality. For the marriage of the future head of state, an exception was made. Bernhard renounced his German citizenship in favour of the Dutch, although he remained a prince of German origin.[39] Historians, linguists, ethnographers, archaeologists, geologists, lawyers and other scientists had for decades already been studying the similarities between different 'Germanic tribes'. The assumption in much of this research was that the Dutch, Flemish and Germans, together with the Scandinavians, shared a 'Germanic' culture. Since the First World War these intellectual efforts had increasingly focused on strengthening the encompassing Germanicness (*das gesamtdeutschen Volkstum*) as well as the preservation of the unity of the German Empire (*die Wahrung der Reichseinheit*).[40] This endeavour seamlessly fitted the National Socialist goal of a Greater Germanic (Third) Reich.

Even though Bernhard distanced himself from his German citizenship, his marriage could still be viewed as a German-Dutch union in keeping with a genealogically demonstrable and long-standing tradition of Dutch-German entanglements. With such an approach the Nazi regime could have made use of the enthusiasm that this fairy-tale union of German and Dutch royalties managed to evoke among wider groups in German and Dutch society. It could have seized on Bernhard's marriage to emphasize the ties between the German and Dutch people. Instead, however, Goebbels and Hitler were guided by their aversion to German royal houses in general and their annoyance about the 'faithless' Bernhard in particular. That was reinforced when Bernhard, in line with his mother-in-law, the then Dutch head of state Queen Wilhelmina, publicly opted for the Allies at the time of the German invasion in May 1940. His attitude rendered him and the royal wedding useless as a symbol of German-Dutch 'unification' within a Germanic Empire. From that moment, the 'safe' story about German-Dutch commitments changed into a 'risky' story about conflicting nations.[41] In the selected letters between Irmgard and her family in Germany the royal couple is no longer mentioned after the invasion of the German troops.

---

39   Cees Fasseur, *Juliana & Bernhard. Het verhaal van een huwelijk. De jaren 1936-1956* (Amsterdam: Balance Sheet, 2008).

40   B. Dietz, H. Gabel and U. Tiedau (Hrs.), *Griff nach dem Westen. Die 'Westforschung' der völkisch-nationalen Wissenschaften zum nordwesteuropäischen Raum (1919-1960)* (Münster: Waxmann, 2003).

41   Johnson, 'Two Ways to Remember'.

Family and Nation Under Pressure

Judging from the letters, at both ends of the correspondence the longing for the mail to arrive remained undiminished. In addition, the postman also brought packages and photos. If the relatives could not be together at special occasions such as birthdays, Christmas, or other festivities where 'the family' manifested itself as a community, gifts were the substitutes: the tangible manifestations of bonding. The same symbolic role was played by pictures. Thanks to their photographic images, the absent loved ones could be included in family life: they were given a visible place on the dresser or on the sewing table, whether or not in the company of relatives who had died. Thus, the distance in time and space – not to mention values – was domesticated within the private domain of the family. 'The big family picture of your holiday in Scheveningen is in front of me as a last greeting from the summer. (...) My thoughts go to Holland so often and through your dear letters the connection remains alive', Eberhard wrote a few months after his comrades had invaded the Netherlands and the National Socialist authorities had taken over in his sister's new home country.[42]

The consistent pursuit of neutrality by the Dutch government before May 1940 certainly contributed to the image of the Dutch as like-minded people in the struggle for a better world – a world that in the eyes of the German Gebenslebens started with the Third Reich. On 1 September 1939, when the Netherlands mobilized after the German invasion of Poland, Irmgard's grandmother wrote that she hoped that 'those poor fishermen of yours' would not suffer much.[43] She apparently considered the bombing of Dutch fishing and merchant ships by German aircrafts a necessary evil for the 'big step forward' towards a joint Germanic future. Irmgard's brother Eberhard also showed himself concerned about the fate of the Dutch: 'you also had to mobilize yourselves and feel the needs and hardships of the war around you, and you may not immediately see why this must all happen'. After what he had experienced in Poland, he was convinced that the German annexation would bring 'progress'. 'Hopefully', he added in his letter, 'you will be able to keep your paradise in Holland. If you only knew how often I think of you, the children, the garden and Amersfoort!'[44] In the months that followed, the relatives in Germany refer

---

42   Eberhard Gebensleben, 5 Oct. 1940, quoted in: Kalshoven-Brester, *Ik denk zoveel*, 304.
43   Minna von Alten, 27 Sep. 1939, quoted in: Kalshoven-Brester, *Ik denk zoveel*, 262.
44   Eberhard Gebensleven, 2 Oct. 1939, quoted in Kalshoven-Brester, *Ik denk zoveel*, Ibidem, 263.

time and again to the tense situation in the Netherlands, the cause of this was always attributed to 'the English' — they were presented as the common enemy, ignoring the invasion of the neighbouring country by their own German troops.[45]

The image of the English as a common enemy was destroyed after the Nazi-German invasion on 10 May 1940 and the hasty flight of the Dutch government and the royal family to London two days later. The bewilderment and fear that the violent attack caused in the Netherlands also applied to the Brester family in Amersfoort. As soon as the invasion started, it was decided that Amersfoort and other municipalities on or near the *Grebbelinie*, one of the Dutch lines of defence, should evacuate their inhabitants. Thus, Irmgard and the children left for Haarlem, while her husband August stayed behind — as a doctor he had to be available at the hospital.[46] Not only did Irmgard fear that her brother would have to fight against 'us', but due to her German origin she also ran the risk of being identified as a potential enemy. During the five days of war in May, quite a few German migrants were interned in the Netherlands as the fear of a German Fifth Column took on hysterical forms.[47] 'On the way to Haarlem the car was often stopped, someone then leaned over to the window and asked us where we lived, which school we were in, we had to say "Scheveningen" and I noticed that my mother concealed her German origin', recalls Irmgard's eldest daughter, fifty years later remembering the tension during that journey. After the Dutch surrender on 14 May 1940, which followed the fatal bombing of the centre of Rotterdam, Irmgard and the children returned to their home in Amersfoort.[48] These war days ended without casualties close to Irmgard, August and the children, but the relationships in Dutch society and between the Netherlands and Germany had changed radically.

The invasion and occupation of the Netherlands put further pressure on relations within the German-Dutch kinship networks. There were indeed Germans and German-Dutch immigrants who identified themselves with Nazi Germany; others looked for ways to keep their National Socialist compatriots at bay. Either way, the new, tense situation meant that many of them had to deal with distrust from their Dutch environment and pressure from the German authorities to show themselves loyal to the Hitler regime. Refusing to receive German family or friends if they were part of the German occupation

---

45   Minna von Alten-Rauch (27 Nov. 1939) and Eberhard Gebensleben (29 Nov. 1939), quoted in Kalshoven-Brester, *Ik denk zoveel*, 270–271.

46   Kalshoven-Brester, *Ik denk zoveel*, 13.

47   L. de Jong, *De Duitse Vijfde Colonne* (Amsterdam: J.M. Meulenhoff, 1953).

48   Kalshoven-Brester, *Ik denk zoveel*, 283.

force in the Netherlands was one of the possible outcomes. Some used their German background and personal ties with Nazi Germany as a cover for resistance activities. Still others kept in touch with their relatives, trying to separate their affinity with the family from their political aversion to National Socialism.[49]

Judging from the correspondence and other information, Irmgard Brester-Gebensleben and her husband followed this last coping strategy, as did their relatives. Keeping up the transnational correspondence was crucial for this purpose, however ambiguous the messages. Thus, joy about the conquests of the Third Reich could go hand in hand with concerns about the fate of relatives in the bombed Netherlands. This is clearly expressed in a letter from Irmgard's German friend Hilde. After the German invasion she wrote with how much interest she had followed 'our advance' in the Netherlands. In the next sentence she immediately adds: 'Our museum in Rotterdam has remained intact, I hope?'[50] 'Our' therefore stands for both Hilde's identification with the German military force that bombed Rotterdam, and for her identification with the admired Dutch heritage attacked by that same military force. The hundreds of civilian casualties remained outside the edges of the writing paper, and whether Irmgard brought them back in when answering Hilde's letter cannot be verified. Still, whatever was or was not mentioned: the letter in itself shows Hilde's continued engagement with her friend Irmgard.

Because the Dutch royal family and the Dutch government quickly fled the Netherlands to settle temporarily in England, it became problematic for relatives in Germany to continue referring to 'the English' as a common enemy, although that still happened initially. In July 1940, Irmgard's grandmother wrote about her concern 'that the English do not leave you alone'.[51] In her anxiety she may have forgotten that the Netherlands was initially bombed and occupied by the German military. Her worries about the family of her granddaughter increased even more after she heard on the radio that English bombs had fallen on Amersfoort on the night of 23 to 24 July 1940.[52] She waited anxiously in Brunswick for the news that her relatives in the Netherlands had

---

49   Henkes, *Heimat in Holland*, 175–195 and 223–128.

50   Hilde Kammerer, 5 June 1940, quoted in: Kalshoven-Brester, Kalshoven-Brester, *Ik denk zoveel*, 287. Indeed, the museum came through unscathed while the collection was moved to safety before the bombing.

51   Minna von Alten-Rauch, 8 July 1940, quoted in Kalshoven-Brester, *Ik denk zoveel*, 293.

52   The allies wanted to destroy the railroad emplacement to hinder the German occupiers. A few bombs ended up in the adjoining Soesterkwartier, a residential area.

survived with only a fright.[53] Despite the Allied bombs that were to hit the Netherlands – deliberately or by mistake – during the war years, the emphasis on suffering from 'the English' on the German side of the correspondence soon shifted to concern about suffering from the more abstract 'war'. That was a point of reference which underlined the shared circumstances and destiny; there were indeed similarities in the suffering of civilians in both countries, the longer the war lasted. But there were fundamental differences, too – if only because the one expansive nation had occupied the other, and had installed a regime with aggressive policies against inhabitants who happened to be identified as Jews, Sinti or Roma, Jehovah witnesses, or mentally disabled, quite apart from the persecution of political opponents.[54] This ensured that most Dutch people experienced the brutality of war differently when it came to the involvement of the Allies against the National Socialist regime.

At the outbreak of war on 1 September 1939, Irmgard's brother Eberhard was quickly mobilised in the *Wehrmacht* and sent to Poland a few days after the invasion. At the end of October he was transferred back to Berlin, where he continued working intermittently as an assessor at the Ministry of Economic Affairs. In the May days of 1940 he was at the Western front on the German-French border, so that he did not have to fight against 'us' Dutchmen, as his sister Irmgard initially feared.[55] However, before long he was sent to the Netherlands to be part of the German-Nazi occupation force. In June 1940, Irmgard wrote in a letter to her grandmother how wonderful it was to see 'our Eberhard' again. It is no coincidence that in the same letter she mentions the 'correct behaviour' of the German military. According to her, most Dutch were 'surprised that the Germans were not the savage Barbarians they had expected them to be'.[56] The first anti-Jewish measures were yet to come, as well as the first public manifestations of resistance.[57] Her observations were in line with the cautious and moderate politics with which the German authorities in the early days tried to win over the population of the Netherlands to National

---

53   Minna von Alten-Rauch, 27 July 1940 and 6 Aug. 1940, and from Irmgard to her grandmother, 5 Aug. 1940, quoted in: Kalshoven-Brester, *Ik denk zoveel*, 295–296.

54   See e.g. Bill Niven, 'Introduction: German Victimhood at the Turn of the Millennium', in: Bill Niven (ed.), *Germans as Victims. Remembering the Past in Contemporary Germany* (New York: Palgrave/Macmillan, 2006) 1–25. See also the references to Tessa de Loo's book in Chap. 2.

55   Kalshoven-Brester, *Ik denk zoveel*, 279. Confirmed by the diary of Eberhard Gebensleben over the period 20 Nov. 1939-11 June 1940.

56   Irmgard Brester-Gebensleben, 13 June 1940, in: Kalshoven-Brester, *Ik denk zoveel*, 290.

57   J. Presser, *Ashes in the wind* (London: Souvenir Press, 2010); originally *Ondergang, deel I en II*. (Den Haag: Martinus Nijhoff, 1965).

Socialism. Most Dutch people, however, continued to view the occupying forces as hostile and National Socialism as reprehensible, despite their tendency to adapt to the New Order.[58]

This attitude was also taken by Eberhard's sister and brother-in-law. As a doctor, August Brester became involved in the resistance against the same occupation force of which Eberhard was part.[59] The mutual joy when Eberhard paid a visit to Amersfoort could not always prevent tempers from rising high. In December 1941 it came close to a breach when Irmgard and her husband made it clear that Eberhard had to get changed into civilian clothes if he wanted to accompany the family. The distrust that his appearance evoked in their immediate surroundings became too much for the Brester couple. After a 'fierce fight' and with pain in his deeply hurt, German national officer's heart, Eberhard finally gave in. From now on he was wearing August's suits when he visited.[60]

Their tough confrontations were sometimes mentioned in Eberhard's letters to August and Irmgard. In October 1941, for example, he wrote positively about the Dutch volunteers who had registered for the Eastern Front: 'I'm sure the two of you will have a little more to say about that, and something completely different'.[61] During his leave in Berlin in January 1942, he wrote: '[T]o avoid having to argue in vain with my dear brother-in-law every two years, I am going to the university library to research the question of how long the Netherlands belonged to the [Holy Roman] Empire'. Irmgard's brother was inspired by the history of the Roman Empire to support the Greater Germanic endeavour.[62] Eberhard came to

58   J.C.H. Blom, 'Nederland onder Duitse bezetting', in: J.C.H. Blom, ed., *Crisis, bezetting en herstel.* (Den Haag: Nijgh & Van Ditmar, 1989) 56–101, at 61 and 68; See also E.H. Kossmann, `De Tweede Wereldoorlog', in: *Winkler Prins Geschiedenis van de Lage Landen. Deel 3: Deel 3: De Lage Landen van 1780 tot 1970.* (Amsterdam/Brussels 1977) 268–286, at 273.

59   For more information about the Dutch doctors' resistance, see Ph. De Vries, *Geschiedenis van het verzet der artsen in Nederland* (Haarlem: Tjeenk Willink,1949); Joost Visser (red.), *Witte jassen en bruinhemden: Nederlandse artsen in de Tweede Wereldoorlog* (Breda: Reality Bites Publishing 2010); https://anderetijden.nl/aflevering/278/Artsen-in-de-oorlog, visited 20 Feb. 2019.

60   Kalshoven-Brester, *Ik denk zoveel,* 324 (including n. 1).

61   Kalshoven-Brester, *Ik denk zoveel,* 321. Some 22,000 Dutch volunteers fought with the *Waffen SS* for Nazi Germany on the Eastern Front against the Soviet Union. For more information about these Dutch volunteers: Geraldien von Frijtag Drabbe Kunzel, *Hitler's Brudervolk – The Dutch and the Colonization of Occupied Eastern Europe, 1939-1945* (New York: Routledge, 2017).

62   As mentioned in the Introduction to this book, his endeavour also shows how tales from different periods and different experiences can touch and lend each other meaning. Although there are no specific references in his letters or diaries, Eberhard might have been inspired by Arthur Moeller van den Bruck's book *Das Dritte Reich* (1923). It describes three

FIGURE 1.7   Eberhard Gebensleben in uniform, visiting his sister Irmgard
              and her family in Amersfoort, June 1940.

the conclusion that from the seventeenth century onwards, 'both sides were
clearly and naturally aware that the Netherlands belonged to the German
Empire'.[63] At the end of his essay he referred to the well-known writer and nationalist Ernst Moritz Arndt, who had emphasized in 1831 that 're-incorporation
of the old Reich countries' should not be enforced, but that a 'rejuvenated and
re-created' Germany had to become so attractive that these countries were keen
to join. With his research and the conclusion that emerged, Eberhard was in line
with the National Socialist pursuit of a Greater Germanic Reich, although his
views on the strategy to achieve this (to urge rather than coerce) differed from
those of the hardliners within the Nazi ranks.[64]

German eras: the first started when the Holy Roman Empire came into existence in 962
and ended in 1806 when the Empire fell apart. The Second Reich started in 1871, when the
German states were united under Prussia, and collapsed with the defeat in the First World
War in 1918; the Third Reich would arise when the Weimar Republic collapsed. This pre-
diction seemed to come true when the Nazis took over power in 1933.

63   Eberhart Gebensleven, 25 Jan. 1942, quoted in Kalshoven-Brester, *Ik denk zoveel*, 325–326.
64   Eberhart Gebensleben, 26 May 1942, quoted in Kalshoven-Brester, *Ik denk zoveel*, Ibidem,
      332–333, including note 1. Eberhard writes that his study was judged favourably by a

Regardless of how his conclusion was judged, such a letter makes clear how much effort Eberhard put into continuing a dialogue with his sister and brother-in-law, and to maintain contact with them and their children. He also did this by regularly expressing how much he loved not only his Dutch relatives, but also 'their' Netherlands.[65] And he did more: when in July 1943 he learned that his brother-in-law August had been arrested for his participation in a doctors' strike, Eberhard took immediate action. He contacted the staff sergeant of the local *Kommandantur* and the next day took the train to Amersfoort, although he feared that 'it would be difficult to get August out because he acts on principle'. On arrival Eberhard was surprised to find August himself answering the door. His brother-in-law had gone into hiding after he had been warned about his impending arrest. Five days later the conflict had been settled and August and his colleagues were allowed out in the open again. 'For me, a great joy but at the same time disappointed since my ideas and efforts were all unnecessary'.[66]

Eberhard's political pursuit of a Greater Germanic Reich that also encompassed the Netherlands was not hampered by his personal involvement with his sister and her family. On the contrary, an integration of the 'Dutch' part of his family within this Germanic Empire could bring them even closer together. The letters from German relatives show how far their identification with the Third Reich and the German nation reached across the Dutch border through the idea that the Netherlands and the Dutch ('our' Dutch) were to be included within a shared Germanicness. For them, the tension between nation and family was resolved by making the family subordinate to a further nation-building project, whereas the letters from the Dutch side show the exact opposite. Irmgard's identification with Germanness was undermined by this expansionism under a 'Germanic' flag, which made a combination with her Dutchness impossible. Under these circumstances her letters were mainly focused on kinkeeping: a desperate attempt to domesticate the profound political-moral differences between herself and her relatives in Germany by fully concentrating on the affective ties that connected them.

---

professor in Berlin, but that it was not published, 'because the conclusion might be offensive elsewhere'. For more information on these different approaches of the Greater German Reich, which split the SS see: Barbara Henkes and Björn Rzoska, 'Volkskunde und' Volkstumpolitik 'der SS in den Niederlanden. H.E. Schneider und seine "Grossgermanischen" Ambitions für den Niederländischen Raum' in: Dietz *et al.*, *Griff nach dem Westen*, 291–323.

65   'Near me is a young pastor who loves Holland as much as I do', Eberhard Gebensleben, 27 Nov. 1942, quoted in: Kalshoven-Brester, *Ik denk zoveel*, 338.

66   Eberhard's diary, 27–29 July and 1 Aug. 1943, quoted in: Kalshoven, *Between two Homelands*, 199.

FIGURE 1.8   Karel and Hedda Brester with their uncle Eberhard Gebensleben
             (not in uniform), Amersfoort June 1943.

Gnadengesuch (Request for Exemption)

Eberhard's commitment to National Socialism not only clashed with the attitude of his sister and her husband in the Netherlands, but his identification
with the Nazi's also came into conflict with his love for a German woman, as
appears from the German-Dutch correspondence and his diaries. It touched at
the issue that had been decisive for Irmgard's aversion to National Socialism:
the antisemitic exclusion policy of the Nazi regime that later turned into
prosecution and murder. In a letter of 25 December 1939 to his sister, Eberhard
first mentioned Herta Euling, a young pianist from Berlin. Eight months later,
Irmgard received a distressed letter from her grandmother. Her brother's new
love had a Jewish grandmother. In the antisemitic jargon of the National Socialists that made 'Fräulein Euling' a *Mischling 2. Grades*; a Jewish 'mixed-
blooded' in the second degree. 'Ohmchen, if that 25% had not been there

[by which he meant the one 'non-Aryan' grandmother], I would marry her immediately', Eberhard had told his own, non-Jewish grandmother.[67]

More than four years after the introduction of the Nuremberg Laws, in particular the 'Law for the Protection of German Blood and German Honour',[68] grandmother Minna knew only too well that there was no blessing on such a relationship in the Third Reich. As Herta Euling had only one Jewish grandparent – who had provided her with only 'a small proportion of Jewish blood', which, according to the Nazi authorities, would fade over generations – she was exempt from many degrading measures such as wearing a yellow star.[69] With the necessary permission, she might even marry a *'Deutschblütigen'* (German-blooded) husband. In practice, however, permission was rarely granted, and certainly not when a government official or a member of the *Wehrmacht* was involved.[70]

Everyone knew that this marriage would do Eberhard's career in Nazi Germany no good, and that the rules could be changed at any time, which made Herta's position and their life together in Nazi Germany uncertain. Minna von Alten-Rausch added that, according to her grandson, his girlfriend had indicated that she could not bear it if Eberhard was in some way hampered by a marriage with her; a statement that made her no less attractive. In the continuation of her letter, his grandmother realized that, one way or another, this situation entailed 'a lot of disappointments' for Eberhard. After listing the obstacles that would result from his marriage to Herta – 'he would have to break off his career, he could no longer be a civil servant, he would have to leave the Party, and what not!' – she asked what Irmgard and her husband August thought about it.[71]

How did Irmgard in the Netherlands deal with this devilish dilemma? Her brother's happiness in life was paramount. Her consideration that the antisemitic measures in Nazi Germany were an established fact, formed the basis

---

67   Minna von Alten-Rausch, 29 Aug.1940, quoted in Kalshoven-Brester, *Ik denk zoveel,* 299.

68   The Nuremberg Laws were antisemitic racial laws enacted by the *Reichstag* on 15 Sep. 1935, forbidding marriages and extramarital intercourse between Jews and non-Jews and the employment of non-Jewish females under the age of 45 in Jewish households. See also Chap. 2 and 3.

69   Beate Meyer, *"Jewish Mischlinge". Rassenpolitik und Verfolgungserfahrung ("Jewish hybrids" Race politics and persecution experience 1933-1945).* (2nd Edition. Hamburg: Dölling and Galitz Verlag, 2002) 30.

70   Meyer, *"Jewish Mischlinge"*, 166–169; 178–179. For *Deutschblutigen* applicants in the *Wehrmacht,* front transfer or demotion threatened, as we will see later.

71   Irmgard Brester-Gebensleben, 29 aug.1940, quoted in: Kalshoven-Brester, *Ik denk zoveel,* 299.

for her reflections on Eberhard's position and the dilemma with which he was faced. She had discussed the problem with August at length. In her final response, Irmgard emphasized how 'dangerous' it was for her brother to give up his 'future and career' for a woman. In his later life, the chances were high that this resulted in reproaches that would not do the marriage any good. The ideas of the Brester-Gebensleben couple about marriage and the responsabilities of man and wife that come with it were in alignment with the then-prevailing perception of the proper gender positions. Both Irmgard and her husband assumed that the future of her brother, as a man, primarily lay with his career and that he could expect his wife to support him in this. They did not consider how leaving Herta to the mercy of antisemitic sentiments in Nazi society might also do real harm to Eberhard's future and sense of self.[72] Given the antisemitic reality in Hitler's Germany, Irmgard and August came to the 'sad conclusion' that Eberhard should not enter into such a commitment. It was up to her grandmother whether or not to give Eberhard their 'honest opinion'.[73]

Despite their aversion to an antisemitic exclusion policy, Irmgard and her husband confirmed the distinction between Jewish and non-Jewish: because of the small grain of Jewishness attributed to her, Eberhard had better keep Herta at a distance. A few days later, grandmother Minna wrote that she had pointed out 'all the dangers' to her grandson. Above all, she hoped that he would uphold 'our Germanness' (*Deutschtum*) and not disgrace 'our ancestors'. To what extent she was referring to a violation of 'racial purity' in the family or to the risk of a missed career for her grandson is not clear; in any case, her concern for Eberhard's future was predominant. The correspondence shows that his personal dilemma did not lead to a political reorientation. On the contrary, Eberhard retained his belief in the Greater Germanic ideal, judging by his voluntary commitment to the army and his studies to show that the Netherlands ought to be part of the Third Reich. Nevertheless, he and Herta Euling stayed together and, without marriage, she took on the role of partner or 'fiancée', as she was called by a *Wehrmacht* officer after Eberhard's death in September 1944 at the Belgium front.[74]

---

72   Even if the exclusion of *Jewich Mischlingen* from Nazi German society was not legally substantiated, they were nevertheless confronted with exclusion by their immediate environment. See for instance Meyer, *"Jewish Mischlinge"*, 266–275.

73   Irmgard Brester-Gebensleben, 5 Sep. 1940, quoted in: Kalshoven-Brester, *Ik denk zoveel*, 300.

74   Herta Euling, 10 Oct. 1944 to Irmgard with an undated transcript of an officer from Eberhard's battery, and a letter from a *Wehrmachtsfuersorgeoffizier*, 12 Oct. 1944 to Irmgard requesting her to contact Frl. Herta Euling for arranging the inheritance, quoted in: Kalshoven-Brester, *Ik denk zoveel*, 359–360.

It is precarious to draw conclusions about what options were and were not considered based on an exchange of letters, certainly in times of enhanced censorship. The same goes for wartime diaries, such as Eberhard's diary entries over the period November 1939-November 1943, which came into the possession of Hedda Kalshoven-Brester after the publication of the German edition of *Ik denk zoveel aan jullie*.[75] They need special attention to significant silences. Reflection afterwards can provide insight into themes that were avoided. For example when Eberhard's niece Hedda realised that her uncle, 'while we loved him', is nowhere mentioned in the diaries that she kept as a teenager in the war years, and neither was the Jewish boy who went into hiding in their household. Her diaries were mainly filled 'with stories about school, and about all the crushes I went through (and which were never answered ...)'.[76] The sometimes extreme events she witnessed or heard about did not fit in with the design of her diary. In another way, a Jewish contemporary explained the slight attention to antisemitism in her journals from the time of the occupation: 'You wanted to continue your pleasant life, but it was often not pleasant. I notice that when I read my diary: that I tried to write down the good things and neglect the negative things'.[77] Such comments show the simultaneous seeing and looking away, knowing and denying, which make drawing conclusions about what people did and did not know based on egodocuments such a delicate matter.[78]

In his diaries, Eberhard was careful not to show the whole story. This applies both to his brief indications of the sometimes difficult conversations with Herta,[79] and to the few words with which he sometimes referred to alarming situations after the first euphoria of the 'brilliant military success' in the spring

---

75   A German collector of journals found two diaries of Eberhard Gebensleben over the period Nov. 20. 1939-11 June 1940, and from 10 Mar. 1942-6 Nov. 1943. Unfortunately, diary entries for the period 11 June 1940-10 Mar. 1942 are missing.

76   Hedda Kalshoven-Brester, e-mail 14 mar. 2014 to Barbara Henkes.

77   Fragment from an interview with Edith Velmans-van Hessen in the documentary series *De Oorlog* (the War), part 2 (http://deoorlog.nps.nl edited by Joris Smeets). See also Edith Velmans-van Hessen, *Edith's story* (New York: Soho Press, 1999) and Barbara Henkes, 'De Bezetting revisited. Hoe van De Oorlog een "normale" geschiedenis werd gemaakt die eindigt in vrede' (The occupation revisited. How the Second World War was turned into a 'normal' history that ends in peace), BMGN 125 (2010) 1:73–99.

78   The controversial approach of diaries in the publication by the historian Bart van der Boom, *Wij weten niets van hun lot. Gewone Nederlanders en de Holocaust* (Amsterdam: Boom, 2012) gave rise to a sharp and insightful debate. See e.g. Ensel and Gans, 'The Dutch Bystander'.

79   Notes from Eberhart's diary, 1 Jan. 1940 about Herta's 'errors and confusion'; 20 Jan. 1940 about a 'lovely evening despite the dissonance of a national socialist discussion' and 'a complicated altercation' with Herta.

of 1940.[80] Antisemitic operations were never mentioned as such, except for the moment when Eberhard – on his way to the Eastern Front in September 1942 – wrote in his diary about the killing of 35–40,000 Jews from Kiev a year before: 'That will be avenged, dear poor Germany'.[81] Even then, he put the Greater Germanic Reich first, although he distanced himself from this antisemitic mass murder. If we compare these notes with the letter he wrote to Irmgard about his visit to Kiev, the mass killing is conspicuous by its absence. Instead, he praised the 'beautiful city', which he perceived 'behind the broken and neglected facades'.[82] Fear and embarrassment have often been found to lay at the heart of what can be called a 'conspiracy of silence', which develops around 'highly conspicuous matters we deliberately try to avoid'.[83] To him, the realisation of the Third Reich as the justified recovery of the former German Empire was key. The tragic 'mistakes' that accompanied the struggle for this aim could still be legitimised as 'collateral damage' by individual mistakes, instead of realising that it was inherent in the Nazi policies.

Eberhard's loyalty to Nazi Germany came first, even before his private love life. As long as he and Herta abandoned their wedding plans, their relationship seemed not to hinder his career in the National Socialist state apparatus. In May 1941 he was promoted to *Regierungsrat*, first-class official at the Ministry of Economic Affairs. Because of 'personal circumstances', the joy of his promotion was 'not entirely happy', he wrote Irmgard in covert terms.[84] After announcing in December 1942 that Herta was pregnant, Eberhard wrote in April 1943 that she had given birth to a stillborn, 'pretty powerful girl of seven and a half pounds'. 'We are so infinitely sad … You don't know how we were looking forward to this baby, just looking forward to it. However, we will also come to terms with this loss'.[85] An official letter shows that Eberhard had submitted a request for exemption ('*Gnadengesuch*') a few months earlier to obtain permission for a marriage with Herta Euling, while retaining his membership of the

---

80   Notes from Eberhart's diary, 8–10 Apr. 1940 in Altenkessel (Saarland). See also 15 Mar. 1940 where Eberhard expresses his satisfaction that he was on reconnaissance as 'one of the vanguards of the whole German front'.

81   Notes from Eberhart's diary of 27 Sep. 1942. For more information about these atrocities at the ravine of Babi Yar: Ray Brandon and Wendy Lower, *The Shoah in Ukraine: history, testimony, memorialization*. (Indiana: Indiana University Press, 2008).

82   Eberhard Gebensleben, 11 Oct. 1942, quoted in Kalshoven-Brester, *Ik denk zoveel,* 336.

83   Zerubavel, *The Elephant in the Room,* 6 and 9.

84   Eberhard Gebensleben, 28 May 1941, quoted in: Kalshoven-Brester, *Ik denk zoveel,* 317. Unfortunately, his diary for this period is missing.

85   Eberhard Gebensleben, 9 Apr. 1943 from Berlin, quoted in: Kalshoven-Brester, *Ik denk zoveel,* 343. Similar phrases can be found in Eberhard's diary entry of 7 Apr. 1943.

FIGURE 1.9   Herta Euling and Eberhard Gebensleben in Berlin, 8 June 1943.

National Socialist Party (NSDAP).[86] That request, on top of his private commentary on the massacre of the Jews in Kiev, indicates that he had his eyes wide shut to the murderous antisemitic operations of the Nazi regime. At the same time, he both noticed and refrained from noticing the consequences of what he himself heard, saw and experienced. Such an attitude was necessary for him to be able to continue supporting the fight for restoration and strengthening of a Germanic community within a Third Reich, despite everything that spoke against it.

---

86   Eberhard, who was hit by a 'nervous breakdown', noted in his diary from Lithuania on Dec. 26, 1942 that he 'successfully (fights) to submit the marriage application to the adjutant'.

His request for exemption was denied: the responsible district leader (*Gau-leiter*) as well as 'the highest court of the NSDAP' were opposed to it, 'considering the strong Jewish impact in the blood of Herta Euling', according to a letter of 7 August 1943. It was added that a Party member who submitted such a request to the Party leadership was 'not worthy to remain a member any longer'.[87] The question is whether and when Eberhard actually received the announcement of his expulsion from the Party. In his diary of 25 October 1943, he indignantly noted that 'the marriage request has been left unanswered somewhere in the department for 4 months!' Apparently, in July 1943, a few months after the death of their child, he had once again made a request for permission to marry Herta Euling. In February 1944, another negative response to his second request was sent.[88] It is likely that his repeated request and the subsequent rejections, together with the announced expulsion from the Party, affected Eberhard's position in the army.[89] By this time *Oberleutnant* Gebensleben had been ordered (*abkommandiert*) to the Western front, where he perished on the Belgian coast in September 1944. Since he had bequeathed his legacy to Herta Euling, she and her parents moved into the Gebensleben's family house in Brunswick after the war.[90]

However, no sense of kinship between his unofficial widow Herta and his sister Irmgard, both suffering from the loss of Eberhard, developed after the war. The two women did not like each other, despite their shared love for the deceased Eberhard and their common passion for music. While Herta had been a pianist before the war and gave music lessons to pupils during wartime, Irmgard had developed into a semi-professional singer.[91] In a letter to her

---

87   Dr. Volkman to the Kanzlei des Führers der NSDAP, Hauptamt für Gnadensachen, quoted in: Kalshoven-Brester, *Ik denk zoveel*, 348–349. Retrieved from the former Berlin Document Centre in Berlin, now part of the *Bundesarchiv*. This had been a general directive, further reinforced from 1942 onwards when the position of so-called *Mischlinge* was deteriorating.

88   Repeated rejection of the *Gnadengesuch* in a letter of 25 Feb. 1944 from the head of the *Kanzlei des Führers* to *Herr Regierungsrat* Gebensleben, quoted in Kalshoven-Brester, *Ik denk zoveel*, 355.

89   Meyer, *"Jewish Mischlinge"*, 178–179.

90   Kalshoven-Brester, *Ik denk zoveel*, 400, n.3. After the German translation was published, Hedda Kalshoven-Brester came into contact with a niece of Herta Euling, who provided additional information about the postwar life of her Aunt Herta.

91   Brester-Gebensleben managed to perform a few times at public concerts, despite her refusal to become a member of the so-called *Kultuurkamer* (Cultural Chamber), which was part of the Nazification of Dutch society. Artists, writers, journalists, musicians, film actors and stage artists had to be affiliated, and thereby declared non-Jewish, to be allowed to work.

husband during a postwar visit to Brunswick, Irmgard wrote about Herta's 'difficult character' expressed in 'distrust and suspicion'.[92] National Socialism, and her disqualification as a Jewish *Mischling 2. Grades* during that regime, will not have increased Herta's confidence in the people around her. In addition, Irmgard was one of the first to have advised against a possible marriage between Herta and her brother. For her part, it appears that Irmgard had little compassion for Herta, who had inevitably been shaped by the dramatic experiences of vulnerability and secrecy during the Nazi period, apart from the loss of her loved one and their child. Like so many people after the war, in both Germany and the Netherlands, Irmgard was mainly focused on reconnecting with her *Heimat*, and leaving the war and the related antisemitism behind as quickly as possible. In a way Herta's presence was an obstacle to such a 'normalization' of the past.[93]

Irmgard had few problems in resuming contact with family members and acquaintances who had supported the Nazi regime. As soon as the postal services with Germany were restored in the spring of 1946, *Heimat* for Irmgard came back to life in correspondences with relatives (two cousins), her parents' former housekeeper, and some of her old school friends. At first, she was hurt by the demands for tea and coffee that showed ignorance about the repression and the shortages the Nazi occupation had caused in the Netherlands. According to Irmgard, too many Germans saw themselves as victims of the sheer misery caused by a regime they themselves had welcomed and supported.[94] This feeling of alienation soon made way for the necessity of restoring and renewing kinship networks after the profound political-ideological and moral crisis. After the death and destruction that the war had caused to them all, they sought consolation and support from each other through letters. When Irmgard finally managed to visit Brunswick in 1949, she was deeply moved by the warm welcome: 'A wonderful feeling, so much love and friendship yet to be found here. That compensates for a lot'.[95]

---

92   Unpublished excerpt from a letter of 21 Sep. 1949 from Irmgard to her husband August during her first postwar stay in BRUNSWICK in Sep. 1949. See also Kalshoven-Brester, *Ik denk zoveel*, 401–403.

93   See e.g. Evelien Gans, 'The Jew as dubious victim', in Remco Ensel and Evelien Gans (eds.), *The Holocaust, Israel and 'the Jew'. Histories of Antisemitism in Postwar Dutch Society* (Amsterdam: Amsterdam University Press, 2017) 62–81, at 72.

94   Fritsche, 'Preface', xix. See also Chap. 2.

95   Irmgard Brester-Gebensleben, 21 Sep. 1949 to August Brester, quoted in: Kalshoven-Brester, Kalshoven-Brester, *Ik denk zoveel*, 401.

Race as the Elephant in the Room

The phrase 'Safe and risky stories in a German-Dutch family context' in the title of this chapter refers to the way in which the Gebenslebens tried to secure their own position in relation to that of others in the kinship network. In their correspondence and contacts, family members were primarily concerned with perpetuating their mutual bond through 'safe' stories. At the same time, those safe stories threatened to become risky, certainly under the pressure of National Socialism. These dynamics can be found in the various narrative strategies used in the letters. One was to emphasize their reciprocal connections: references to a holiday with the grandchildren, or a joint outing to the colourful tulip fields, helped to put aside the divide around racist exclusion policy in the country of origin. But when the famine during the last year of the war was combatted by eating sugar beet and tulip bulbs, those same tulip fields would take on a different meaning and lose their innocence. Another narrative strategy for confirming their mutual bond was to present the rapprochement between representatives of both countries as proof of German-Dutch interdependence. The marriage between the German Prince Bernhard and the Dutch Crown Princess Juliana lent itself well to this purpose, although the fairy tale story was cruelly disrupted by the outbreak of a war between the two countries. Then we see how a 'safe' story turned into a 'risky' story because of the critical attitude of Dutch royalty towards Nazi Germany. The royals were no longer fit to represent both countries' common grounds and disappeared from the correspondence.

Yet another strategy for negotiating tensions within the family about Nazi German politics was to postulate the common origins of both nations. For example, Eberhard Gebensleben referred to the Holy Roman Empire of Germanic peoples to convince his relatives in the Netherlands of the desirability and legitimacy of the National Socialist endeavour to fuse the two nations within a Greater Germanic Empire. He was not heard, because in practice this endeavour meant that the Netherlands was annexed and subordinated to the 'loving' or greedy hold of the expansionist German. Reich Nevertheless, Eberhard's research into the common roots of both countries in the Holy Roman Empire was an attempt to turn a risky story about annexation into a safe story about the restoration of a historic unity that could benefit the Dutch as well. That he in so doing ignored the violent policy of excluding all who were defined as non-Germanic – including the woman he loved – shows how strong his desire was for safe stories, with which both the pursuit of a strong nation and a close family network could be expressed.

The publication of the correspondence and other egodocuments from the legacy of the German-Dutch Brester-Gebensleben family, as well as the memories of Hedda Kalshoven-Brester, offer multiple perspectives on the experiences of a dramatic episode from twentieth-century history. Moreover, they shed a clear light on 'doing' or 'constructing' and maintaining family as a community that is never independent of national and political identifications. But there is more to say about the publication of the selected documents in *Ik denk zoveel aan jullie*. Nearly half a century after the end of the war, Hedda Kalshoven-Brester joined the line of kinkeepers. By delving into the old correspondence, by transcribing it from Gothic to Latin script, followed by a careful selection and explanation, she made the correspondence accessible. Thus, she showed the entanglement of the histories of her National Socialist parents in Germany with those of her anti-National Socialist parents in the Netherlands.

Since the 1970s, and more specifically with the inaugural lecture at the University of Amsterdam of historian Hans Blom in 1983, an impetus was given to get away from 'the spell of right and wrong' in the Dutch historiography about the Second World War.[96] Hedda Kalshoven-Brester took this call one step further by presenting the contacts, dialogues, confrontations, contradictions and guidelines running across the political and national border between the Netherlands and Germany. By publishing the long-term exchanges of divergent views and practices in her book, Kalshoven-Brester shows which different positions were taken by relatives in the Netherlands and Germany, and which multiple responsibilities were weighed against each other in an transnational context. This created room for an ambivalent narrative about the negotiations within the Gebensleben family and with their beloved ones to maintain their emotional bonds despite their acceptance and rejection of the violence inherent in the racist policies implemented by National Socialism.

This long-term exchange of letters made it possible to follow how the Gebensleben relatives managed to keep their mutual bonds intact. After Irmgard's open criticism of antisemitic measures in 1933 and the painful deliberations surrounding her brother Eberhard's fiancé, it seems that the theme of 'race' – in the sense of Germanic, Slavic or Jewish – became the 'elephant in the room' in the correspondence: the number one theme that was carefully avoided over

---

96   J.C.H. Blom, 'In de ban van goed en fout? Wetenschappelijke geschiedschrijving over de bezettingstijd in Nederland', in: Blom, *Crisis, bezetting en herstel*, 102–120. The indications of the attitudes during the occupation in oppositional terms of *goed* and *fout* is translated as either 'right' or 'wrong', or 'good' and 'bad'. I will use both options, depending on the context.

and over again, not only because of censorship and illegality, but certainly also because of the irrevocable alienation that this political-moral theme could cause. Race became an all-determining category under National Socialism, also in the lives of individuals and families who were defined as Aryan or Germanic. This was true both for Eberhard, who as a Nazi remained loyal to his 'mixed Jewish' lover, and for his sister and brother-in-law who got involved in the doctors' resistance and offered a hiding place to a prosecuted Jewish child. In order to gain some insight into the meaning of race as an element in mutual contact, it was necessary to read between the lines with a sharp eye for what is *not* written down on paper. The unexpectedly surfaced diaries of Eberhard Gebensleben offer compelling material that can be compared with his letters. They help to understand the complex and highly contradictory negotiations around Nazi politics in this transnational family, and their rather heroic efforts to stay together.

Whereas in this chapter the emphasis was on doing *family* in relation to national identifications and political positions, in the following chapter the emphasis shifts to doing – and, indeed, undoing – *nation*. The focus there will be on negotiations around multiple national identifications, that define how the actors see themselves in relation to others, and to politics of inclusion and exclusion.

"If War Comes, I will be Tossed to and Fro"

Literature as a Home for an Immigrant from Germany

She sits in front of her bookcase filled with the works of Franz Kafka, Max Brod, Joseph Roth, Ernest Hemingway and others of the most politically engaged writers of modern world literature.[1] During our conversations Mrs. Ton-Seyler will regularly refer to these and other well-known authors, as she does in her letters and autobiographical writings. When I ask her who has had an important influence in her life, her reaction is: 'Living people? You must not forget the literature!'[2] In one of her letters she comes back to this: 'I have always been guided by books, they are a part of my life, I find so much in those books that was already there, but that I could only recognize after reading about it. For example, the books of Arnold Zweig, such as *Junge Frau von 1914* (Young Woman of 1914), *Erziehung vor Verdun* (Education before Verdun), and *Einsetzung eines Königs* (Crowning of a King). They belong to a cycle called *Der grosse Krieg der weissen Männer* (The Great War of the White Men). Those books and others have made me so anti-war'.[3]

Mrs. Ton-Seyler, Rie or Tonnetje for intimates, has from early on always been a true bookworm (*'Leseratte'*), as she calls it. The way she talks and writes about her life is steeped in references to famous German, English and Dutch books, as if the writers and their main characters are her close family or intimate friends. The self-evident way in which she includes authors' names and book titles in her stories shows her literacy. In addition, she allows the Dutch language to flourish in an expressive way, with an inflection that unmistakeably reflects a German background. In her choice of words, too, the German language is part of her narrative, especially when she draws on her childhood memories. At those moments her Dutch is peppered with German words and expressions. She herself likes to write: letters in response to statements or

---

1 This chapter is a re-working of my contribution 'Rie Ton-Seyler: een Duitse in Nederland, een Nederlandse in Duitsland', in: Wim Willems, mmv. Annemarie Cottaar, Barbara Henkes en Chris Keulemans, *De kunst van het overleven. Levensverhalen uit de twintigste eeuw*. Den Haag (SDU) 2004: 30–55.

2 Conversation of Barbara Henkes and Mrs. Ton-Seyler (hereafter: Conversation Henkes and Ton), 19 July 1987.

3 Letter Ton-Seyler of 28 Sep. 1987. Arnold Zweig's *Der grosse Krieg der weissen Männer* consists of books: *Der Streit um den Sergeanten Grischa* (1927), *Junge Frau von 1914* (1931), *Erziehung vor Verdun* (1935), *Einsetzung eines Königs* (1937), *Die Feuerpause* (1954) and *Die Zeit ist reif* (1957).

© BARBARA HENKES, 2020 | DOI:10.1163/9789004401600_004

FIGURE 2.1
Rie Ton-Seyler in front of her bookcase,
Heemstede, c. 1948.

announcements in the media,[4] as well as letters intended to maintain and
deepen existing contacts in the pre-internet age. Diaries form another genre
that she used to document her experiences for herself; these were later taken
up for autobiographical writings about three episodes in her life: *Volkach*,
about her childhood between 1917 and 1923 (in German from c. 1985); *De Oorlogsjaren* (The War Years *1940-'45*) from 1987, and a report of her first visit to
devastated postwar Germany in 1946, entitled *Kom vanavond met verhalen*
(Come with Stories Tonight) from 1975, both in Dutch.[5] Our dialogues always
produced new questions, followed by new memories with accompanying emotions and reflections.[6]

---

4 That is how she contacted me after seeing an announcement of my historical PhD research
   into the arrival and settlement of German maids in the Netherlands. Henkes, *Heimat in Holland*, 20–21.
5 Copies of Ton-Seyler's autobiographical writings are in my possession. Her diaries and the
   many letters she exchanged with family and acquaintances in the Netherlands, Germany and
   abroad are not accessible.
6 Our first meeting took place on 20 Sep. 1986. In this chapter are incorporated recordings and
   transcripts of our conversations then and on 19 July 1987, and notes on our meetings and
   telephone conversations, as well as the correspondence between us until her death in 1998.

Marie Seyler came from Germany to the Netherlands in 1933. Unlike Irmgard Gebensleben's arrival, hers was not a consequence of the First World War, nor of the Hitler regime that came to power that same year. Nor was it love that drew her to the Netherlands, although a reckless flirtation with the son of her German employers contributed to her departure. Marie Seyler had best be characterized as a labour migrant: like many tens of thousands of unmarried German women, she travelled to the Netherlands during the interwar period to earn money as a maidservant and to broaden her horizons.[7] The way back to Germany remained open, although that route was no longer obvious after she married a Dutchman in 1937. Like many Germans who had settled in the Netherlands, with the rise of National Socialism Rie Ton-Seyler found she needed to reconsider her connection with both the country of origin and the recipient country. In this way political engagement became embedded in her personal life and would never let her go. We can follow how that process took shape and what consequences it had for her identification with German and Dutch society, as well as with her relatives in both countries, thanks to her autobiographical writings and her oral memory work.

Longing for the 'Good' Germany

In 1912, Rie Ton was born as Marie Klara Seyler in Achern, a village near Strasbourg in the then German part of Alsace. Only a year later her father died. When her mother remarried, Mariechen was lodged from the age of five to eleven with 'Uncle' Josef and 'Aunt' Aurelia, a childless middle-aged couple who ran a hotel in the southern German town of Volkach.[8] Sun, play and festivities dominate her memoirs of her early childhood in 'the small Franconian wine city (*fränkischen Weinstadt*)'. Even the painful memories of being beaten at school with a cane and her exclusion from Catholic events as a Protestant

---

Mrs. Ton's daughter Vally Ton provided me with additional information in Aug. 2003. Both the recordings and the transcripts are stored at the International Institute for Social History (IISH) in Amsterdam.

7   Barbara Henkes, 'German Maids in the Netherlands in the Interwar Period', in: Klaus J. Bade, Pieter C. Emmer, Leo Lucassen and Jochen Oltmer (eds.), *The Encyclopedia of Migration and Minorities in Europe. From the 17th Century to the Present Cambridge* (Cambridge: Cambridge University Press, 2011) 419–420.

8   Rie Ton-Seyler, *Volkach* (n.p., n.d.), unpublished manuscript. Shortly before our first meeting, Mrs. Ton had finished typing this manuscript about her childhood between 1917 and 1923 based on diary entries, supplemented with her own memories of that time.

are remembered with a hint of melancholy. The First World War passed by almost unnoticed, she realizes afterwards.[9] A French prisoner of war who had to work on the land, the faded photographs in prayer books of soldiers who died, and the death on the battlefield of her aunt's youngest brother pass as an organic part of everyday life. The subsequent 'Revolution' did not have any consequences either: 'here in the quiet little town there were no socialists (*Sozies*)'. The rebellion of the red Spartacists as well as the failed *Kapp Putsch* left the predominantly Catholic inhabitants of Volkach untouched, as far as the memories of the young Rie Seyler stretch.[10]

Mrs. Ton-Seyler remembers how the interwar developments in Weimar Germany first dawned on her through her hairdresser: the much-coveted bob cut (*Bubikopf*) remained out of her reach time and again, because the money saved with so much effort turned out to be insufficient for the desired cut.[11] The postwar inflation, however, had a much more dramatic effect on her life, when her mother and stepfather's business went bankrupt. They could no longer afford their daughter's boarding expenses and school fees, which meant that Marie did not return to the warm world of Uncle Josef and Aunt Aurelia after the Christmas holidays of 1923. 'In the book of a wonderful childhood the wind had turned the pages, it was over', she ends her memories of her time in Volkach.

'Then I went, well, not from heaven ... but when you look back on it, it looks like from heaven into hell, Mrs. Ton-Seyler says more than sixty years later.[12] While she had felt cherished by her foster parents in Volkach, back with her own mother and stepfather she felt more like 'a real Cinderella'. In addition to her compulsory school hours, she had to clean the house because her mother was suffering from a heart disease. '*Herzklappenfehler*, she has always blackmailed me with that, Mrs. Ton remembers. On top of that, she mentions casually that her stepfather couldn't keep his hands off her. She points to these negatively loaded memories of her parental home as a post-hoc explanation of why she wanted to leave the village in the *Rhön* region where her mother and stepfather had then settled. But there was more to it: 'The world over there was really nailed shut. There was nothing. Yes, wonderful scenery, but what can you do with that when you are sixteen?'[13] Previously she had given a romantic description of the landscape in Volkach as the backdrop to her beautiful

---

9   Conversation Henkes and Ton, 19 July 1987.
10   Ton-Seyler, *Volkach*: 8–9.
11   Ton-Seyler, *Volkach*, 15–16.
12   Conversation Henkes and Ton, 20 Sep.1986
13   Conversation Henkes and, 20 Sep. 1986

childhood, but in her memories of her adolescent experience the unspoiled nature with wooded hills near Struth serve as a metaphor for her isolation in the province.

Marie Seyler was not the only one who wanted to exchange life in the province for city life. Many of her peers looked for work and entertainment in the city, even if they got on well with their relatives at home. At the beginning of the twentieth century, living and working in a household offered young women an approved opportunity to take the leap into the city.[14] In Germany there were not only cleaning women and live-in maidservants, but also the so-called *Stütze der Hausfrau* (literally: 'support of the housewife') or *Haustochter* ('house daughter'), comparable to what we now call an au pair. In exchange for food, lodging and some pocket money, they worked in the household to learn the tricks of the trade, but were also used as cheap labour.

Thanks to the mediation of a woman from Frankfurt who came to Struth for a summer holiday, the sixteen-year-old Marie was hired as a *Stütze der Hausfrau* in the household of a doctor's family, the Stiebs. 'I remember how I sat there, with my thick legs, calves and relatively thick arms and round face. Then Mrs. Stieb said: "She is strong, she will be able to work hard (*Sie ist kräftig, die kann tüchtig arbeiten*)". I felt as if I was being inspected at the slave market. That didn't sound nice. I had already read *Uncle Tom's Cabin*'.[15] With this reference to the much-translated classic in world literature, Mrs. Ton introduces her identification with others who found themselves in a difficult situation because of poverty, discrimination, persecution or violence. That identification will run like a red thread through her life story.

Although the first encounter with Mrs. Stieb made her fear the worst, Marie had a 'great time' in Frankfurt. In the Stieb household she was entrusted with light tasks, there was a woman for heavy-duty cleaning, and during her five-years' stay she got involved in family life: 'I ate with them at the table and went with them to the theatre; I was a kind of niece who helped, you could say. […] it was my home'.[16] Her memories of this period breathe emotional security and tell of much intellectual stimulation, thanks to the open-minded atmosphere amongst the Stieb family. In the summer of 1933, an impossible flirtation with

14   Barbara Henkes, 'Maids on the move. Images of femininity and European women's labour migration during the interwar years', in: P. Sharpe (ed.) *Women, Gender and Labour Migration. Historical and global Perspectives.* London/New York (Routledge) 2001: 224–243.

15   Conversation Henkes and Ton, 20 Sep. 1986. The book first appeared in 1852 as *Uncle Tom's Cabin or Life among the Lowly*. In the same year, translations appeared in several countries, including Germany and the Netherlands. The book, which was of great significance for the anti-slavery movement, has remained in print to this day.

16   Conversation Henkes and Ton, 20 Sep. 1986.

the son of the house and the need for new vistas and more financial scope
made Marie Seyler decide to go abroad. 'Unfortunately, I cannot say that I left
because of Hitler, Mrs. Ton says, changing the perspective from which she approaches her choice from the past to the present. 'Politics was not the number
one interest in my life at the time. Yes, I had my opinions, but not like now,
when I do think it is number one: the most important as regards influence on
people, on countries, on life. At the time I thought more about boys and
Schlagers (hit songs) and films and all that'.[17] With the distinction between the
'young' and the 'older' Marie, she marks the process of her growing political
awareness, which was accompanied by a radical reorientation with regard to
her country of origin and her Germanness.

Into the Blue

Without friends or relatives who had preceded her, Marie Seyler depended on
intermediary agencies or advertisements to find a job abroad. In 1933 it was
no longer that simple. The Wall Street Crash of 1929 had had an immediate
and profound effect on the German labour market. Soon, many Germans –
including many young women – were looking for work and income abroad. But
the economic malaise also took hold of the surrounding European countries:
rising unemployment led to measures limiting the inflow of foreign workers.
When Marie Seyler responded to an advertisement for a job in the household
of a Cambridge family, it turned out that she was no longer allowed to enter the
United Kingdom. At the British consulate in Frankfurt she was told that only
specialized workers were granted a permit; domestic work was not included. In
the Netherlands, the implementation of restrictive measures for maidservants
from abroad took longer, due to a shortage of Dutch domestics and a strong
lobby of Dutch housewives.[18]

Marie Seyler advertised in one of the largest liberal newspapers in Germany,
the *Hamburger Fremdenblatt*. The Dutch-German Handl family from Amsterdam responded, and on Sunday 1 October 1933 Marie, 21 years old, left by train
for the Netherlands. 'I kind of went into the blue. I would equally have liked to
go to Denmark, or rather to France, because I had been taught French at school,
and I really preferred to go to England, but that didn't happen. Mr. Stieb warned
me before I left for the Netherlands: 'Mariechen, what are you going to do
there? They clean the outsides of the houses!' His story about this sparkling

---

17   Conversation Henkes and Ton, 20 Sep. 1986.
18   Henkes, *Heimat in Holland*: 193.

clean nation was in line with a then widespread image of 'Holland' in Europe.[19] Stieb's warning did not promise much good for Mariechen's workload in the Dutch household, but she was not to be restrained by it. 'Completely unprepared' she took the train to Amsterdam.[20] Her new employer was waiting for her at Central Station and took Marie on a boat trip on the river IJ. The sight of large sea-going vessels and the smell of tar increased her expectations of her stay in Amsterdam: 'I had just read Joseph Conrad and I saw a large Scandinavian sailboat ... I was very romantic about harbours and the sea, or what they implied'.[21]

The city of Amsterdam with its harbour and ships offered Marie 'a gateway to the world', but she certainly did not experience the Handl household in those terms. Everything was just small, tight and frugal. This applies to both the Amsterdam upper floor apartment with the narrow staircase, and the suppliers with bills she had to show the door with the message that 'Madam is not at home'. The limited leisure time also offered little opportunity to get to know others, although there were many German colleagues in her immediate surroundings: 'the entire Euterpestraat was populated with German girls', Mrs. Ton remembers, but a chance to go out together hardly ever occurred.[22]

She soon realized that her position as a domestic with the Handl family in Amsterdam was very different from what she had been used to as a *Stütze der Hausfrau* with the Stieb family in Frankfurt. Marie had to do rough work, such as cleaning windows and floors. Her opinion was never asked, let alone appreciated and – what for her was most humiliating – everyone addressed her with the informal *Du* instead of the polite form *Sie*. In short: she was approached as a 'real' subordinate maid, who had to invisibly adapt to the family life of her employers and certainly was not expected to object to the tasks assigned to her. 'At the slightest thing they threatened with the alien police: "Oh, it is easy to have a German girl put across the border when you say that she is without a

19   E.g. a cluster of travel accounts of the Czech author Karel Capek, published under the title *Obrázky z Holandska* (1932). In the same year the German translation appeared, *Liebenswertes Holland. Erlebnisse einer Reise*. The book was also translated in English as *Letters from Holland* (London: Faber and Faber, 1933).
20   Conversation Henkes and Ton, 20 Sep. 1986.
21   Conversation Henkes and Ton, 26 Sep. 1986. The Polish-British writer Joseph Conrad (1857-1927) drew on his own experiences as a sailor and exile. His work first appeared in German translation in 1926 as *Jugend. Drei Erzählungen*, which also included his most famous novella *Heart of Darkness* from 1899.
22   Conversation Henkes and Ton, 20 Sep. 1986.

job"'.[23] That was no idle threat. As the call for measures against foreign workers increased in the course of the 1930s, the Dutch police was much stricter with German maidservants who had become unemployed. On the basis of the Aliens Act of 1849 they could be evicted from the country – which did indeed happen.[24]

At the time a form of support was provided by so-called German Girls' Protection Associations in Dutch cities and places where many girls had found work. Most of these organizations were associated with German Catholic or Protestant churches and endeavoured to care for young women who had come to the Netherlands on their own. In addition to mediation they organized weekly meetings where the young German women could exchange experiences and ask for advice in their own language. Many participants valued these associations as a second *Heimat*, a safe meeting point where they gathered around a cup of tea to share joys and sorrows under the watchful eye of a German-speaking *Fürsorgerin*, priest or pastor. Occasionally they ventured into a dance around a gramophone, or an outing was organized to Volendam or the tulip fields. Visits to cinema, dance halls or contacts with the opposite sex were taboo. If girls wanted to enjoy such activities, they had to organize it themselves, which many of them did.[25]

The activities of these Girls' Associations were unknown to Marie Seyler. But even if she had been aware of it, the question is whether she would have felt at home in such an environment. She was more interested in the adventurous side of city life, while these gatherings were meant to keep their participants away from any exploits. For Marie Seyler the spontaneous meeting with Dutch bookkeeper Roel Ton in front of a cinema offered an opportunity to escape the limited world of servant life. He spoke to her on a Sunday afternoon when she was absorbed in reading the poster for a new film with the German film actor Conrad Veidt. 'I didn't understand Dutch at the time, because everyone spoke German to me, so I said, "I don't understand you"'. Roel Ton immediately switched to German. 'We then talked extensively about films, because I knew a lot about them. I was a cinema fan. And then we arranged a date and that's how our relationship came about'.[26] After a year, Marie resigned from the Handl household and found a new job in the vicinity of Haarlem, where her boyfriend lived.

---

23   Conversation Henkes and Ton, 20 Sep. 1986.
24   Henkes, *Heimat in Holland*, 122.
25   Henkes, *Heimat in Holland*, 98–99.
26   Conversation Henkes and Ton, 20 Sep. 1986.

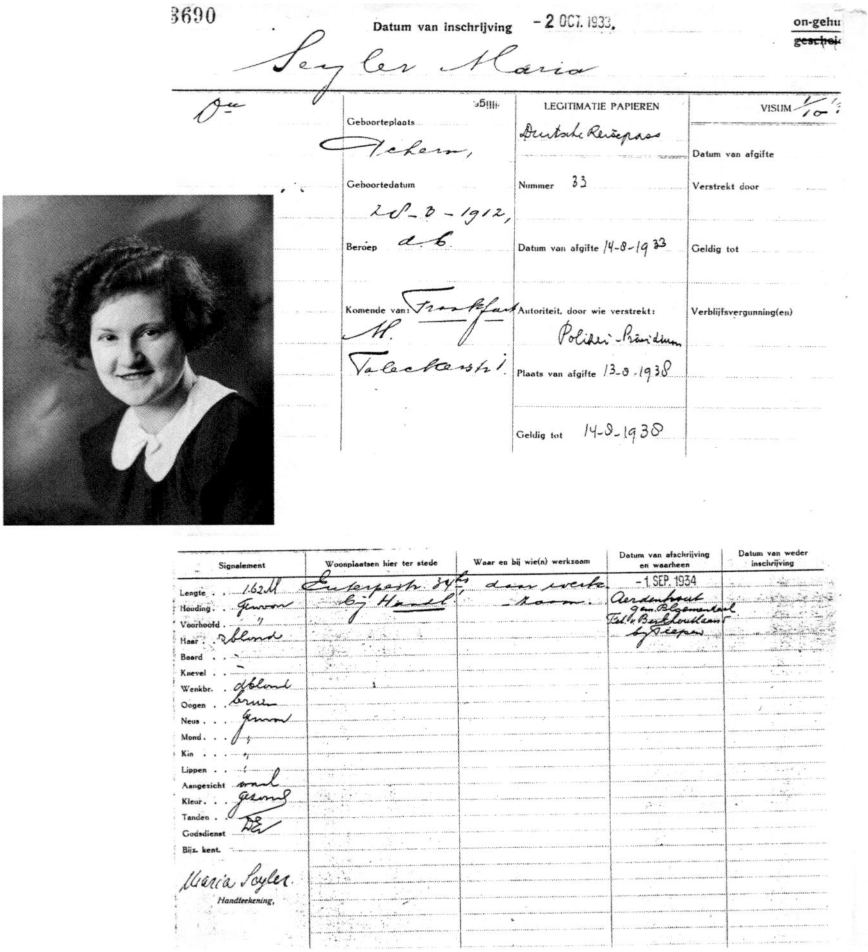
3690 Datum van inschrijving - 2 OCT. 1933. on-gehu
Seyler Maria
LEGITIMATIE PAPIEREN VISUM
Geboorteplaats Achern, Deutsche Reisepass Datum van afgifte
Geboortedatum 28-8-1912, Nummer 33 Verstrekt door
Beroep d.b. Datum van afgifte 14-8-1933 Geldig tot
Komende van: Frankfurt a/M. Autoriteit, door wie verstrekt: Polizei-Präsidium Verblijfsvergunning(en)
Plaats van afgifte 13-8-1938
Geldig tot 14-8-1938

Signalement	Woonplaatsen hier ter stede	Waar en bij wie(n) werkzaam	Datum van afschrijving en waarheen	Datum van weder inschrijving
Lengte 1.62 M; Houding gewoon; Voorhoofd "; Haar blond; Baard –; Knevel –; Wenkbr. d.blond; Oogen bruin; Neus gewoon; Mond "; Kin "; Lippen "; Aangezicht ovaal; Kleur gezond; Tanden "; Godsdienst Ev	Euterpestr. 34 bij Handel	dienstmeisje	- 1 SEP. 1934 Aerdenhout	

Maria Seyler. Handteekening,

FIGURE 2.2 Excerpt from the Amsterdam population register. *Stadsarchief* Amsterdam; Marie Seyler, 1934.

'I was really unlucky', concludes Mrs. Ton about her unfortunate experiences as a German domestic in several lower-middle class Dutch households. Within two years she changed her job three times, until in 1936 she was employed as a housekeeper by the widow Groenhof, a teacher at the Montessori school in Haarlem with two sons.[27] She liked it there, but she was not to stay for long. Marie was three months pregnant when she married Roel Ton in July 1937: the

27 Announcement of the appointment of Mrs. W.A. Groenhof-Wanrooij at the primary school for Montessori education in *Haarlems Dagblad,* 4 Mar. 1937.

FIGURE 2.3
Marie Seyler and Roel Ton on their wedding day,
Haarlem 21 July 1937.

German Marie Seyler became the Dutch Mrs. Rie Ton.[28] However, they first
had to be able to prove that neither she nor her future husband were Jewish. With the introduction in September 1935 of the Nuremberg laws 'for the
protection of the German blood and German honour', a marriage between a
Jewish and a non-Jewish partner was prohibited in Nazi Germany. Because
both the Netherlands and Germany had signed the 1902 International Marriage Convention, whereby the participating countries agreed to respect
each other's marriage laws, these racist laws also penetrated the Dutch legal
system. Germans in the Netherlands who wanted to marry a Dutch partner
had to prove that they, like their future spouses, were of 'Aryan' origin. If they
were unable to do so, the German civil service was not allowed to issue a Certificate of Marriageability (*Ehefähigkeitszeugnis*).[29] And without permission
from the German authorities in the form of such a certificate, there was a serious problem executing the formalities necessary for a wedding, as we will
see in the next chapter. Thanks to the church archives Roel Ton and Marie
Seyler were able to demonstrate their 'untainted' Protestant and non-Jewish
origins.[30] This legal measure and the time-consuming formalities it involved
were mainly experienced as a nuisance, also because of Marie's early pregnancy. They did not realize at the time that these formalities were an antisemitic
measure.

---

28   Notice of marriage of R.J. Ton and M.K. Seijler [sic], registry Heemstede 16 July 1937, fol-
      lowed by a notice of the marriage two weeks later.
29   Barbara Henkes, '"Hausmädchenheimschaffung" aus den Niederlanden. Gender, "Volksge-
      meinschaft" und Migrationsregime in der Zwischenkriegszeit', in: Jochen Oltmer (Hrg.),
      Nationalsozialistische Migrationsregime und 'Volksgemeinschaft (Paderborn: Verlag Ferdi-
      nand Schöningh, 2012), 205–217.
30   Conversation Henkes and Ton, 20 Sep. 1986.

A *Heimat* in Holland?

'Looking back', says Mrs. Ton, 'I was not in love with my husband. He was the one who was kind to me and who wanted me. Then I took him. But really to say, "he is my man, he is the one!" ... no. I wanted to have a home, I wanted someone who was good to me'.[31] Her marriage provided protection against both exploitation as maidservant and against expulsion as a foreign worker. Her husband took good care of her and their child, and so offered security. However, that is not the same as a place to feel at home. Rie Ton-Seyler never experienced the feeling of belonging in a new national and local community. In the company of her Dutch Reformed family-in-law she was confronted with an anxious kind of conformism. 'It was so terribly important that you didn't go to church with the same hat too often and things like that. I couldn't stand it'. Mrs. Ton characterizes their lifestyle as 'petty bourgeois', which she sets off against a more liberal or bohemian lifestyle.[32] She longed for the openness and 'grandeur' she remembered from the Stieb household in Weimar Germany, instead of her in-laws' habits of 'the miserly one biscuit' presented with tea, and the sandwiches taken along in a box for lunch at work.[33]

When Mrs. Ton refers to her identifying with a certain lifestyle, she shows how nationality, class, religion, gender and marital status were inextricably intertwined and gave each other meaning. In this phase in her life story she identifies herself more with a form of Germanness than with a form of Dutchness. The image of the Netherlands that she evokes is partly derived from postwar Dutch literature in which these petty bourgeois environments are described in uncompromising terms as 'suffocating'.[34] However, she does not fail to put that image immediately into perspective again when emphasising her own process of adjustment and increased Dutchness: 'It certainly had its attractions, but it was ... stuffy. In the meantime, I have become the same myself, as happens. I myself keep every rubber band and bring sandwiches with me on an outing'.[35] The sandwich box as a metaphor for a thrifty, 'Dutch' lifestyle is proverbial.

---

31   Conversation Henkes and Ton, 19 July 1987.
32   For these families the term '*kleine luyden*' ('small people') was coined in the 19th century by the founder of the Anti-Revolutionary Party (ARP), Abraham Kuyper, to underline the humility of his followers. The mostly strictly devout middle classes, farmers, workers and lower officials organized themselves under his leadership in their own churches, schools and a political party. This remarkable emancipation process of the Protestant lower middle classes during the first half of the twentieth century is closely related to what has been called the process of 'pillarization' in Dutch society. See also Chap. 5, n. 90 of this book.
33   Conversation Ton and Henkes, 19 July 1987.
34   See e.g. the work of Jan Siebeling, Gerard Reve and Jan Wolkers.
35   Conversation Henkes and Ton, 19 July 1987.

It took a long time before Rie Ton-Seyler could find her place in the pre– and postwar 'pillarized' Netherlands, when Dutch society was to a large extent organized through politico-denominational networks or 'pillars', according to different religions or political allegiances.[36] She experienced this *hokjesgeest* ('sectarianism'), as she calls it, as a hindrance in social intercourse. Neither her Protestant origin, nor religion or church community in general, gave her a point of identification with the people around her. Her sense of being an 'outsider' was further strengthened by her past employment history as a domestic, which made her part of the working class. The erudition and keen political interest she had developed did not fit the image of maidservants in the Netherlands. Rie Ton-Seyler was or became well aware of this, judging from the following anecdote she presented during one of our conversations.

Her husband wondered why she immediately informed people she had just met that she had been a housemaid. His observation made her think. Her conclusion, she says, was 'that I did so to avoid disappointment'. Because of her literacy, many people placed her in a 'higher' rank and when it turned out that she had come to the Netherlands as a domestic, many felt uncomfortable. '[Then] I thought: "here we are, I'll tell them straight away, so that they don't have to be nice at first and then drop me anyway". By now, it has become a bit more democratic, but in the past it was like: "Oh no, she was a maid".[37] Eventually Rie Ton-Seyler found a charming solution for this problem: 'If I am asked nowadays how I ended up in the Netherlands, I will say: "*Else Böhler*". With this reference to the famous novel by the Dutch author Simon Vestdijk, about a German maid in pre-war The Hague, her past as a domestic is revealed, and at the same time she links it to her knowledge of Dutch literature. The literary figure of Else Böhler is, as it were, the connecting link between her positions as former German housemaid and erudite Dutch housewife.[38]

---

36   The notion of 'pillarization' was first introduced by the sociologist Arend Lijphart in *The Politics of Accommodation. Pluralism and Democracy in the Netherlands* (Berkeley: University of California Press, 1968) to characterize the organisation of Dutch society in politico-denominational networks that manifested itself from around the beginning of the 20th century and gradually disappeared after the 1960s, when secularisation got the upper hand. There is much debate about the use of this concept to characterize the specific political culture of Dutch society in these years. When it comes to the way in which people could position themselves by simultaneously opposing and identifying with specific groups on the basis of lifestyle and beliefs, the concept can be useful. For recent debates on the usefulness of and confusions around this notion: Peter van Dam, *Staat van verzuiling: over een Nederlandse mythe* (Amsterdam: Wereldbibliotheek, 2011).

37   Conversation Henkes and Ton, 19 July 1987.

38   Simon Vestdijk, *Else Böhler, Duitsch diensmeisje* (Rotterdam: Nijgh & Van Ditmar, 1935), since 1959 followed by many reprints.

FIGURE 2.4
Simon Vestdijk's *Else Böhler, Duitsch
dienstmeisje*. Third edition. Design
Joan McNeill. The book was banned
by the Nazis as anti-German during
the occupation.

There is more to her reference to the novel. Vestdijk situates *Else Böhler* in The
Hague's petty bourgeois milieu. The environment that he so ruthlessly portrays
shows remarkable similarities with Mrs. Ton's characterization of the world in
which she ended up as a maidservant and (future) wife of a Dutch Reformed
accountant. Remarkably, the character Else Böhler returns to Nazi Germany
before the outbreak of the war and, according to the novel, joins the National
Socialists. Marie Seyler, on the other hand, turned against National Socialism
in the Netherlands. During postwar conversations *Else Böhler* offered her an
opening to emphasize that she – unlike Else – had distanced herself from Nazi
Germany.

After her marriage in 1937, Dutch citizenship protected Rie Ton-Seyler from
a forced return to Germany, something that many German men and women
abroad faced at the end of the 1930s. In the early morning of 14 December 1938,
the Dutch national newspaper *De Telegraaf* reported on an imminent Nazi
government decree to recall all German (and Austrian) maidservants to their
'fatherland'. The same day other newspapers confirmed this news about the
planned '*Hausmädchenheimschaffungsaktion*'. As the official reason for this

far-reaching measure the prevailing shortage of domestic staff in Germany was given. But other motives certainly had equal weight: the Netherlands acted as 'poison' on politically uninformed and uninhibited young German women. They often preferred the 'completely alienating influence' of Dutch organizations instead of joining the National-Socialist oriented local German community (*Reichsdeutsche Gemeinschaft*), as German National Socialists in the Netherlands wrote in their letters to the authorities in Berlin. Besides, many of the German maidservants were supposed to hold 'morally or economically unworthy' positions. When employed by Jews, communists, or poor people, they formed an 'easy prey' (*Freiwild*) for 'Jewish boys and certain Dutchmen' (*Judenjungs und bestimmte Holländer*).[39] The warnings against moral dangers that have always been associated with the migration of unmarried women thus became drenched in fierce antisemitism.

The negative image of the Netherlands, which had already deteriorated further due to the economic crisis, was now further intensified along the lines of the 'Germanophobic (*deutschfeindliche*) and Judaised (*verjudete*) Netherlands'. Only in their own country could the German maidens be saved as the future mothers for the German people (*Volkstum*). Also, in Belgium, England, Switzerland and other countries, German women under the age of forty had to deal with coercive measures intended to make them return to the *Heimat*. If they refused they would lose their German citizenship.[40] The many written requests for dispensation, as well as the applications for naturalization in the Netherlands and the reports about 'a rush to the town hall' to get married to a Dutchman, indicate that the enthusiasm for a return was not great. German girls who had not yet returned to Germany in 1938 rarely felt addressed as future 'mothers for the fatherland'. They preferred to stay in the Netherlands. While they sought every possible way to evade the forced return, their Dutch employers thought about possible solutions to the imminent loss of their domestics. There were voices calling for extended access to the Netherlands for those Jewish girls from Germany who wanted to work in Dutch households. Since many Dutch girls no longer wanted to become maidservants, they caused no 'harmful competition on the labour market'.[41]

The cruel humiliations and murders of Jewish Germans during the so-called Crystal Night (*Kristallnacht*, also called Night of Broken Glass or November Pogroms) in November 1938, intensified the pressure on the Dutch government

---

39   Based on correspondence from the German Archive of the Ministry of Foreign Affairs (*Auswartiges Amt*), cited in Henkes, *Heimat in Holland*, 155–157.

40   Henkes, 'Hausmädchenheimschaffungsaktion'.

41   The liberal newspaper *Het Algemeen Handelsblad* of 21 Dec. 1938, quoted in Henkes, *Heimat*, 158.

to open the borders to Jewish refugees. Mrs. Ton-Seyler remembers how she, too, was shocked by the reports about the antisemitic violence in her country of origin. Without much knowledge of the restrictive policy applied by the Dutch government towards Jewish refugees, she wrote to her Jewish school friend Ruth Bamberger – 'Ludwigstrasse 33 in Bad Kissingen, the address is still engraved in my memory' – to come to the Netherlands. Her letter was returned to her with the message on the unopened envelope: 'The Jews over here are gone, all left for Palestine' (*'Die Juden sind bei uns heraus, allen nach Palestina'*).[42] The relief that Ruth and her family had escaped barely made up for the disgust that this scribble evoked.

'You are no Longer German'

A sense of belonging to the country of origin is not necessarily cancelled by establishing oneself in a new country and acquiring the corresponding citizenship. Mrs. Ton-Seyler makes this clear when she remembers another incident in the autumn of 1938, shortly after the birth of her first and only child: 'Then Chamberlain was in Munich and it was broadcast on the radio. Vally had already been born, I was knitting baby clothes. It was really scary. I thought, "My God, if it comes to war, I might be tossed to and fro". It was my country, after all, and it was my people, my compatriots. Well, ex-compatriots ... but I did not feel it that way yet'. When she recalls this moment, Mrs. Ton primarily refers to her own ambiguous identifications with both the German and the Dutch nation. Neither her German relatives, nor the son of the Stieb family who, like the brother of Irmgard Brester-Gebensleben,[43] may have taken up arms against her new homeland and her Dutch countrymen, are mentioned in her narrative.

Although Mrs. Ton-Seyler barely mentions her personal relationships with family or acquaintances in Germany, contacts with them had not been completely broken off. In 1936 she crossed the border with Roel Ton to present her fiancé to her mother and stepfather. In the autumn of 1938 she packed her bags again, after receiving a telegram about the death of her stepfather: 'Papa tot, komm sofort'.[44] She presents a lively account of this journey. After a transfer in Frankfurt, she shared the compartment with a group of German soldiers on their way to their garrison: 'There was mobilization. They had been pulled out

---

42   Conversation Henkes and Ton, 20 Sep. 1986.
43   See Chap. 1.
44   Conversation Henkes and Ton, 20 Sep. 1986.

FIGURE 2.5 'Take care when talking. The enemy is listening'. White enamel shield from 1935.
            Photo: Auction house Franke, Nuremberg, for auction on 14 January 2016.

of their civilian existence and – as one could clearly see – they were really nervous. I sat there like a black crow in the middle of the green-grey of their uniforms. They spoke about various types of drinks in the world. They were talking
about *saki* and *arak* and *jenever* (gin), which they said was distilled from rice.
And I am such a blabbermouth, so I said: "No, that is distilled from grain". In
perfect German, of course. "What makes you think that?", one of them asked.
He knew exactly: gin was made out of rice from the Dutch colonies. I said, "No,
really, I know, I am from Holland". "You are from Holland? I don't believe that".
I pulled out my pass. Silence. Nothing more was said. At first, I did not understand, but then I saw those posters with warnings at the stations: 'Take care!
The enemy is listening' (*Vorsicht! Feind hört mit*). They were completely silent.
So, I was also a possible spy. Then I realized: "Oh dear, you are no longer German". At that moment a valve shut somewhere in my mind. I thought, "Yes,
that's true, I am Dutch, I don't belong to you lot anymore". I didn't even have to
choose; that had already been done for me'.[45]

     Not only in our conversations, but also in her memoirs this incident appears
several times in almost the same words. Rie Ton-Seyler opens her written
memories of *De Oorlogsjaren* (The War Years) with this 'key event', as she calls
it.[46] That was the moment when for her the war started emotionally, and when
for the first time she felt primarily Dutch. Back in the Netherlands, it was not
long before mobilization was called. A company of conscripts was stationed in
the school next to the Ton family house. At the Tons', the coffee was ready for
them and the letterbox bulged with 'soldier's letters', because the military field

45   Conversation Henkes and Ton, 20 Sep. 1986.
46   Rie Ton-Seyler, *De Oorlogsjaren*, (1987) 1–2. After I asked in a letter about her memories of
       specific events and experiences during the war period, Ton surprised me a month later in
       June 1987 with the 16-page story of her war experiences, partly based on diary entries.

post did not function properly. Despite her German accent, Mrs. Ton cannot remember that she was confronted with mistrust at the time, though the hospitality with which she opened her house to the Dutch soldiers may have been inspired by a feeling that she had to prove herself trustworthy and loyal to the Dutch cause. 'I have that accent, so I had to prove my reliable Dutchness again and again. But that was no problem because the people I knew, well, they knew I was okay. Although there were those who after the May days of 1940 assumed that I was happy with the German victory'.[47]

It was mainly after the German occupation that Rie Ton-Seyler encountered distrust and hostility. At that time there were many people who behaved 'ever so patriotically' and were afraid 'to burn themselves on cold water', as she characterises their attitude. To her astonishment, the headmaster of the school next door greeted her on the day of the liberation in May 1945: "'Are you free?' I say, "What do you mean, free?" "Are you not interned then? You are German, aren't you?!"[48] Her German origin had not prevented Rie Ton from turning against the occupying forces. In fact, she was well able to use her former nationality and her perfect command of the German language as a cover for resistance activities.[49] When, due to the stricter measures around forced labour service (*Arbeitseinsatz*), her neighbour was in acute danger of being arrested on the street, she was asked to take on the distribution of the illegal magazine *Je Maintiendrai*.[50] 'That wasn't much, mind you, twenty-five or thirty copies', she adds hastily. Not long afterwards, the same man – referring to her German origin, which would make these activities easier for her[51] – asked if she would also be willing to convey secret messages for the resistance. 'Those things had to be put to me by others, as it were', she says about this development. In the sequel, she cycled every week to Bennebroek and from there to Santpoort with envelopes in her bra.[52]

When we first met, Mrs. Ton only casually referred to her involvement in the resistance: 'I had a small district to distribute illegal magazines to and a little courier work'. Later, at my request, she would write and tell me more about it. Time and again she emphasizes how little her commitment to resisting the Nazi regime entailed: 'I have not experienced those great events, I did not

---

47   Ton-Seyler, *De Oorlogsjaren*, 2–3 and conversation Henkes and Ton, 20 Sep. 1986.
48   Conversation Henkes and Ton, 20 Sep. 1986.
49   As a German by birth, Rie Ton-Seyler was known as *Volksdeutsche*, or *Auslanddeutsche*. The National Socialist authorities assumed that these would identify with Nazi-Germany and its goal of a Third Reich. See also: Henkes, *Heimat*, 187–190.
50   H. van den Heuvel en G. Mulder, *Het vrije woord: de illegale pers in Nederland 1940-1945* (Den Haag: SDU, 1990).
51   Ton-Seyler, *De Oorlogsjaren*, 10a.
52   Conversation Henkes and Ton, 19 July 1987.

know Hanny Schaft', she begins the story of her illegal activities.[53] Hanny
Schaft was immortalized by the famous, then communist Dutch author Theun
de Vries in his often reprinted novel *Het meisje met het rode haar* (The Girl with
the Red Hair, 1956). Schaft was a young woman who was active in the communist resistance in the area around Haarlem, for which she paid with her life.[54]
Against the hero status of Hanny Schaft Mrs. Ton sets her own 'small' and 'relatively safe' involvement, which 'accidentally' came her way. 'You had Dutch
Reformed resistance people, you had communists, and you had freelancers. I
don't really know what group I was involved in, I got assignments and I didn't
know anything else about it. Those things, really, it was not very spectacular, it
was simple. I really didn't risk anything, or only in an exceptional case, but no,
no, really no risks'.[55]

A Sprinkling of Sand in the Gears

The story about Rie Ton's attitude during the Nazi regime in the Netherlands is
characterized by her emphasis on the limited significance of her own efforts.
The topos of 'modesty' often appears when women of her generation talk
about their independent thinking and acting against existing rules and expectations.[56] If they participated in the organized resistance, they often held a
position that was an extension of the usual gender roles and the division of
labour between the men and women involved. This led women to mainly
transport illegal messages, counterfeit papers, and ration coupons in their bras
or corsets, or conceal weapons at the bottom of prams. Care for people in hiding was often also their responsibility. Men in the resistance were more likely
to take on the organization of illegal networks and to lead spectacular actions
such as burning the population register, liberating political prisoners, or assas-
sinating traitors and high Nazi officials. For a long time, women received hardly any recognition for their indispensable but 'unremarkable' contributions to
the resistance. That omission in Dutch historiography influenced personal

---

53   Conversation Henkes and Ton, 19 July 1987.
54   *Het meisje met het rode haar* belongs to the Dutch classics and had a 20th edition in 2013.
      In 1981 the novel was made into a successful film by Ben Verbong.
55   Conversation Henkes and Ton, 19 July 1987.
56   Jil Ker Conway, *When memory speaks. Exploring the Arts of Autobiography* (New York: Vin-
      tage Books, 1999) 12–14, points out that Western European women's autobiographies have
      often been produced within a religious framework, in particular the author's relationship
      with God. In such a discourse a sense of agency – of independent consideration and
      action – was hard to develop.

memories and caused women to often downplay their efforts. When their husbands, other family members or friends reminded them of their responsibilities as wives and mothers, it was all the more desirable to emphasize their modest role and the low risk of their efforts.[57] As these gender arrangements were re-asserted after the war, many women were inclined to present their resistance activities as just coincidental, and hardly dangerous.

This is also reflected in Mrs. Ton's story, which she starts with the memory of the neighbour who was in danger of being caught for the *Arbeitseinsatz,* and the question whether she wanted to take over his task. Once she had said 'yes' to this request, she was asked to take on another assignment. As a woman and as a former German, she felt compelled to do 'something' against the Nazi occupation forces, despite her husband's objections. Roel Ton did not like his wife's illegal escapades and appealed to her responsibilities to family life. 'He thought it was a bit dangerous, for me and for his bike, because I was riding his bike. And yes, the household was slightly disrupted, it was a bit *rommelig* (messy)'.[58] Dutch households became messy anyway, as the occupation lasted.

The increasing scarcity of foodstuffs and other primary necessities required permanent talent for improvisation. Bedspreads were unpicked to knit socks, sand served as scouring powder, and in the garden the flower beds were replaced by potato bushes and string beans. In addition to her riding out to farms to search for the necessary food supplies, Rie Ton also did bicycle rides for the resistance. 'Then my husband said: "Think about your child". And he always said: "You only do that for the excitement and for the adventure". That was not true, but it did add an extra element. I don't even want to say "the danger", but you know: you got out of the treadmill for a moment, got away from that rotten little emergency stove and you had the feeling, if only to an extent, that you did something about it, to pour a sprinkling of sand in the gears'.[59]

For Rie Ton-Seyler, under those circumstances, her responsibility for the wellbeing of her husband and child was balanced against her need to act, exactly because she was a woman of German origin, in her aversion to the Nazi

---

57 Only at the end of the 1970s, parallel to the second feminist wave and the rise of women's studies at the universities, did an interest in the role of women and the significance of gender in the resistance against National Socialism arise. The involvement of women and the gender division of labour in organised resistance in the Netherlands were first thematized by Bob de Graaff and Lidwien Markus, *Kinderwagens en Korsetten* (Amsterdam: Bert Bakker, 1980), Marjan Schegman, *Het stille verzet: vrouwen in illegale organisaties in Nederland 1940-1945* (Amsterdam: SUA, 1980), and Barbara Henkes, 'Levensgeschiedenis om het verleden van huis uit te leren kennen', *IPSO-cahier 6. Over de geschiedenis van de CPN* (1981) 110–118.

58 Conversation Henkes and Ton, 19 July 1987. See also Ton-Seyler, *De Oorlogsjaren,* 13.

59 Conversation Henkes and Ton, 19 July 1987. See also Ton-Seyler, *De Oorlogsjaren,* 13.

regime – apart from the opportunity to step out of the routine and boredom of a housewife's routine during wartime. The fact that Roel Ton did not value the political commitment of women in general, and Rie's in particular, is also implied in her recalling a discussion about the 1935 Italian invasion of Ethiopia. The newspaper photos of African soldiers killed by Italian mustard gas had made both of them indignant. 'My fiancé said, "Wait till the League of Nations gets involved!" I didn't understand. What could the League do? I wondered. Then my future husband became furious and claimed that women simply do not understand politics and had better stick to their knitting'.[60] She did not, although Mrs. Ton emphasizes more than once that she herself had not helped persecuted Jews or political refugees, whereas others risked their lives for them.[61]

Although her opposition to National Socialism developed only after her departure from Germany, Mrs. Ton links her rejection of the Nazi-politics to her German 'guardian angels', who shaped her into an independent and critically thinking person. She mentions Mr. Stieb, 'who was really a pan-European' and *Frau* Berg, the socialist charwoman in the Stieb household who 'enjoyed the respect of everyone'.[62] Even her mother and stepfather come under a more favourable light when remembered from this perspective. They had a communist friend, who answered all her questions about the 'how and why' with much patience and understanding.[63] Thus, she also counts her parents among the people who laid the foundation for her aversion to National Socialism, despite the 'shameful' way in which they treated her. 'I sometimes thought: if I had grown up in a sympathetic, nice family and they had patched up their bruised self-esteem after the lost war in 1918 with slogans such as "We Germans shall again …", all those things Hitler promised them … should I have been sensible enough to see through that? Could I have resisted?'[64] Rie Ton-Seyler was spared the dilemma that Irmgard Brester-Gebensleben faced.

---

60 Conversation Henkes and Ton, 19 July 1987. The second Italian-Ethiopian War lasted seven months and led to the occupation of the Empire of Ethiopia by the fascist regime of Mussolini. The raid was labelled by the League of Nations as an aggressive act by Italy, but the sanctions were ineffective.

61 But even if women did risk their lives, as Irmgard Brester-Gebensleben did by taking in a Jewish child in hiding (see Chap. 1), it was often considered a 'self-evidently' private matter rather than a political act of resistance.

62 Conversation Henkes and Ton, 19 July 1987.

63 Conversations Henkes and Ton, 20 Sep. 1986 and 19 July 1987, and a letter of 28 Sep. 1987 from Ton to Henkes.

64 Conversation Henkes and Ton, 19 July 1987.

Mrs. Ton is aware of how loyalties within a kinship network may hamper a moral stance and limit the scope for political action. In her case this seems not to have played a role, as she believes that neither her mother or stepfather, nor the Stieb family, felt attracted by National Socialism. Nevertheless, despite the poor relationship with her next of kin in Germany and her disgust with the Nazi regime, her sense of connectedness with her country of origin remained intact. In Mrs. Ton-Seyler's life story, her favourite German writers, such as Kurt Tucholsky, Berthold Brecht and Thomas Mann, represent the 'other', cosmopolitan, anti-National Socialist Germany, with which she continued to identify. In addition, she expresses her contempt for the many Dutch people 'who turned around' and opted for the Nazi regime: 'you don't have to be a hero, but you can still remain decent'.[65] In this way Mrs. Ton-Seyler is able to put in perspective the opposition between the 'bad' Germany and the 'good' Netherlands and connect her Germanness and her Dutchness.

6   Guilt and Shame

Yet, the significance Mrs. Ton attaches to her German origin remains ambivalent. Since the collapse of the Third Reich she has been reminded of her Germanness and has felt the burden of the National Socialist past weigh on her shoulders. Despite, or perhaps because of her resistance to the Nazis, her connection with Germany was strengthened, albeit in a paradoxical way. With some bewilderment she remembers how in West Germany immediately after the war people resumed their lives as soon as possible, without dwelling too long on the dramas that had taken place in their name. When in December 1946 she got permission to visit her sick mother in Germany – 'the Political Investigation Service (*Politieke Opsporingsdienst,* POD) had declared me spotless'[66] – she kept a diary. Some thirty years later she revisited this diary and presented the information as a memoir, with a motto from the poem *Vrede (Peace)* by the Dutch-Jewish poet Leo Vroman: *Kom vanavond met verhalen – hoe de oorlog is verdwenen – en herhaal ze honderd malen – alle malen zal ik wenen* (Come tonight with all those tales/ of how war at last has died/ and repeat them a hundred times/ every time again I'll cry).[67]

---

65   Conversation Henkes and Ton, 19 July 1987.
66   Marie Ton-Seyler, *Kom vanavond met verhalen* (1975) 1. Straight after the liberation the POD was tasked with tracing members of the NSB, and other collaborators with the Nazis. A German origin was already suspicious at the time (see n. 46 above). Around 120,000 people were arrested and imprisoned.
67   Leo Vroman, 'Vrede', in: *De Gids,* Vol. 117 (1954) 5.

FIGURE 2.6   The old opera house in Frankfurt was bombed and burned to the ground in
             March 1944.

In it she describes the 'city of the dead' Cologne with its Schillerian hollow
window openings (*öden Fensterhöhlen*) that she passed on her journey. The
boys who were begging for a cigarette on the railway platform could still count
on her sympathy, unlike the young ladies (*Fräuleins*) at the Frankfurt station
who stepped through the snow on the arms of black American soldiers. With a
paradoxical indignation she wrote: 'So soon the concept of 'miscegenation'
(*Rassenschande*) has been erased'. Regarding the ruined opera house in Frankfurt, of which only part of the facade, with the inscription *Dem Wahren Schönen
Guten*(The true, beautiful, good) was still standing, she noted that 'they', her
former compatriots, had deviated very far from that motto.[68] After the war, Rie
Ton-Seyler struggled with the continuing memory of the mass killing of so
many innocent people: a genocidal murder that was committed in the name of
'the German people' of which she still felt part, in the language that was so dear
to her.

---

68   Ton-Seyler, *Kom vanavond*, 1–2.

Once in Germany she used her travel permit for the allied zones not just to visit her mother. In Frankfurt, she made a stopover at the Stieb family, who welcomed her warmly. She also went to the village where Gerard Groenhof, the son of her last Dutch employer, was killed during the advance of the French Allies. He had been sent to southern Germany with the forced *Arbeitseinsatz* to work on the land. Rie Ton hoped to be able to take his suitcase, letters and other tangible memories back to his mother, but his legacy was limited to some old clothes.[69] Her memoir about this harsh journey through defeated Germany ends with a retrospective in December 1975, in which she notes that there had met only one person who – looking at the ruins of Würzburg – had said: 'Yes, that is our fault, yes, we are to blame for that'.

During our conversations she will regularly refer to her postwar experiences in Germany, where the ruins were soon replaced by new houses (*Wirtschaftswunderhäuser*): 'I have spoken with so many people there, but I am the only person, also among my family and acquaintances, that was and still is ashamed of what happened there. Most of them will say: "We didn't know" (*Wir haben es nicht gewusst*). Or they say, "That is so long ago ...".[70] Her personal observations about the collective denial of responsibility for the war atrocities tie in with the findings of German historians such as Stefan Berger, who emphasize that 'a strong victims' discourse was present in postwar West and East Germany'.[71] A similar pattern can be seen in the historiography of the postwar Netherlands, where the invasion by Nazi Germany allowed for a victim discourse. That in turn proved to be an obstacle to a critical self-evaluation of the way in which a majority of the Dutch had accepted and thereby enabled a space to isolate and persecute Jews.

Neither in Germany nor in the Netherlands did Rie Ton-Seyler find a setting in which she could share her confusion about her own degree of complicity in the crimes of Nazi Germany. In the Netherlands, too, people went about their business as usual. She herself was left with what she calls 'an inferiority complex' about her German origin. How uncomfortable she is with the German Nazi past becomes clear when I come back to her involvement in the Dutch resistance: 'I knew that it didn't matter much but doing something ... (was important). Yes, maybe because of my feelings of guilt'. Later she adds, with an anachronistic term: 'I believe that the wish for reparation (*Wiedergutmachung*)

---

69   Ton-Seyler, *Kom vanavond*, 2–6
70   Conversation Henkes and Ton, 19 July 1987.
71   Stefan Berger, 'On taboos, Traumas and Other Myths: Why the debate about German Victims of the Second World War is not a Historians Controversy', in: Bill Niven (ed.), *Germans as Victims. Remembering the Past in Contemporary Germany*, (New York/Basingstoke: Palgrave Macmillan 2006) 210–224.

dominated my underground activities'. According to Mrs. Ton, her husband never understood: 'Afterwards, when I was so ... I was actually ashamed of my German origin. I'm still ashamed. Then he said: "Woman, what has that got to do with you? If there is anybody who doesn't have to worry about that, it's you"'.[72]

Roel Ton's level-headed reaction was well meant, but he ignored Rie's ambiguous identification with both the executors and the victims of National Socialist policies, and therefore had no eye for the complex feelings of responsibility and solidarity with which his wife struggled. Even though she has been told 'a hundred times', in the words of Leo Vroman, that the war was over and that she was not personally responsible for the persecution of the Jews, Mrs. Ton continues to weep internally for her own failure to act and from disappointment about the attitude of her fellow human beings, both in Germany and the Netherlands. She is all too aware that, despite her involvement in the resistance, she has not been able to save persecuted human beings. As such she was an 'implicated subject', who in spite of herself got embroiled in histories and events beyond her reach. Rie Ton-Seyler felt burdened by the shame of the crimes committed by Nazi Germany, but there was no setting in which she could undertake a shared reflection on the Nazi past that might have brought about some kind of closure.

Shortly after the war, the process of dealing with that violent past was limited to the prosecution of a small group of Nazi war criminals, in the postwar Federal Republic as well as in the Netherlands and other occupied countries. Alongside the first condemnations of high-ranking Dutch Nazis and a few German officials who were captured in the Netherlands, attention was focused on 'the' Dutch resistance: a 'safe' story by which the 'good' Dutch were juxtaposed to the 'bad' Germans in order to repair and strengthen a national community that had suffered from the Dutch involvement in collaboration, betrayal and murder. Because of this nationalistic and dualistic frame, Rie Ton-Seyler felt addressed as a former German, despite the assurances of her friends that they did not mean her when they talked about 'those Krauts'.[73] And her uneasiness did not go away after the sheer scale of Dutch collaboration penetrated Dutch historiography and Dutch collective memory from the 1980s onwards.

With her German origin, Mrs. Ton-Seyler carried with her a historically anchored sense of guilt that complicated her social encounters, certainly when it concerned victims of the Holocaust. When she became a member of the local section of the *Humanistisch Verbond* (Humanist Union) shortly after

---

72   Conversation Henkes and Ton, 19 July 1987.
73   Conversation Henkes and Ton, 19 July 1987.

its foundation in 1946,[74] she got in touch with Dr. Cohen, who had been in Auschwitz. 'I used to think: "O God, how awful for those people to sit at the table with me, with that German accent". I was always very careful. My husband said: "You are crazy". But then I tried to explain: "Look Roel, it's like this: if it had been my brother who had killed Dr. Cohen's wife ...?" That is how I felt towards the Jews. I didn't have a brother and his wife was still alive, but ...'.[75] By introducing an imaginary brother who might have killed Jews in the service of National Socialism, Mrs. Ton literally creates a community, imagined now in a very strong and literal sense, within which national origins and family overlap. In this way she tries to explain how impossible it was for her to separate her Germanness – in the sense of being born and raised in Germany, in the German language and culture – from the acts of violence committed in the name of Nazi Germany.

Compared to the statements of Irmgard Brester-Gebensleben, who at the time of the German invasion wondered whether her brother should fight against 'us' Dutch,[76] Rie Ton-Seyler faced a different kind of dilemma. From the outset, Irmgard was positively embedded in Dutch society. Her identification with Dutchness helped her to formulate her despair about the German invasion in the first place in terms of her actually existing, uniformed brother. After all, he was part of those who turned against her new home country and her Dutch compatriots, even though her brother and other National Socialists were convinced that they were acting in the best interests of the Netherlands as a 'Germanic' neighbouring country. Rie Ton's stories and writings, on the other hand, give the impression that despite her pre-war marriage and her difficult relationship with her mother and stepfather in Germany, she never really felt at home in the Netherlands, while German society was not an option either. Yet her youth in Germany and certainly the formative time in the Stieb household in Frankfurt remained crucially important for her self-image.

She was all too aware of the sensitivities that her unmistakeably German origin could evoke in the Netherlands, in particular among those who had been persecuted on behalf of Nazi Germany. That uncomfortable consciousness was decisive for how she presented herself in the postwar Netherlands, and later in her life stories when we met. Her embarrassment about the Nazi crimes goes hand in hand with an identification with Jewish victims, as becomes clear when I ask her about the meaning of the concept of 'fatherland': 'Fatherland

---

74   From a report in the *Haarlems Dagblad*, 28 February 1950, it appears that Mrs. Ton-Seyler
      was elected to the board of the *Humanistisch Verbond Haarlem*.
75   Conversation Henkes and Ton, 19 July 1987.
76   See Chap. 1.

in the sense of borders drawn at random and for which one should die? Fatherland in the political sense? No, that doesn't mean anything to me. Anyway, that word, I have erased that long ago'. She adds that she does believe in a connection with 'the familiar lines of the landscape'.[77] During our conversation she comes back to literature: 'As far as you can speak of a fatherland, or something like a sense of belonging, that for me is in Jewish literature, also books by American Jews. I really feel at home there'. The relationship that she creates, through a detour, between the concept of 'fatherland' and the world literature co-created by Jewish authors, refers to a transnational community with its own political-moral narrative. The words of Mrs. Ton are at the same time a tribute to that literary world and a mourning of its partial, cruel destruction.

Her stories and her bookcase show that the literary landscape in which she feels at home is certainly not limited to Jewish authors. German and Dutch, as well as English, French, Russian and American writers, both Jewish and non-Jewish, together form a collection of politically and socially engaged literature, in which historical events are represented together with various forms of exclusion and inequality in world history. The main theme of this collection is the need for critical reflection on recent social and political developments. Rie Ton took this need to the local branch of the Humanist Union in Haarlem. In addition to organizing lectures by famous Dutch authors and meetings on themes such as social justice, the upbringing of children and the relationship between humanism and religion, she became intensively involved in the organization of the so-called 'children's transports' in the late 1940s. Through the Humanist Union, young children from Germany and France were brought to Dutch foster homes near the sea to recuperate for a while. She devoted herself fully to this opportunity to build a bridge between the postwar Netherlands, Germany and other countries in Europe through the care of 'innocent 'children, at a time when Germany and the Germans were still too often linked to everything that was 'bad' and barbaric.

The dividing line between the 'good' Netherlands and the 'bad' Germany was not the only opposition that Rie Ton-Seyler found problematic. The way in which communism was presented as the enemy of postwar Western society did not sit well with her either. Had not communists been at the forefront of the fight against National Socialism? That was quickly forgotten in the heat of the Cold War. When the communist takeover in Czechoslovakia in 1948 was defended by the Dutch Communist Party with reference to the threat of a reviving fascism, Rie Ton was confronted in the Humanist Union with the

---

77   Letter Ton-Seyler, 21 Oct. 1986.

expulsion of a communist board member who was dear to her. This incident, followed by strong reactions to the Hungarian uprising in 1956, certainly contributed to her joining the newly founded Pacifist Socialist Party (PSP), in 1957. This political party recruited an important part of its support especially among the politically homeless on the left, including other members of the Humanist Union who in these years refused to choose between 'East' and 'West'. Rie Ton felt at ease among this group of people united in a radical socialist approach, although she did not simply adopt the pacifist principle. 'I am so anti-war because it is accompanied by madness, dirt, hunger, blood and the wiping out of achievements, such as the belief in humanity, tolerance and a little integrity. But I do sometimes think: "if only they'd cleaned up those guys – like that rat catcher from Braunau ...", referring to Hitler, who was born in the Austrian border town of Braunau.[78]

At the time of our conversations Mrs. Ton was mainly concerned with identifying and criticising ideologies or stereotypes that threatened to exclude groups of people, whether it was the fundamentalism of 'those Ayatollahs', the Apartheid policies in South Africa, or the homophobia of the Roman Catholic Church. Until the end of her life, even when her weak health kept her housebound, Mrs. Ton followed the news and remained involved in what was going on in the world. In addition to literature, television – initially rejected as the great leveller of culture – had become an indispensable window to a world that, after the fall of the Wall and the release of Nelson Mandela, for a short time seemed to assume the contours of a post-national, multiracial and multicultural community.

In 1995, three years before her death, she sent me the novel *De Tweeling* (The Twins) by the Dutch writer Tessa de Loo.[79] Just as in our conversations and correspondence, the Second World War is a central theme in this novel, which is approached from two different perspectives. To this end, the author created the twin sisters Anna and Lotte Bamberg. Born in pre-war Germany, they were separated at the age of six. Lotte grew up in the Netherlands, while Anna stayed behind in Germany. The two sisters happen to meet again at the age of 74 in the Belgian town of Spa. In this 'neutral' place, neither German nor Dutch, they tell each other about their lives and especially about their experiences during the war. It turns out to be a painful confrontation. Lotte, who helped Jews in hiding

---

78   Conversation Ton and Henkes, 19 July 1987. See also Ton-Seyler, '*De oorlogsjaren*', 15.

79   Published in Dutch in 1993; translated into German (*Die Zwillinge*) in 1995, and in English (*The Twin*) in 2000. The book was also translated into other European languages. Ben Sombogaart made the book into an Oscar nominated film and the story was also presented in the form of a musical.

FIGURE 2.7   Rie Ton-Seyler (in the right-hand corner) at a meeting organised by a local
Anti-Apartheid Movement, published in *Ede Stad*, 18 April 1979.

during the Nazi occupation and lost her Jewish fiancé, looks back through the
perspective of the Dutch collective war narrative about the 'good', peaceful
Dutch versus the 'bad', violent Germans. On the other hand, Anna sets out
from the perspective of German citizens, in her case that of a young war widow, who also became a victim of the same war her compatriots had started.

Through the life story of Anna, the author invites Lotte's understanding
(and that of the reader) for Anna's painful experiences in Nazi Germany. De
Loo makes a sincere, albeit somewhat clichéd and much-criticized attempt
to show how individuals suffer from a self-destructive system originated from
their 'own' national community. The success of the book in the Netherlands
and Germany indicates that it has provided a welcome shift of perspective,
opening up awareness of – and recognition for – the German suffering from the
Nazi regime. In post-Apartheid South Africa, too, De Loo's book was received
with enthusiasm. The literary scholar W.F. Jonckheere points to the 'touching
tales'[80] in this narrative about the interaction between the two sisters that

---

80   See the Introduction to this book.

could promote an exchange of experiences and hence mutual understanding. He wonders if De Loo's 'thought-provoking literary model' could be useful in post-Apartheid South Africa to encourage former enemies to engage with each other.[81] However, like De Loo's, his argument is framed in terms of oppositions between *equal* groups, ignoring the violence as a result of structural racial inequality during National Socialism as well as during Apartheid, and its longlasting effects in the present. Then there is the danger of an a-historical and a-moral narrative in which all people involved are equated. Nevertheless, at the end of her life De Loo's narrative offered Mrs. Ton-Seyler a framework by which she could reconcile herself with her German origin. *De Tweeling* figured as a metaphor for a unity pulled apart by a violent political regime, and this made it possible for her to acknowledge her own identification and disidentification with both Germany and the Netherlands.

In Rie Ton-Seyler's life story, politically engaged world literature forms a continuous guideline. Around that literary universe, where reality and imagination touch in a powerful manner, she found a transnational and multicultural community where she felt 'at home'. In the narratives that were created and shared, she recognized herself, her ideas and emotions; literature offered her a frame of reference to determine and further develop her own position in the world. She never felt homesick, Mrs. Ton says. But in her bookcase and her own writings and stories one notices the yearning for the broad-minded Germany populated by Jewish and non-Jewish *Denker und Dichter* that was taken away from her by National Socialism. In world literature, with both the authors and the characters who populated their books, she ultimately found recognition and experienced a sense of belonging. For Lukas Plaut, the Jewish protagonist in the next chapter, it was not so much world literature as the worldwide starry sky that accommodated him, after National Socialism had pulled the rug from under him and his wife and children.

---

81   W.F. Jonckheere, 'Een dilemma van percepties: De tweeling van Tessa de Loo' in het *Tydskrif vir Nederlands en Afrikaans* 3 (1996) 1. See also: Luc Huyse, *Alles Gaat Voorbij, Behalve Het Verleden*. (Amsterdam: Van Gennep, 2006).

'Even After the War we will Stand Alone'

Letters as Drops in an Antisemitic Ocean

Lukas Plaut (1910-1984) came to the Netherlands in 1933.[1] He had been born 23 years earlier in the Japanese city of Kumamoto, where his father Joseph worked as a private teacher and later as a trader in Eastern art. The German Joseph Plaut and his wife Catherine Lewy gave their children a liberal upbringing in which Jewish rituals such as circumcision, Bar/Bat mitzvah or regular synagogue visits were not on the agenda.[2]

As teenagers, Lukas and his twin brother Ulrich continued their education at a boarding school in southern Germany; their sister Eva, five years their junior, later followed to her grandparents' home in Berlin.[3] With the diploma of the *Real-gymnasium* in his pocket, Lukas went to Berlin to study at the Friedrich-Wilhelm University. In 1931, after graduating in mathematics and physics, he acquired a place at the Neubabelsberg observatory near Berlin. A year later, according to a preserved certificate from the Prussian magistrates

---

1 This chapter is a re-working of my contribution 'Het vuil, de sterren en de dood'. Lucas Plaut en Stien Witte: portret van een 'gemengd' huwelijk, in: C. van Eijl et al. (red.), *Jaarboek voor Vrouwengeschiedenis 18: Parallelle Levens*. Amsterdam (Stichting beheer IISG) 1998: 91–116. Also published in ICODO-info 15 (1999) 3/4: 20–39.

2 Conversation Barbara Henkes and Mrs. Plaut-Witte (hereafter: Conversation Henkes and Plaut-Witte), 21 Apr. 1997. During our conversations, Mrs. Plaut-Witte provided letters and other documents she had saved. Unless stated otherwise, the documents are from her private collection (now with her children). Copies are in the possession of the author. See also the biographic information about Lukas Plaut's sister, in: Sabine Richter, *Einblick in ein kunstpädagogisches Skizzenbuch. Leben und Werk von Eva Eyquem* (Erlangen: FAU University Press, 2017), Part 1, at 27.

3 Richter, *Einblick,* 37–38. In 1937 Eva Plaut continued her studies at the art academy *de la Grande*-Chaumière in Pars, where she met the medical student André Eyquem. They got married in Sep. 1939 and during the Nazi occupation Eva Eyquem-Plaut survived in South West France, where she gave birth to a son. In 1946 the family returned to Paris. See also: https://www.pasteur.fr/infosci/archives/eyqo.html: André Eyquem (1916-2013) Notice biographique. For more genealogical information on the Plaut kinship network: *Descendants of Abraham PLAUT*: https://jinh.lima-city.de/gene/chris/Descendants_of_Abraham_Plaut_from_Willingshausen. PDF dated 9 Jan. 2016, prepared by Christopher Kuehn (hereafter: Descendants of Abraham PLAUT). The same source indicates that Lukas's brother Uli married the Jewish Lilly Falkenstein in Shanghai in 1935. Pre-war letters from Joseph and Catherine Plaut-Lewy show that Uli and Lilly went from there to the US in 1939. A large community of German Jewish refugees had formed in Shanghai. Cf. James R. Ross, *Escape to Shanghai: A Jewish Community in China*. (New York: The Free Press, 1994).

© BARBARA HENKES, 2020 | DOI:10.1163/9789004401600_005

FIGURE 3.1
Lukas and his twin-brother Uli with their
Japanese nanny. Kumamoto, Japan, 1913.

Court, he renounced Judaism (*das Judentum*).[4] The document shows that he felt the need to officially distance himself from a Jewishness others imposed on him, at a time of growing antisemitism. However, this could not prevent Lukas from being hit by the antisemitic measures taken by the newly elected National Socialist government.

'Under the present circumstances, I find myself compelled to give you notice of the termination of your room at the observatory on April 15, 1933'.[5] With this brief statement, two weeks after the Nazi boycott of Jewish businesses (*Judenboykott*),[6] the observatory director made it clear that he was going to conform to the increased antisemitism in those days. His talented student was given a week to pack his belongings. Lukas Plaut could not at will detach himself from his forced identification as a Jew, and as a German Jew his position and civil rights were undermined. Germanness and Jewishness became two mutually exclusive categories in Nazi Germany: Jews could not be 'true'

---

4 Certificate, issued 1 Nov. 1932.
5 'Unter den zurzeit obwaltenden Verhältnissen sehe ich mich gezwungen, Ihnen das von Ihnen bewohnte Zimmer auf der Sternwarte zum 15. Apr. 1933 zu kündigen'. Private collection.
6 See also Chap.1, p. 32.

Germans and true Germans were by definition non-Jewish, or 'Aryan'. This meant – as the history of Eberhard Gebensleben and Herta Eulings showed in Chapter 1 – that measures were taken to avoid 'damage' to German society by the 'non-Aryan' race. Lukas Plaut tried to escape the antisemitic obstacles by leaving for the Netherlands. There, he was eventually overtaken by National Socialism: from the moment that Nazi Germany invaded the Netherlands in May 1940, Jewishness became an inevitable, all-determining category in his own life and that of his wife Stien Witte and their children.

After the death of her husband, Stien Plaut-Witte (1911-2007) carefully preserved his letters and papers, as well as some letters from the correspondence with a dear uncle and aunt of hers, and occasional letters with others who got involved in the fate of Lukas and his family. All documents testify to the mutual loyalty and struggle for survival of the Plaut-Witte couple, not only during but also after the end of the Nazi-German occupation. The voice of Lukas Plaut, as it resonates from his letters, is combined with the memory work done by his wife at the end of the 1990s. This links her contemporary memories with written accounts of herself and her husband at the time. Their letters, to each other and to others, show how they tried to bridge the forced dividing lines between Jewish and non-Jewish or Gentile, between Dutch and German, and between the male and female domains in their lifetime.

Marriage Certificate

At the insistence of his mother, who travelled from Japan to Europe and visited the Leiden observatory with her son, Lukas moved to the Netherlands. A few years later that would have been much more difficult, if possible at all. From 1934 onward the Dutch admission policy became ever more restrictive in order to prevent 'undesirable aliens', especially the many Jewish refugees, from coming to the Netherlands.[7] Financially supported by his parents, Lukas Plaut was able to continue studying in Leiden with Professor J.H. Oort and the director of the Leiden observatory, Professor E. Hertzsprung. He learned Dutch in no time and re-took his BA degree (*kandidaatsexamen*) before obtaining his doctorate in 1938. That same year he married the Dutch Stien Witte. A year later, he obtained his PhD with a dissertation on variable stars, and in September 1939 his

---

7   Corrie Berghuis, *Joodse vluchtelingen in Nederland, 1938-1940: documenten betreffende toelating, uitleiding en kampopname* (Kampen: J.H. Kok, 1990) 11.

first child was born.[8] It looked as though Lukas Plaut had settled down safely in the Netherlands with Stien, who was herself lucky with her kind, educated and attractive husband.

The image Mrs. Plaut-Witte presents of her late husband in those pre-war years is in stark contrast to that of her father. Gerhard Witte ruled as a *pater familias* over his wife and five children. His Lutheran background dominated her mother's Catholicism, and his political conservatism left no room for progressive ideas. As far as he was concerned, his daughters' education need not be more than a housekeeping training. Stien felt more at home with her socialist Aunt Cor and Uncle Thé van Woerkom, at whose house she immersed herself in the socially engaged contents of their bookcase.[9] She found support from the socialist director of the Rotterdam School for Housekeeping, Hélène Heijermans,[10] who ensured that Stien did a follow-up training in childcare and pedagogy. Subsequently, she exchanged her work as a kindergarten teacher for a position as an apprentice nurse at the Leiden University Hospital. To the displeasure of her father she got involved in the Social Democratic Youth Movement, the *Arbeiders Jeugd Centrale* (AJC). At this point in her life story Stien Witte comes across as a studious and socially minded young woman who followed her own path. Apart from her uncle and aunt, the rest of the family no longer appears in the remainder of her biographical trajectory.

In Leiden she met Lukas Plaut: 'He gave a talk and I went there with a friend. I can't remember what it was about, but we were interested [...] When we arrived a little late for his lecture, he noticed me, and [later he told me that] I reminded him of his girlfriend in Germany who had died ... and that's how it started'. Stien was charmed by Lukas: 'he was a handsome young man; he was really nice also in the way he acted. I was socially engaged and so was he'. She took Lukas to folk dances and on tours to the houses of the Friends of Nature Association, although he never joined the *AJC* or the Dutch Social Democratic Workers' Party. Lukas helped Stien with the exams for her nursing course and

---

8   L. Plaut, *Photografische photometrie der veranderlijke sterren CV Carinae en WW Draconis* (Leiden 1939).

9   Mrs. J.C. van Woerkom-Witte (1898-1965) was honoured in 1964 for her dedication 'to very different areas of social life, driven by a great deal of social concern' (the local *Nieuwe Stadsblad van Schiedam* and surrounding areas of 1 Sep.1964). Her husband Th. van Woerkom (1895-1975) was a head teacher, chairman of the Dutch Education Association and active in many other organizations. (See e.g. the Social Democratic daily newspaper *Het Vrije Volk* of 23 and 24 Dec. 1960).

10   She was the daughter of the Rotterdam journalist and social democrat Herman Heijermans Sr., and the sister of the socialist Jewish writer; Herman Heijermans.

FIGURE 3.2   Lukas Plaut and Stien Witte, 1936.

supported her in difficult situations, for example when her flute teacher became too obtrusive and could not keep his hands off her. From then on Lukas accompanied her and they had flute lessons together.[11] Although in Nazi Germany Lukas had been forcibly labelled as Jewish, this was not the first category that he identified with. Stien also saw her friend primarily as politically and culturally like-minded, not in terms of race (Jewish) or nationality (German).

After completing her training in Leiden, Stien Witte successfully applied for a job as a nurse at the Amsterdam Wilhelmina hospital. There she became involved with the socialist Commission *Hulp aan Spanje* (Aid to Spain), which supported the struggle against Franco's fascists.[12] She remembers that she had

11   Conversation Henkes and Plaut-Witte, 7 Oct.1997.
12   There were more nurses in the Wilhelmina hospital who left for Spain in 1937, including Stien's roommate Noortje Diamant, who, like her, had been a member of the AJC. See also: the brochure *Spanje helpen is werken voor de vrede* (Amsterdam: Commissie Hulp aan Spanje, 1938) and *Wij werkten in Spanje: Ervaringen van het Hollandse medische personeel in Spanje, met bijdragen van B.H. Sajet, A. Blauw, N. Diamant e.a.*, Medisch-Hygiënisch Comité van 'Hulp aan Spanje', 1939. For more information about this *Hulp aan Spanje* Commission: H. Dankaart, J.J. Flinterman, F. Groot en R. Vuurmans, *De oorlog begon in Spanje. Nederlanders in de Spaanse burgeroorlog 1936-1939* (Amsterdam: Uitgeverij van Gennep, 1986) 121 and www.spanjestrijders.nl (hosted by the International Instite for Social History (IISG), Amsterdam.

FIGURE 3.3   The Spanish ambassador in the Netherlands says goodbye to Dutch nurses prior
             to their departure to the Spanish front; The Hague, April 1937. Stien's colleague
             Noortje Diamant is on the left of the ambassador.

already signed up to travel to Spain as a nurse, when Lukas's mother visited the
Netherlands. 'She said indignantly: "Lukas has been through so much and now
you rush into a war voluntarily?!"'[13] Lukas had never raised any objections to
her plans and she apparently had not imagined that as a nurse she could be
killed.

Finally, she decided to stay in the Netherlands. Soon afterwards plans were
made for their wedding. But when Lukas and Stien wanted to give notice of
their marriage in 1937, they encountered a serious problem. The official refused
to perform the marriage, because the German Nuremberg laws had their repercussions in the Netherlands.[14] These laws made it impossible for Lukas Plaut as
a 'non-Aryan' German Jew to marry an 'Aryan' woman. Without permission
from the German authorities in the form of a certificate of marriageability

---

13   Conversation Henkes and Plaut-Witte, 7 Oct. 1997.
14   See also Chap. 2.

(*Ehefähigkeitszeugnis*), the Dutch official felt compelled to refuse to perform their wedding ceremony.[15]

Lukas Plaut and Stien Witte were not the only couple that unsuccessfully applied to the local Civil Registry during these years. When it became clear that antisemitism, as enshrined in the Nuremberg laws of September 1935, also penetrated the Netherlands through the International Marriage Convention, Minister of Justice Van Schaik opted for a pragmatic arrangement. The Treaty was not cancelled, but a German *Ehefähigkeitszeugnis* was no longer an absolute requirement for marriage. If such a document was refused by German officials, and the Dutch civil servants or, ultimately, the judge thought that this had been done unjustly, the wedding could still take place. Thus, the minister placed the responsibility with the civil servants and the judiciary. In practice this led to arbitrary actions whereby much depended on the individual attitudes of the officials involved, the inventiveness of lawyers, and the perseverance of the bride and groom. The wedding couple had to be prepared to take their marital commitment to the court, or outside the Netherlands in a country that had not signed the Convention.[16]

Stien Witte and Lukas Plaut enlisted the help of the Leiden lawyer Tj. D. Schaper, who was able to use the space left by the government's half-hearted guidelines. A favourable statement from the highly esteemed Professor of astronomy J.H. Oort helped: the marriage was performed 'as quietly as possible' on 18 July 1938.[17] Remembering her wedding day, Mrs. Plaut says: 'It was so bizarre (...) the lawyer called me at my work in the hospital and said: "you have to get married immediately, because the licence can be declared invalid at any moment"'. So, I ran to the town hall in my nursing outfit, and my husband, or rather my future husband, also came quickly, and that's how we got married, without a party or whatever. So that wasn't so nice'.[18] Stien did marry in white, but it was not the wedding gown she had in mind. For romance there wasn't much space, not on their wedding day, nor afterwards – or it might be the romance of living faithfully together 'till death us do part'.

---

15   Henkes, "Hausmädchenheimschaffung".

16   See Henkes, *Heimat in Holland*, 166–168 with references to the *Nederlandsch Juristenblad* en the *Nederlandsche Jurisprudentie*, Sep. 1935.

17   J.H. Oordt, 6 May 1938 on letterhead paper of Tj.D. Schaper, and Schaper's postwar letter, 4 May 1984 after a request of Mrs. Plaut-Witte, explaining the legal course of affairs regarding her marriage.

18   Conversation Henkes and Plaut-Witte, 21 Apr. 1997.

Stateless

According to Dutch regulations Stien Witte had to adopt both the family name and nationality of her husband. If she had been a man and Lukas a woman, Lukas would have received the Dutch nationality from Stien. And if Lukas had been a Dutchman and Stien a German woman, she would have taken her husband's Dutch nationality, as the experiences of Rie Ton-Seyler and Irmgard Brester-Gebensleben in the previous chapters indicate. But now that Lukas was categorised as a male German Jew, a problem arose. Although they got officially married in the Netherlands, their 'mixed' marriage was not valid in Nazi Germany. By marrying a German Stien had to give up her Dutch citizenship, while as an Aryan woman she had no access to German citizenship because she married a non-Aryan German. A combination of the antisemitic exclusion policy of Nazi Germany and the gender-specific admission policy regarding Dutch citizenship ensured that the two of them ended up between 'Dutch' and 'German' — which meant that they both became stateless.

Shortly after their marriage Stien Plaut-Witte planned to accompany her husband on a trip to an international congress of astronomers in Sweden. However, she was unable to get a passport. Mrs. Plaut vividly remembers the official's reaction to her request for a new passport: 'He said: "you will not get a passport, because you do not exist". I said: "Sir, I am standing right before you!" Then he said: "You will not get a passport, because you are stateless".'[19] At that time Lukas still had a valid German passport, although he had to take care it would not be taken at the German border. To avoid that risk, he went by boat to Göteborg and from there by train to Stockholm. The day after Stien had taken her husband to the train for Antwerp, from where the ship to Sweden was leaving, she was informed by her lawyer that the necessary papers were ready for her at the Ministry of Foreign Affairs. 'I said to Mr. Schaper: "What good is it to me now? Everyone has already left, and my husband is on the boat".' On Schaper's advice she went to The Hague, where a friendly official handed her the travel document. It was made out under her maiden name and only valid for three months. If Stien (Plaut-)Witte were to travel through Germany, she needed to hide her married status. The following morning she left for Stockholm via Germany. In Sweden, she stood on the station platform waiting for her husband when he arrived.[20]

---

19   Conversation Henkes and Plaut-Witte, 21 Apr. 1997.
20   Conversation Henkes and Plaut-Witte, 21 Apr. 1997. This was the Congress of the International Astronomical Union (IAU), founded in 1919 to promote international cooperation and coordination in the astronomical field, in August 1938 in Stockholm.

Although Stien and Lukas Plaut ran a legally recognized, joint household in the Netherlands, voting in Dutch elections was no longer possible for the politically committed Stien. In the spring of 1939 she tried unsuccessfully to regain Dutch nationality in order to be placed on the electoral roll for 1939-1940.[21] In spite of the increasing political tensions in Europe and the loss of their citizenship, in 1938 the Plaut-Witte couple seem to have looked to the future with confidence. At the Leiden observatory Lukas was appreciated as a promising astronomer. Although they lived on an allowance from his parents, after completing his dissertation in 1939 there was a good chance that Plaut would find a place in the international academic network of astronomers.[22] The developments in and around Nazi Germany gave enough cause for concern, but Mrs. Plaut – notwithstanding her political engagement – cannot remember that she and her husband were (or wanted to be) aware of the threatening events in Nazi Germany.[23] Lukas Plaut, whose grandmother lived in Germany, apparently kept his worries to himself, or his wife was unable to grasp their significance at the time. It seems that before May 1940 both Lukas and Stien ignored the threats posed by National Socialism as much as possible. In the last year before the Nazi-German invasion of the Netherlands, they focused mainly on his dissertation and their (then imminent) parenthood.

After May 1940 it was no longer possible to ignore the antisemitic policies that were soon implemented in Dutch society. In the first few months of the installation of the Nazi regime these seemed not as severe as expected, but from September 1940 one anti-Jewish measure followed another, with Jewish 'foreigners' (often a euphemism for refugees) being the first to be hit. Lukas Plaut could no longer escape the antisemitism that declared him a *persona non grata* and thus outlawed him as a Jew. A written order was delivered on 5 September 1940 to the address of the Plaut family in Leiderdorp, signed by the head of the local police. Plaut had to leave the municipality of Leiderdorp before 9 September as a 'non-Aryan foreigner'. From that date Leiderdorp was forbidden

---

21   In Mar. 1939 Lukas Plaut still had a valid German passport, according to an unsuccessful request to the Mayor and City Council of Leiderdorp to place Stien Plaut-Witte on the electoral roll for the Dutch elections.

22   Plaut, *Photografische photometrie*.

23   Postwar notes from Mrs. Plaut-Witte (undated), probably in connection with the application for a war pension from the Foundation 1940-'45 (private collection). This information is at odds with Stien's memory of Lukas's mother's statement about the misery her son had experienced in Germany. Besides, in the Netherlands the anti-fascist struggle against Nazi Germany was linked to that against the Spanish fascists under Franco in the Spanish Civil War.

territory to him, as were a series of other places, ranging from Ameland to Amsterdam and from Bennebroek to Oude Tonge.[24] The city of Groningen was not mentioned in the page-long list of place names, which made Lukas rush north to continue his research at the university's astronomical laboratory. A few days later he was followed by Stien and their baby Irmgard. She first had to arrange their forced departure from Leiderdorp: 'The whole house had to be empty. In the meantime, my husband would be seeking shelter in Groningen', explains Mrs. Plaut in retrospect.

His marriage to the Dutch Stien Witte and his work at Leiden University offered Lukas Plaut access to a national community as well as to an international circle of peers and other scholars. But as a man with a German passport, he was not eligible for Dutch nationality, and as a Jew he lost his position at the Dutch university soon after the Nazi-German invasion. The 'nation', in the form of 'being German' or 'becoming Dutch', offered him no protection or guidance in these circumstances. The transnational kinship network of which he was part was also under constant pressure from the Nazi regime. Since the Nazi-German occupation of the Netherlands, neither his parents in Beijing,[25] nor his brother and sister-in-law in Los Angeles or his sister in Paris, let alone his relatives in Germany, were able to help him and his family in the Netherlands.

'A Man I had to Protect'

When Stien arrived at Groningen station 'with an eleven-month-old baby and a basket of nappies on my arms', Lukas was waiting for her. She remembers: 'There he stood at the gate. Very sad. And he says: "Stien, I have nowhere to go". There I stood, with a man I had to protect, a child I had to care for, and myself of course. Yes, there we were ...'[26] Mrs. Plaut presents this reunion as a turning point in her life. Marking a 'turning point' helps to bring order in what otherwise might seem a chaotic series of events – and to recover some form of agency within a narrative about a situation where she and her family were at the mercy of the Nazi authorities and the help of others.[27] In addition to its ordering capacity, a turning point also provides a dramatic impact, whether it is

---

24   List in the possession of Mrs. Plaut-Witte. See also Presser, *Ashes in the wind*, 222.
25   From a letter from Lukas Plaut's father, Joseph Plaut, 16 Dec. 1936 it appears that around 1936 Lukas's parents moved from Japan to Beijing in China.
26   Conversation Henkes and Plaut-Witte, 21 Apr. 1997. See also her postwar notes (no date).
27   Jan Fontijn, 'Over radicale bekeringen en plotselinge inzichten' & 'Nogmaals keerpunten in een leven Identificatie of objectivering', *Biografie Bulletin*, Vol. 11 2001/1: 97–106 & 224–229.

about religious conversion, affiliation with a political movement, or other events that are experienced as a significant moment in time. It is always about an unexpected new insight into one's own social position. This indeed applies to exactly this point in Mrs. Plaut-Witte's life story. She relates the event several times, and time and again she emphasizes that from then on she was the one who had to guard their family life. Although Lukas shared in the care of their household during wartime, her narrative marks the moment Stien Plaut fully realized how defenseless her husband was and that her marriage had put her, too, in an extremely vulnerable position. Since National Socialism had extended to the Netherlands, the gendered positions of the Plaut-Witte couple switched: the social standing, protection and care that Lukas Plaut had offered his wife and child at an earlier stage had vanished. Instead, Stien had to protect her husband and their household from the far-reaching consequences of the antisemitic policies of the Nazis.

It is not clear to what extent Stien Plaut was already aware of this at the time. She does recall how she took matters in hand: 'I am a practical woman and we had to go somewhere, so I said: "Surely there is a professor here, Lukas? Then let's go there"'. They rang the bell at the house of Professor of astronomy P.J. van Rhijn and his wife. 'But even for one night there was no room for a woman with a child. I did indeed blame them for that. Not for long, because this was still at the beginning of the war. The people were not yet aware of the measures against the Jews.[28] But at that very moment I did of course blame them. You are simply powerless. (…) Then we thought … well, we didn't think anything because we were in such a state of despair: where could we go?!' Van Rhijn did show them the local newspaper, in which rooms were offered for rent. The Plaut family rented a damp basement on Parklaan, where they celebrated the first birthday of daughter Irmgard on 26 September 1940.[29]

While Stien focused on the everyday survival in the here and now, Lukas was mainly concerned with surviving National Socialism in the near future. This is aptly illustrated by two letters of 4 October 1940 to Uncle Thé and Aunt Cor in Rotterdam. The Plaut couple each wrote their own letter of thanks in response to the birthday present for their daughter Irmgard. 'For the money I'll buy cloth for a dress for Irmchen', Stien wrote. 'We have had so many expenses that I can

---

28   Although Mrs. Plaut-Witte states that people were not yet well-informed, an announcement had already been made by the city council of Groningen on 1 July 1940 with a call to all 'non-Aryan foreigners' to report to the head office of the police. Stefan van der Poel, *Joodse stadjers: de joodse gemeenschap in de stad Groningen, 1796-1945* (Assen: Gorkum BV, 2004) 134.

29   Conversation Henkes and Plaut-Witte, 21 Apr. 1997. See also her handwritten note 'Voorgeschiedenis' (author and date unknown).   ■ Please provide content for footnote 29.

FIGURE 3.4   Lukas Plaut with his daugther Irmgard, Groningen 1942.

use the money very well. I can't make ends meet with 80 guilders, and I do everything as economically as possible. Our clothing wears out so quickly, which
confronts us all the time with new expenses. Fortunately, I can sew, otherwise
we couldn't make it'. Then a jubilant description of her daughter follows, in
which her great affection for her husband shimmers through: 'It is such a small,
sunny creature with her beautiful eyes, which absorb everything. I believe she
is a real Plaut in appearance and character and I am happy about that'.[30]

In turn, Lukas Plaut also wrote a thank-you note, in which he immediately
touched on the anti-Jewish measures that caused him the most concern: 'Today I read in the newspaper that from now on Jews will no longer be appointed
or promoted to official positions'.[31] He foresaw that more of such measures
would follow. 'Under these circumstances, the possibility of finding a more or
less permanent job is much smaller or it is completely gone'. In the rest of his
letter he refers to his brother, who had sent an official document from the

---

30   Stien Plaut-Witte, 4 Oct. 1940.
31   See also A.J. Herzberg, 'Kroniek der jodenvervolging' (Chronicle of the persecution of the
      Jews), in: *Onderdrukking en verzet. Nederland in oorlogstijd*, Vol. 3 (Amsterdam: J.M. Meu-
      lenhoff, 1949) 44–49; Presser, *Ashes in the wind*, 16–29; L. de Jong, *Het Koninkrijk der Ned-
      erlanden in de Tweede Wereldoorlog*, Vol. 4 ('s Gravenhage: Staatsuitgeverij, 1972) 780–781.

oUnited States with which Lukas could apply for an immigrant visa. 'If I make the decision to go there, I now have the opportunity to follow all the official steps, i.e., to obtain visas for all countries in between, book a place on the boat, etc'. After mentioning the different travel options, Lukas continues: 'As the options are better now than if we should wait, it is time to decide to either stay here permanently or to do everything we can to leave for America. That is precisely the difficult and crucial decision, and I would like to ask your opinion about this'.[32]

If and what Uncle Thé and Aunt Cor answered is not known, but documents show that Lukas took the initiative on 22 November 1940, together with Stien and Irmgard, to register with the American Consulate in Rotterdam. The application was accompanied by a number of documents from the United States stating that Lukas's brother Ulrich and his wife Lilly, who now lived in Los Angeles, vouched for their relatives from the Netherlands.[33] On the Dutch side, the Leiden professors Oort and Hertzsprung had issued statements about Lukas Plaut's qualifications and talent in the field of astronomy. 'Dr. Plaut is what one might call an astronomer by birth, not simply by profession', wrote Oort, and added his great appreciation for his 'most likeable character'.[34] His colleague Hertzsprung – who had previously arranged a modest grant of 80 guilders a month after the allowance of Lukas's parents could no longer be transferred – described Plaut as an 'eager, quiet and modest worker'.[35] Both also added that, as far as they knew, Plaut had not engaged in any political activities, an addition referring to the prevailing fear among American policy makers that there might be National Socialist or communist sympathizers amongst the Jewish refugees of German origin who entered the country.[36]

Despite the positive assessments from high-ranking professionals and the guarantee of Lukas's brother and his wife, the application was refused.[37] Fifty-seven years later Mrs. Plaut could not remember what might have been the

---

32   Lukas Plaut, 4 Oct. 1940. The information is confirmed by surviving documents with which Ulrich Plaut and his wife Lilly Falkenstein request permission to have their relatives from the Netherlands come to the US.

33   Written statements of June and July 1940 from the employers of Ulrich and Lilly Plaut in Los Angeles, mentioning the Plauts' merits and indicating that they would like to keep them permanently employed. They had already brought Lilly's parents from Germany to Los Angeles.

34   J.H. Oort, 26 Apr. 1941.

35   E. Hertzsprung, 12 May 1941.

36   Saul S. Friedman, *No haven for the oppressed: United States policy toward Jewish refugees, 1938-1945* (Detroit: Wage State University Press, 1973) 105–128.

37   'Mutti', Lukas Plaut's mother Catherine Plaut-Lewy, 19 May 1941 in reaction to the news that Lukas and his family did not obtain permission to emigrate to the United States.

reason.[38] In any case, the limitations of the American admission policy for Jewish refugees posed a hindrance, and from the Nazi side Jewish emigration from the occupied Netherlands was only rarely permitted. The loss of their citizenship will not have helped the Plaut family either.[39] More than six months after the rejection of their request for emigration to the United States, a new regulation by the Nazi authorities came into effect in December 1941: all non-Dutch Jews had to report to the *Zentralstelle für jüdische Auswanderung*, a German institution led by the head of the security police (*Sicherheitspolizei*) F.H. Aus der Fünten. In response, once again numerous forms were filled in by Lukas, Stien, and on behalf of the little Irmgard.[40]

Afterwards we know that this measure was the prelude to the later deportation of almost all Jews, Dutch, German or otherwise, with or without a request for emigration. According to the historian Jacques Presser, German Jews under the age of 45 made up the lion's share of those who were taken away on 15 July 1942 with the first transports.[41] Because under National Socialism Jewishness and Germanness excluded each other, the German origin of Jews worked against them: they were the first to be eligible for antisemitic expulsion procedures in the occupied Netherlands. An exception was only made for the 'mixed' married among them. Thanks to his marriage to a non-Jewish woman, Lukas Plaut was exempted from expulsion for the time being.

Growing Isolation

Slowly but surely, fear grew and personal liberties diminished during the Nazi occupation. From the end of 1941, Lukas and Stien Plaut were increasingly confronted with new, far-reaching antisemitic measures. Lukas was no longer allowed access to the astronomical laboratory and the university library in Groningen. The public library, too, was declared prohibited ground for Jews. These were pre-eminently the places he needed to keep the permanent threat of the Nazis at bay. He lost not only his job, his future prospects, and his freedom of movement, but also his status as an academic and breadwinner. Stien Plaut was also hit by these measures. Going out together was no longer possible since the means of transport and public spaces had become forbidden

---

38   Conversation Henkes and Plaut-Witte, 7 Oct.1997.

39   Friedman, *No haven for the oppressed*; Evelien Gans, *Jaap en Ischa Meijer. Een joodse geschiedenis 192-1956*. Amsterdam: Uitgeverij Bert Bakker, 2008) 139.

40   According to documents of Mrs. Plaut-Witte, she and her husband applied for emigration on 5 May 1942 at the *Zentralstelle für jüdische Auswanderung*.

41   Presser, *Ashes in the wind*, 222.

territory to Lukas Plaut. In a society where so many social activities were con-
centrated around family life and where the man was perceived as the head of
the family, it was difficult for Stien to build and maintain a social life in a new
residence from which her husband was excluded. Only just arrived in Groningen, the Plaut couple had hardly been able to build up a reliable circle of
friends and acquaintances before the antisemitic prosecution started.[42] Whom
could they trust, and whom could they not? They fell into a rapidly growing
isolation, causing them to become more and more dependent on each other
and to get caught up in each other's fears.

At the end of 1942 Stien Plaut became pregnant again. When asked if the
pregnancy was desired, she replied: 'No, I don't think so. In fact, I can't remember. Life was so complicated'. However, the events around the birth on 7 July
1943 are etched in her memory: 'There were all those humiliations. I can still
clearly remember the letter that said: "The Jew Lukas Plaut is allowed to accompany his wife to the hospital". That was the Roman Catholic hospital on
Herenweg. When I arrived, they asked the name of our first child. I said: "Irmgard". "A German name?!" Irmgard was named after my husband's first girlfriend who had died. "The second child certainly has a Dutch name?" I said: "If
it is a girl, her name will be Käthe". "Oh, Keetje!" I say: "No, not Keetje but Käthe,
with an a and an Umlaut. She will be named after Käthe Kollwitz". That woman
did not know at all who Käthe Kollwitz was'.[43]

Naming their daughter after the German artist who was famous for her visual denunciations against war violence was a statement. To them, Käthe Kollwitz was a representative of that 'other', socially and culturally engaged Germany. With this name Lukas and Stien expressed their hope for peace and a
better life in the near future. As the German occupation continued and Dutch
society became more and more polarized along nationalist lines – in which everything that was 'German' was associated with the National Socialist enemy –
the naming of children became more and more politically charged. That explains why so many girls were named after the Dutch Princesses of Orange

---

42   Postwar notes from Plaut-Witte (undated), probably in connection with the application
      for a war pension from the Foundation 1940-'45.
43   Conversation Henkes and Plaut-Witte, 21 Apr. 1997. Käthe Kollwitz (1867–1945) was a Ger-
      man painter, print maker, and sculptor whose work offered a searing account of the hu-
      man condition, and the tragedy of war, in the first half of the 20th century. In 1933, after
      the establishment of the National-Socialist regime, the Nazi Party authorities forced her
      to resign her place on the faculty of the *Akademie der Künste* following her support of the
      Dringender Appell in July 1932 This was a joint call to protest against National Socialism.
      Her work was removed from museums and banned from being exhibited. Cf. M. Klein and
      H. Klein, *Käthe Kollwitz: Life and Art* (New York: Holt, Rinehart and Winston, 1972).

FIGURE 3.5   Käthe Kollwitz, *Die Mütter* (The Mothers), 1921–1922, Art Gallery of Ontario.

during and shortly after the Nazi occupation.[44] Whereas for the Dutch nurse a German first name seemed to indicate a 'bad' political position, Stien Plaut insisted on her daughter being named after the German artist. When asked about books that were important during her lifetime, Mrs. Plaut immediately takes a collection of sketches by Käthe Kollwitz from the shelf: desolate, penetrating images of women and children, seriously affected by the consequences of the First World War.

The day after Käthe's birth Lukas Plaut made his appearance at the hospital. Later a friend told Stien that Lukas had first given her some money to buy flowers, because he wasn't allowed to do so as a Jew recognizable by his mandatory badge in the form of a yellow star. The visiting hour started: 'And who came in first ...? An SS man in uniform!', Mrs. Plaut vividly remembers the terror of that moment. 'There were four of us in the room and his wife was in the bed opposite me. Lukas was coming. He could stand in that doorway at any moment,

---

44   'Corpus of First Names in The Netherlands', Meertens Instituut, Amsterdam: http://www
         .meertens.knaw.nl/nvb/english, retrieved 3 June 2019.

and indeed that was what happened. There stood the Jew, and there the SS man, and there I was with the baby, right in the middle'. Although Lukas Plaut had permission to visit his wife that did not diminish Stien's panic: 'That SS man was in any case his enemy! I told Lukas to leave as soon as possible, because he was in danger, and he did. But I was shaking in my bed'. As it turned out, the visiting hour in the hospital provided a risky 'contact zone', because both visiting fathers were sharing the same social space with the one a potential victim of the other's antisemitism.[45] After the visiting hour was over, Stien was transferred to a single room to calm down. The crib was placed next to her bed, and the same nurse who had reacted with such indignation to the baby's German name apologized and assured her that she could stay in that room as long as she needed to regain her strength. 'That was so wonderful. It will stay with me all my life. I was there for three weeks, then I had to go home at some point. Yes, and then of course there were more anti-Jewish measures to come'.[46]

Lukas Plaut was still living at home with his wife and children. But for how long? And what would happen to their young daughters, since they were registered as 'half-breeds' (*Mischlinge*)? In July 1942 the systematic deportations of Jews from the Netherlands had begun. Although the deportation of 'mixed' married Jews with children was postponed, they felt threatened by the opaque antisemitic policies as much as other Jews did. According to the historian Loe de Jong many of them wondered whether it made sense to get divorced on behalf of the non-Jewish partner and the children.[47] Mrs. Plaut cannot remember whether she and her husband ever talked about this possibility; she would never have considered it herself.[48] This applied to many more non-Jewish partners, precisely because their marriage offered some protection to their Jewish partner. However, for how long?

The wearing of a yellow star alone, which had been obligatory since May 1942, was enough to qualify for deportation. Every convinced Nazi police officer could charge any now visible Jew for any violation, real or fictitious. If they ended up as 'criminal cases' in one of the concentration camps, their fate was extremely uncertain.[49] The Plauts were also unsure about what awaited them when they were at home in Eerste Willemstraat, where they had taken up residence. J.L. Keijer, the Dutch chief of the Groningen Special Investigation and in

---

45   Pratt. *Imperial Eyes*, 8. See also the Introduction to this book.
46   Conversation Henkes and Plaut-Witte, 21 Apr. 1997. SS stands for the paramilitary Nazi organisation Schutzstaffel.
47   L. de Jong, *Het Koninkrijk*, Vol. 6, 291.
48   Conversation Henkes and Plaut-Witte, 29 Oct.1997.
49   In his 'Kroniek der jodenvervolging' (128), Herzberg indicates that the number of 'mixed' married amongst the so-called criminal cases was disproportionately high.

that capacity part of the Nazi Security Service (*Sicherheitsdienst*, SD), lived two houses away from them. 'He came by our house every evening to walk his dog. (...) We had a small bedroom on the street side and when he stopped at the door, we held our breath as we feared that he was going to ring the bell to fetch Lukas'.[50]

Terrified

In retrospect it is surprising that almost all of the more than 9,000 'mixed' married Jews in the Netherlands escaped the macabre death dance of the anti-semitic persecution policy. By way of explanation historians such as Presser and De Jong note that the attitude towards this group was a point of contention between different Nazi authorities in Berlin and in The Hague.[51] However, this did not mean that they and their families were left alone. After all, it was necessary to prevent more Jewish descendants from coming into the world. In the Netherlands, *Reichskommissar* H.A. Rauter proposed the most radical solution: as far as he was concerned, these Jews, their non-Jewish partners and their children should all be deported to Eastern Europe. 'Otherwise we will always have difficulties with these cases', Loe de Jong quotes the commander of the German and Dutch police as saying.[52] Rauter considered the definitive *Entjüdung* (deportation of all Jews) of the Netherlands a top priority, and a condition for a National Socialist final victory. When he did not receive enough support for his far-reaching deportation plans, he introduced an alternative measure.

In the spring of 1943 it became known that the National Socialist authorities were considering sterilising 'mixed' married Jews in the Netherlands. Such a measure had already been introduced in Germany in order to prevent 'Aryan' blood being contaminated with 'non-Aryan' blood.[53] First the Jewish partners had to gather in camp Westerbork; a 'voluntary' sterilization campaign was

---

50   Conversation Henkes and Plaut-Witte, 21 Apr. 1997. Keijer was killed in Apr. 1944 by a Groningen resistance group https://www.tweedewereldoorlog.nl/nieuwsvantoen/razzia-rondom-bedum/, retrieved 3 June 2019.

51   Presser, *Ashes in the wind, 313–316*; De Jong, *Het Koninkrijk*, Vol. 6, 290–294 and Vol. 7, 284–296. They estimated the size of the group at around 12,000; later research settles on a number of c. 9,000. See Coen Stuhldreher, *De legale rest. Gemengd gehuwde Joden onder de Duitse bezetting* (Amsterdam: Boom, 2007) 233–234.

52   De Jong, *Het Koninkrijk*, Vol. 7, 275.

53   See for instance N. Stoltzfus, *Resistance of the Heart. Intermarriage and the Rosenstrasse Protest in Nazi Germany* (New York 1996) 10–17 and 104–106.

planned from there. Those who submitted to sterilization no longer had to wear the yellow star, were free again to enter reading rooms, cafés, cinemas and shops, and so on. If they refused, they were threatened with deportation. The studies by Presser and De Jong, as well as by the journalist Philip Mechanicus, give a poignant picture of the impossible choice with which a first group of more than one hundred childless 'mixed' married Jews were faced at the end of May 1943.[54] However, when the authorities tried to carry out these forced sterilizations, there was so much protest and sabotage that the sterilization program was replaced in the spring of 1944 by a different approach to the 'problem of mixed marriages': Jewish men who were married to non-Jewish women were sent to labour camps.[55]

The sterilization measures passed the Plaut couple by, but Lukas did not escape forced labour in camp Havelte, where an airport had to be constructed.[56] He left on 14 March 1944, leaving Stien with four-year-old Irmgard and Käthe, less than a year old. The same day he wrote a card home in which he indicated that he would be able to come home every four weeks, and that 'the people here say that there is no need for anxiety'. 'Do everything at home as usual', he advised Stien.[57] In the remainder of his letter, Lukas described some of his fellow internees with whom he shared the barrack: a digger from Oude Pekela, a bank clerk from Assen, and a German suspenders manufacturer. He thought it was 'a nice combination' and he could imagine them as 'models for a caricaturist'. His writings give an impression of the way in which Lukas tried to put heart into both himself and his wife: 'You write that you are so scared, but Stieneke you shouldn't be. I'm brave and so are you. And we are all four together, although I am here now. In my mind I am always with you and hold

---

54   De Jong, *Het Koninkrijk*, Vol. 7, 287–288; Presser, *Ashes in the wind, 195–202*; P. Mechanicus, *In Dépôt. Dagboek uit Westerbork* (Amsterdam 1985 – first print 1964), 40, 43–44.

55   The Protestant and Catholic churches played an important role in the protests against sterilization measures, while the actual sabotage was committed by the doctors involved. See: De Jong, *Het Koninkrijk*, Vol. 7, 288–291; Presser, *Ashes in the wind*, 195–202 and Stuldreher, *De legale rest*, 277–317.

56   More information about camp Havelte: Michiel Gerding, 'Fliegerhorst Havelte, het vliegveld dat niet van de grond kwam' in: themanummer 'Landschap in de Tweede Wereldoorlog', *Noorderbreedte* 2005, http://www.noorderbreedte.nl/onder.php3?artikel=2612, retrieved 3 June 2019. See also Peter ter Haar, 'Tijdlijn Flugplatz Havelte': https://www.google.nl/search?q=kamp+Havelte+van+gelderen&oq=kamp+Havelte+van+gelderen&aqs=chrome..69i57.13906j0j8&sourceid=chrome&ie=UTF-8], retrieved 3 June 2019.

57   Lukas Plaut, 29 Mar. 1944. In total, this correspondence comprises 92 surviving letters and cards for the period between 14 Mar. and 4 Sep. 1944, when the German authorities left the camp on 'Mad Tuesday'. The correspondence from Stien's side was unfortunately not preserved after Lukas's unexpected flight from Havelte.

you tight'. Almost daily he hugged his wife and children with his pen. Aside from his reassuring words, the constant stream of postcards and notes in itself constituted an expression and confirmation of their strong bond.

In the occupied Netherlands, his marriage offered Lukas Plaut some protection, but the racist distinction between Aryan and non-Aryan nevertheless cut right through his family life and tore his household apart. Letters helped to bridge the dividing line. From his prison camp Lukas wrote himself back into his close family. Although he was subjected to a strict regime of heavy physical labour, and a primitive life in barracks without privacy,[58] he managed to express a certain confidence in the future. He seemed to draw strength from the company of other men in similar circumstances, as well as from the small pay for his work and the limited freedom of movement in the open air. Outside the camp, Stien found herself in an isolated position with the care of two small children and an imprisoned spouse. Lukas recognized her distress when he wrote on the second day of his captivity in Havelte: 'I would like to know how you manage on your own with Irmchen and Käthe. It must be lonely'. In the same letter he reported about his 'mates', almost half of whom were 'also former Germans'; the German soldiers who had to guard them were, according to Lukas, 'even more fiercely anti-Nazi than the Jews'.[59] Just like the German first names of his daughters, his statements show a sense of identification with a pre-National Socialist Germany. Although in the occupied Netherlands he was excluded both as a Jew and a stateless German, his Germanness nevertheless offered a point of identification and communality within the camp, even with some of the guards.

In addition to 'very friendly' people, Lukas also describes 'not too pleasant' inmates, and the noise of 25 men in one room he found hard to endure. Yet he felt no worse there than he had felt at home under the difficult circumstances, if we are to believe his letters. His head and stomach aches disappeared – 'that will be due to the open air' – and he describes the food as 'good and enough'. In his letters to Stien the main complaints about his condition were fatigue and a flu, and he emphasized several times that he wrote her 'just as it is, so you don't have to think it's worse than I let you know'.[60] Apparently, Lukas Plaut

---

58   Presser, *Ashes in the wind* (378–379) mentions, on the basis of a document of the Amsterdam *Hauptabteilung Soziale Verwaltung* of 29 Feb. 1944, that work was being done 'in groups of sixteen men from 8 o'clock in the morning to 6 o'clock in the evening, with a one and a half hour break in which they could have a warm cup of soup to buy for 5 1/2 cents.' The pay was 47 cents per hour and the work consisted of digging sand. The food provided in the evening was better than the afternoon soup.

59   Lukas Plaut, 15 Mar. 1944.

60   Lukas Plaut, 22 Mar. and 8 June 1944.

experienced a kind of relief after leaving his isolated position indoors. It helped him not to burden those he had left behind with any difficult experiences on his part. Others took a different attitude, as for instance Jacob Mozes van Gelderen, who sketched a much less favourable picture in his letters from camp Havelte to his 'dear wife and children'. According to his description, the men went to bed with all their clothes on, and 'while shivering and trembling' tried to fall asleep on straw and under a thin blanket, while the wind shrieked through the chinks between the boards of the barracks. Van Gelderen makes the fatigue that Lukas mentions concrete by referring to the exhausted men, who 'almost succumb to the hauling of rails and sleepers'.[61] How much hardship Lukas Plaut has suffered in the camp cannot be deduced from his letters. Nevertheless, he took comfort from the nature surrounding him. He also tried to communicate that on paper to his 'dearest Stieneke', with whom he had previously enjoyed nature outings together: 'It has become spring over here as well. Along the way dandelions and shepherd's purse are already blooming. But the best thing here is always the sky with the clouds', Lukas wrote to Stien on 24 April 1944.

In the following months he regularly referred to the indomitable zest for life that he found outside in the springtime. 'Yesterday one of us found a very small bird's nest in the heather, perhaps a bullfinch's. There were very small birds in it, completely naked without feathers, barely a centimetre in size. They opened their beaks very far, as they certainly thought they were being fed. You can find that in the middle of an airport'.[62] Two weeks later he brought up the bullfinch nest again: 'They had grown considerably, with brown-gray feathers, and as a bunch they almost burst out of the nest'. Lukas describes how he is often all alone on the edge of the forest and enjoys the birds singing. 'The beauty of nature gives me strength. (...) Everywhere the flowers are in bloom and in the middle of the airport, you can still find the most beautiful little beetles crawling out of the sand'.[63] His descriptions of indestructible life on the bare plain, sometimes illustrated with drawings of a 'blistering buttercup' or a 'wild bertram', can be read as a metaphor for his own struggle to survive.

They also had the function of a safe story with which he tried to steer clear of the risky story on which it was based. Besides this, Lukas wrote to his wife about prosaic matters, such as his weekly wages and his dirty laundry. Stien, for

---

61   Jacob Mozes van Gelderen, 19 Mar. 1944 from (uploaded by Pieter Kruijt): https://www.joodsmonument.nl/nl/page/548003/jacob-mozes-van-gelderen, retrieved 5 Mar. 2019. Cf. De Jong, Vol. 7: 414, where he calls the treatment at camp Havelte 'fairly good'.
62   Lukas Plaut, 24 Apr. 1944.
63   Lukas Plaut, 6 May, 18 May, 6 June and 11 July 1944.

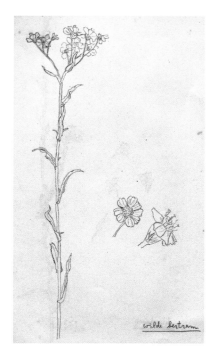

FIGURE 3.6
A 'wild bertram' in one of Lukas Plaut's
sketchbooks.

her part, sent letters and packages of food, according to Lukas's responses: 'But
you shouldn't send cheese, otherwise the children will not have enough. I certainly get enough over here'.[64] Socks, razor blades, a flora or a single book, including *Wat leeren ons de wolken*? (What do the clouds teach us?) by the me-
teorologist H.G. Cannegieter, were the things that Lukas asked for, or which
Stien suspected he would like to have.[65]

Despite their isolation, disturbing reports of persecution and violence
reached the internees. Following a raid among Jews in the city, Lukas Plaut
wrote in one of his letters that it is 'much safer in Havelte than in Groningen'.[66]
This relative safety came to an end when the prisoners, following their guards,
hurriedly left the camp on 5 September 1944. This *dolle dinsdag* ('mad Tuesday'), as it is remembered in the Netherlands, came about when the allied
forces successfully advanced to the north. Shortly before these were stopped at
the big rivers that cut the Netherlands in two, many Nazis had fled to Germany
in a panic. It gave Lukas Plaut the chance to return to Groningen, where he
went into hiding with the help of one of the university professors, J.G. Van der

---

64   Lukas Plaut, 25 Mar. 1944.
65   Lukas Plaut 15, 21 and 24 Mar. 1944.
66   Lukas Plaut, 2 Apr. 1944.

Corput, who was involved in the resistance.[67] Again, his wife was on her own, but this time without the constant stream of his encouraging letters. Stien was not allowed to know where he was. Apart from the courier who regularly came by to pick up clean laundry for Lukas and to provide financial support, Mrs. Plaut cannot remember much of this period. 'I do not know anymore. We lived under very heavy pressure'.[68] On 23 February 1945, Lukas Plaut was arrested at his hiding place. Not as a Jew – he was uncircumcised – but because of his forged ID as a non-Jewish agricultural engineer from Wageningen. He was seen as one of the many 'work refusers' who had withdrawn from the obligatory digging of pits for the German forces to counter the advancing allies. 'Stien, do nothing to get me out', Lukas wrote in a note that she got through a reliable police officer to prevent her from revealing his legal identity. Stien remained where she was and Lukas was taken, under his false identity, to the Fürstenau prison camp in Lower Saxony, not far from the Dutch border. His wife had no clue what had happened to him.[69] She did not hear from him for months, until in May 1945 he unexpectedly stood before her. Lukas Plaut had returned on foot from Germany to the city of Groningen.[70]

Together and Yet Alone

Nazi Germany was defeated, Lukas Plaut was back with his wife and children and, like everyone else, they were looking forward to 'just' picking up the thread of a 'normal' life again. In the postwar reconstruction period, most people wanted to get on with their lives and forget about the war and the Nazi regime. However, for Jewish survivors and their loved ones that was an

---

67   Van der Corput was part of the national and Groningen professors' resistance, which was formed in the course of 1943: Klaas van Berkel, *Academische Illusies. De Groningse universiteit in een tijd van crisis, bezetting en herstel, 1930-1950.* (Amsterdam: Uitgeverij Bert Bakker, 2005), 376 and 401.

68   Conversation Henkes and Plaut-Witte on 21 Apr. 1997. Undated notes from Plaut-Witte in which she states that only after her neighbour contacted a resistance group on behalf of her and her family she received financial support to pay the rent and other primary necessities of life.

69   Conversation Henkes and Plaut-Witte, 21 Apr. 1997 and information based on L. Plaut's naturalization file. (National Archive, (NA), Archief Min van Justitie (MvJ), Naturalisatie-dossier (Naturalization file) nr. 740–355/896. van L. Plaut, with a State of Information (Staat van Inlichtingen) dated 30 July 1948). Hereafter 'Naturalization file Plaut'. Fürstenau is about 65 km from the border at Ter Apel.

70   Document dated 26 Apr. 1945 of the Military Authority with information about the repatriation of Lukas Plaut.

impossible task. 'Even after the war, it will still be very difficult, and with our memories we will be alone among the other people', Lukas foresaw in a letter to Stien from camp Havelte on 18 August 1944. What he experienced in Fürstenau is unknown. After his return Lukas Plaut was not only physically weakened by the imprisonments, but also mentally in a bad state.

For the time being he had no appointment at the university, and six years after his PhD his future as an astronomer was still uncertain. The much-praised 'modesty', which Lukas Plaut demonstrated immediately after his flight to the Netherlands, had not diminished in the years of his persecution. Making himself invisible had become second nature to him, reinforced by the advice to the few Jews who had survived not to draw attention, 'to show modesty, and to be grateful'.[71] With the defeat of National Socialism Dutch society was by no means 'cleansed' of antisemitic stains – on the contrary. The pre-war policy to block the arrival of Jewish refugees, and the antisemitic measures of the Nazi-German regime in the Netherlands, created new dividing lines between Jews and non-Jews, which revived a range of anti-Jewish prejudices.[72] As the number of refugees from Germany increased in the course of the 1930s, Dutch admission policy became increasingly restrictive. From May 1938 every refugee was regarded as an 'undesirable alien'. The Dutch authorities believed that the national community needed protection against the arrival of 'too strange an element', as refugees were referred to in policy documents.[73]

In a memorandum of February 1940, a high official, *referendaris* Van Lier of the Ministry of Social Affairs, used a German term to outline the problem: 'From a political point of view, the inclusion of large groups of persons of foreign race and foreign nationality could pose the danger of *Überfremdung* (foreign domination)'. Van Lier also made a distinction between so-called 'Eastern' and 'Western' Jews (German Jews and Jews who originated from Eastern Europe but were born in Germany 'who have the character of Western Jews

---

71   Dienke Hondius, *Terugkeer. Antisemitisme in Nederland rond de bevrijding* ('s Gravenhage 1990) 95–96. Translated in English as *Return: Holocaust Survivors and Dutch Anti-semitism* (Westport: Preager/ABC-CLIO, 2003). These opinions found a fertile breeding ground in the postwar 'survival guilt' among many Jews. For an analysis of the complex relationships between Jews and non-Jews in postwar Netherlands, see the rich *oeuvre* of the Dutch historian Evelien Gans.

72   Evelien Gans, '"Vandaag hebben ze niets – maar morgen bezitten ze weer tien gulden." Antisemitische stereotypen in bevrijd Nederland', in: Conny Kristel (red.), *Polderschouw. Terugkeer en opvang na de Tweede Wereldoorlog. Regionale verschillen* (Amsterdam: Uitgeverij Bert Bakker, 2002) 313–353, and '"The Jew" as Dubious Victim', In Remco Ensel and Evelien Gans, *The Holocaust, Israel and 'The Jew'. Histories of Antisemitism in Postwar Dutch Society* (Amsterdam: Amsterdam University Press, 2017) 61–81.

73   Berghuis, *Joodse vluchtelingen*, 9.

Joodsche vluchtelingen aan een gesloten grens.

FIGURE 3.7 'Jewish refugees on a closed border'. A train with refugees from Nazi Germany
who fled after the so-called *Kristallnacht* was stopped at the Dutch border.
Winterswijk, November 1938.

through blood mixing'). The former, according to him, had 'a very different
mentality' and 'stood on a lower cultural level than the Western Jews'. He therefore warned against the naturalization of 'foreigners who remain alien to our
national character and lack the sentiment to actually experience Dutchness' –
although at this point it remains unclear what that national character and
Dutchness might have entailed.[74]

The then Prime Minister Colijn also contributed to this anxiety, shortly after
the *Kristallnacht* in November 1938, by warning against an 'unlimited flow' of
Jews from abroad, which could 'undermine the mood among our own people
towards the Jews'.[75] Such statements by senior officials and statesmen show
that a distinction based on nationality, race and culture was commonplace and
that antisemitism was also manifest within Dutch society. The introduction
of an absolute dividing line between Jewishness and non-Jewishness at the
time of the National Socialist occupation and the complex attitudes towards

74   Document Van Lier, Feb. 1940, cited in Berghuis, *Joodse vluchtelingen*, 152. My italics.
75   Speech by Prime Minister Colijn during the General Debate on the State Budget for the
       year 1939, 15 Nov. 1938. Acts of the Lower House, 1938, 262. Cited in Berghuis, *Joodse
       vluchtelingen*, 25-2.

antisemitic measures varying from assent to repugnance, followed by ambivalent feelings of guilt, did not reduce anti-Jewish sentiments before, during or after the war.[76] In addition, Dutch nationalism had only grown in the years prior to the German invasion under the influence of the Nazi regime. After the liberation, there was a great need to present 'the' Dutch as a people of resistance and to brand Dutch people who had stood on the side of the German Nazis as 'non-Dutch'. In this way, the stain of these 'bad' Dutch could be rubbed away from the nation's immaculate blazon. The image of the 'good' Dutch was further reinforced by opposing it to the 'bad' Germans: anyone with German nationality or from German origin, regardless of their political position or experiences of persecution, was faced with suspicion.[77]

Earlier we saw how on the day of the liberation Rie Ton-Seyler was confronted with a form of distrust because of her German origin; Lukas Plaut also had to deal with it. After collecting all the necessary papers in 1946 and depositing two hundred guilders into the account of the Ministry of Justice, he had to wait for another six years before doubts about his 'loyal Dutchness' were resolved. In 1952 he at last acquired Dutch citizenship,[78] after it was finally recognized that as a Jew of German origin he could make a sufficient contribution to the Dutch national community (*Volksgemeenschap*, as it was called in the postwar Netherlands).[79] Plaut himself wanted badly to fully participate in Dutch society: to the Groningen Public Prosecutor he referred to his marriage to a Dutch woman as an indication of how much he was 'established' in the Netherlands. According to the State of Information section in his naturalization file, he also had contacts with 'good', well-known Dutch families. Nevertheless, the Groningen Head of Police S.W. Moolenaar in 1948 had obstructed Plaut's application. Although Plaut had been opposed to the National Socialist regime during the occupation, 'there is no evidence that he served Dutch interests at that time', according to his statement.[80]

---

76   Gans, 'Vandaag hebben ze niets'; Gans, '"The Jew" as Dubious Victim'.

77   About the initial policy of forced eviction. See Jan Sintemaartensdijk and Yfke Nijland, *Operation Black Tulip. De uitzetting van Duitse burgers na de oorlog* (Amsterdam: Boom, 2009); Bogaarts, M.D., 'Weg met de Moffen'. De uitwijzing van Duitse ongewenste vreemdelingen uit Nederland na 1945. *BMGN – Low Countries Historical Review* 1981, Vol. 96 (2) 334 – 351.

78   Law of 17 Jan. 1952, published in the *Staatsblad van het Koninkrijk der Nederlanden* no. 25.

79   In the postwar Netherlands too, the term *Volksgemeenschap* was used in relation to the desire to restore a national unity. See: Martin Bossenbroek, *De Meelstreep. Terugkeer en opvang na de Tweede Wereldoorlog.* (Amsterdam: Bert Bakker, 2001), 183–284. See also the introduction to this book.

80   Naturalization file Plaut.

This reasoning touches on existing stereotypical images of Jewish cosmo-politanism and the related doubts about their loyalty to national interests.[81] The statement also indicates the poor understanding of or empathy for the precarious position of the Jews at the time of the National Socialist regime, and the heartbreaking consequences of the Shoah for its survivors. Partly at the insistence of the aforementioned Professor Van Rhijn, the procedure for the naturalization of Lukas Plaut was cranked up again in 1950, after which the same Head of Police came to realize that it was 'not surprising' that during the occupation Plaut kept himself 'passive': 'Apart from his natural attitude, he needed to cope with the dangers to which a German Jew was exposed at the time'. Echoing others, he described Plaut as 'a very modest man, who is completely absorbed in his science. He will never push himself forward'.[82] The question remains if the whole procedure could have gone faster with slightly less modesty. Modesty has a downside for a man who had to regain a position, both within the Netherlands and within an international academic environment.

Stien Plaut-Witte realized this all too well. She knew what astronomy meant for her husband and for their family. In August 1945 she made a bold decision. She wrote a letter to the Leiden Professor Oort about the unhappy situation in which Lukas found himself at that time: 'My husband is seriously ill (jaundice). This is otherwise an annoying disease, but innocuous. However, my husband has absolutely no mental reserves (...) For a long time he has been worrying about his future (...) Now I would like to ask you: isn't there any one in the en-tire astronomical world who can help this man? I would not ask you this, but you know what a fine person he is and if there is no change, he will be lost. My husband has been persecuted for nearly twelve years and he does not feel like starting all over again in another country. I have fought for five years to keep going, but you will understand that I, too, can no longer bear this situation. If it's not too much to ask, could you please write him a short letter as soon as possible? My husband does not know that I have written to you, so do not men-tion this'.

With 'many cordial greetings, also to your wife', Stien Plaut signed her emer-gency call.[83] The personal bond and loyalty between her and Lukas had contin-ued unabated under immense political pressure. At the same time, this letter

---

81   Cathy S. Gelbin and Sander L. Gilman, *Cosmopolitanisms and the Jews* (Ann Arbor: Uni-versity of Michigan Press, 2017).

82   Statement dated 16 Nov. 1950 from the Head of Police S.W. Moolenaar in: Naturalization file Plaut.

83   Leiden University Library, Oort archives, nr. 98B.

confirms a substantial change in their relationship. In hindsight, Mrs. Plaut marks the start of this change with the scene at Groningen station at the beginning of the occupation, when her husband changed from a caring breadwinner to a dependent spouse. This process threatened to become irreversible in the aftermath of the Shoah. Knowing how important his work as an astronomer was to him, Stien Plaut called on an influential colleague of her husband to reverse the downward spiral in which Lukas (and hence she herself and their children) was caught. She successfully entered the risky domain were private and public life overlap.

Professor Oort responded with an encouraging note, for which Lukas Plaut thanked him on letterhead paper from the astronomical laboratory in Groningen. His letter of 30 August 1945 begins with an apparently sober sketch of the state of affairs. He had been working at the astronomical observatory for a week, and there were discussions about a possible appointment as an assistant of Professor Van Rhijn. However, before Van Rhijn was going to take further steps with the Board of Trustees and the Board of Restoration, he wanted to be certain about Plaut's future after the end of the assistantship, for example because there was a real possibility of Plaut's going to the United States. That was why Lukas had written his brother in Los Angeles to apply for a visa. 'It is a pity that the decision has been postponed, so that I will be in uncertainty for some more time', he added cautiously. Immediately afterwards he continued his letter with an enthusiastic report of his findings based on 'the literature of the past years' and his plans for an improvement of the Schneller catalogue of variable stars.[84]

Lukas Plaut's future, which was so cruelly interrupted by National Socialism, was primarily related to his work. He had said goodbye to Germany, and when his prospects looked doubtful in the postwar Netherlands, he turned to the United States. The variable stars – sparkling quietly and brightly above the different nations – gave him something to hold onto. Eventually he was offered a view of the starry sky from the Groningen observatory. After he was appointed as an assistant in the astronomical laboratory on 1 October 1945, he continued to work there as a curator, (chief) scientist assistant, and from 1964 as holder of a special chair.[85] A successful career at first sight, but because a regular professorship passed him by, his wife thought differently.

---

84   Leiden University Library, Oort archives, nr. 98B.

85   Notes and copies regarding the appointment of Lukas Plaut at the University of Groningen. (Private collection). Cf. a necrology of Plaut by his colleague A. Blaauw, 'Leven en werk van Lukas Plaut', in: *Zenit* 11 (Apr. 1985) 152–153.

FIGURE 3.8 Lukas Plaut (fourth from the right) in the procession of professors walking across
the Grote Markt in Groningen on the occasion of the opening of the Academic
Year 1965.

She felt that her husband was overtaken by his colleagues. Addressing Uncle
Thé van Woerkom, her confidant, she expressed her disappointment about the
fact that 'the most cheeky people take centre stage, but the smartest and most
modest people are driven into a corner'.[86] Her experiences during the Nazi regime resonated with her later assessment: she was disappointed with a society
that had offered so little protection to fellow humans, Jewish compatriots and
refugees alike; a society that, even after the peace was signed and the persecutions had stopped, offered little or no support to the survivors of the Holocaust.
Lukas did not have any illusions in that regard. In August 1944 he foresaw that
after the war he and his wife would stand alone among the people around
them; a letter to his doctor from May 1978 underlines his position: '(...) an occasional depression is no more than normal, or simply a consequence of the
present state of society, as far as you can speak of a real society. (...) The only

---

86   Stien Plaut-Witte, 6 Dec. 1962.

thing we can do is to live as decently as possible and to realize how little we humans signify in the infinite universe'.[87]

'One Cannot Say: It Belongs to the Past'

Neither Lukas Plaut nor Stien Witte noticeably identified with a nation state, whether the German or the Dutch. Stien's political engagement almost took her to Spain to fight on the Republican side in the Spanish Civil War. Also, with her choice of the Social Democratic Workers Party, and Lukas's sympathies they both expressed their commitment to a community that was driven by international solidarity with the poor and oppressed, without participating in Dutch party politics.[88] Lukas felt connected to a form of Germanness that was quite different from nationalist sentiments. His kinship network spread throughout Asia, America, and Europe, and he himself preferred to focus on the starry sky, which offers all nations one shared roof. However, the significance of citizenship and the risk of exclusion from a national community were imposed on both Stien and Lukas Plaut from the moment he was identified as 'Jew' and his Jewishness was declared incompatible with his Germanness.

Antisemitic measures in Nazi Germany made Lukas's German nationality a serious obstacle to his marriage in the Netherlands. After he and Stien had managed to get married despite the antisemitic obstructions they both lost their citizenship. The relative and at the same time crucial importance of citizenship in their lives is also apparent from their unsuccessful attempt to emigrate to the United States. Their statelessness, in combination with the restrictive American immigration policy, prevented them from gaining access to the United States, despite personal guarantees and recommendations.

It was not only Lukas but also his wife who lost the rights and protection of citizenship. After her marriage she was no longer allowed to vote in the Dutch elections, but even worse was the disconcerting experience that after May 1940 her husband was cut off from Dutch society in no time. Through their marriage they shared a common destiny, as they both experienced how they were left to

---

87   Lukas Plaut, 20 May 1978 to ' Dear Olaf ' (his doctor Olaf Kersch).
88   See: *Wat wil de SDAP?* (What does the SDAP want?), the election programme of the Social Democratic Labour Party (SDAP) from 1937. Whereas the 1933 programme still talked about striving for 'disarmament, national and international', the disarmament position was no longer mentioned in the 1937 election programme. The Party did, however, emphasize 'strong defence of democracy, threatened by National Socialists and Communists'.

FIGURE 3.9   Stien and Lukas Plaut-Witte, c. 1970.

their own devices by most people around them.[89] The pain that came with this experience was not limited to the period of the Nazi regime in the Netherlands but remained palpable for the rest of their life. In that sense, Stien had become alienated from Dutch society.

In the shared history of Lukas Plaut and Stien Witte, the significance of having access to a national community is directly linked to the racialised, antisemitic exclusion and persecution policy of the National Socialists in both Germany and the Netherlands. Although Jewishness was hardly a category of significance for the young Lukas Plaut, nor for his (future) wife, it was irrevocably forced upon them since Hitler's rise to power and the Nazi invasion of the Netherlands.[90] Any tensions that stemmed from identification with the Nazi

89   That was even true for Uncle Thé who, following a visit of Lukas and Stien in August 1965, wrote in August 1965 about his regrets that he and Aunt Cor, while living with the tensions of bombardments and illegal work during the war years, had never realised what horrors Lukas and Stien had been through.

90   Lukas's mother, Catherine Plaut-Lewy writes on 17 Feb. 1939, that she visited Grandmother Plaut during her journey through Europe. Less than three and a half years later Ernestine Plaut-Löwenthal was murdered in July 1942 in Theresienstadt. In *Descendants of*

regime within the kinship network were absent from the history of the Plaut-Witte family. But, as in the life stories of Irmgard Brester-Gebensleben and Rie Ton-Seyler described in the preceding chapters, the Nazi regime did not prevent Lukas from maintaining a strong attachment to 'another' Germany he had come to know before 1933: the people, places, language and culture that had grown familiar to him.

The 'mixed' history – in terms of race, nation and gender – of the Plaut-Witte family is primarily marked by the antisemitism of the National Socialist regime, which cut through German and Dutch society alike. Most non-Jewish people could afford to focus on surviving the bombardments and hunger in these years and ignore the deadly racist persecutions. As far as the Dutch opposed the Nazi authorities, it was mostly driven by a nationalist urge to combat the infringement of national self-determination. The struggle against racism and the rescue of persecuted Jews in Dutch society was less obvious. After the war was over, the initial lack of a public discussion – let alone grief – about Dutch involvement in the dramatic fate of the Jews, the Sinti, Roma and other victims of Nazi racism might be defined as a form of national 'aphasia': an inability to find words for the collective failure of Dutch society and most Dutch people to protect their fellow humans.[91] The result was that both Lukas and Stien Plaut were still 'alone among the other people' after the antisemitic persecutions were over.

From his imprisonment in camp Havelte, Lukas Plaut was able to write himself back into his small family circle, creating a 'home' and a family to live *by*. After the end of the Nazi regime, when the extent of the atrocities that he had managed to escape became known, it was hard to live *with* his family in the shadow of the Shoah.[92] While her husband sought consolation and beauty in

---

Abraham PLAUT (see n. 2) we read that of the seven uncles and aunts on Lukas's paternal side at least two aunts were killed in Auschwitz. Letters from his mother indicate that his brother and sister-in-law succeeded in bringing Lilly Falkenstein's Jewish parents from Germany to the United States.

91   See Ann Laura Stoler, 'Colonial Aphasia: Race and Disabled Histories in France', in: *Public Culture* 23:1(2011) 121–156, in which she invokes the term 'aphasia' to supplant the notions of 'amnesia' or 'forgetting', in order to explore an occlusion of knowledge about a violent past, and a difficulty generating a vocabulary that associates appropriate words and concepts with appropriate experiences.

92   When analysing 'doing family' in *A World of their Own Making* (see also the introduction to this book) Gillis distinguishes between 'the family we live by' (in our imagination) and 'the family we live with' (we deal with in daily life). Gilles stresses that the latter is more complicated, fragmented and therefore less stable than the former. In the case of Lukas Plaut and other survivors of the Shoah one may wonder whether the former is not equally fragmented and complicated – which inevitably has its consequences for the latter.

FIGURE 3.10   'Forbidden to Jews'. Sign in the window of café *Huis 'de Beurs'*, Groningen 1942.

the vast universe with his astronomical quest, Stien Plaut-Witte tried to continue life with her own memories, fears, and unfulfilled wishes. In contrast to
Lukas's unspoken grief, Stien expressed her overt indignation. Looking back on
her life, Mrs. Plaut still feels a powerless rage about the fate that took hold of
Lukas and hence herself, their children and so many others. 'How do you erase
the text 'forbidden to Jews' from your memory?', Stien Plaut wrote many years
after the defeat of National Socialism.

And following the debates in 1972 about the release of three Nazi war criminals sentenced to life imprisonment, she sighed in a letter to her Uncle Thé:
'One cannot say, it is over. You just have to learn to live with it'.[93]

93   Stien Plaut-Witte, 15 Mar. 1972.

PART 2

Apartheid Across the Dutch-South African Border

∵

CHAPTER 4

'Can we Build a Future on this?'

An Epistolary Love Affair Between the Stamverwante *Netherlands and South Africa*

Pim Valk (1929) was just sixteen years old when Nazi Germany was defeated in May 1945 and the National Socialists in the Netherlands were imprisoned, put on trial, or had fled to Germany.[1] 'It wasn't easy here during the war', Pim wrote a year later in his letter to fourteen-year old Lena Dusseljee in South Africa. He had responded to a call in the illustrated Christian weekly *De Spiegel* of July 1946: 'Find a pen pal in South Africa'.[2] The editors sent him Lena's address. In his first letter he introduced himself as 'a Calvinist boy'. A small black and white picture that he included in the envelope showed himself and his immediate family: father, mother, three brothers and three sisters. They lived in Domineeslaantje in Breukelen, close to the Merwede canal with 'a beautiful view' of all the ships passing by. In his letter he also recalled the hunger trips he had undertaken during the last months of the war, together with his sister Willie. 'We sometimes cycled about 100 to 120 km a day, and at every farm we asked for some rye'. After about ten days their bags were full and they headed home. 'And then: skinny, skinny that we were. Skin and bones!'[3]

The Second World War in Breukelen and Bloemfontein

Apart from the gnawing hunger, the orthodox-Protestant Valk family with six children did not suffer any losses during the Second World War. The eldest son Freek (1927) had successfully evaded the forced labour service (*Arbeitseinsatz*) in Germany, and the Allied bombing of the strategically located Breukelen had not affected the Valk household. The signs with texts such as 'Jews not wanted' that were placed in Breukelen in the spring of 1941, had either escaped Pim's

---

1 This chapter is a re-working of my article '"Mag ons daarop 'n Toekoms bou" Transnationale identificaties in en door brieven tussen Nederland en Zuid-Afrika, 1946-1952', *Tijdschrift voor Sociale en Economische Geschiedenis* 7:3 (2010), 56-86. At the request of Pim Valk, he and his relatives are referred to by pseudonyms.

2 See the announcement in *De Spiegel*, 20 July 1946, no 41, 10.

3 Letter Pim Valk to Lena Dusseljee (hereafter: Valk), 18 Aug. 1946. On Breukelen during the war: Henk J. van Es, 'Breukelen in oorlogstijd', *Tijdschrift Historische kring Breukelen* 10: 2 (1995) 67-92.

© BARBARA HENKES, 2020 | DOI:10.1163/9789004401600_006

attention or he couldn't remember them.[4] The Valk family had nothing to do with the three Jewish families in Breukelen, and apparently their fate was not a topic of conversation within the family or the broader kinship network.[5] Neither did Pim have any idea of the involvement of his former teachers at the local Christian school in the resistance against antisemitic measures that excluded teachers, board members and school children of Jewish descent.[6] His letters to his South African pen friend show that his memories of the occupation in the years following were dominated by hunger and a nationalistic aversion to the 'Krauts'.[7] Anti-German sentiments were cherished in the postwar Netherlands for many years, long after mutual relations between the two countries had been restored.[8]

Pim Valk describes his life in the liberated Netherlands in positive terms, despite the prevailing scarcity. In the late summer of 1946 consumer goods such as meat, tobacco and coffee were still rationed, but writing paper and envelopes were available. Pim let Lena know in Dutch that he was looking forward to 'a long, pleasant correspondence'.[9] In response to his first letter and picture, Lena wrote in Afrikaans and sent photos of herself with her parents, her two sisters and their live-in grandmother. She herself attended high school (*Hoërskool*), and describes her father as a policeman in Bloemfontein, the capital of the Orange Free State.[10] In her letters she never wrote about her experiences during the Second World War in South Africa. It was not until much later that she – by then Mrs. Valk-Dusseljee – told me about the difficult situation in which her father and his family found themselves after the outbreak of war.

In those days, feelings ran high about whether South Africa should remain neutral or take the British side. This dilemma was closely related to the tensions

---

4   In Apr. 1941 Nazi-German orders required that at the entrances to the village of Breukelen signs with the text *Juden Nicht Erwünscht* (Jews not allowed) should be fixed. At the entrances of hotels and cafes this kind of sign, including a Dutch translation, also had to be shown. The Mayor reported on 19 April 1941 that this had happened. In June 1941, the Mayor had to make a list of all the names and addresses of Jews residing in his municipality and hand it over to the Nazi *Sicherheitspolizei* in Utrecht. He did so on 7 June 1941. Van Es, 'Breukelen in oorlogstijd', 70-74.

5   Valk, e-mail, 28 Apr. 2017.

6   In his e-mail of 28 Apr. 2017 Mr. Valk refers to the weekly services conducted by pastor W.O. Bouwsma during the war years. Bouwsma had made efforts to release two teachers who had been arrested for participating in the schools' resistance. David A. Manten and Henk J. van Es, ' 'Het protestants-christelijk onderwijs in Breukelen en de Tweede Wereldoorlog', *Tijdschrift Historische Kring Breukelen* 10: 2 (1995), 93-101, at 93.

7   Valk, 9 Feb. 1947. See also his letters of 9 Mar. 1947; 20 July 1947; 9 May 1949.

8   See also Chap. 2 and 3 in this book.

9   Valk, 18 Aug. 1946.

10   Letter Lena Dusseljee to Pim Valk (hereafter: Dusseljee), 24 Nov. 1946.

among the White European settlers. Since the arrival of Jan van Riebeeck and his European crew at the Cape in 1652, Dutch, German, and Scandinavian sailors, French Huguenot vine growers, Scottish Protestant pastors and many others had settled in the wake of the ships of the Dutch East India Compagny (VOC). The authority of Europeans over the local Khoisan and enslaved Asians and Africans was soon enshrined in laws. After Dutch rule was definitively transferred to the British in 1806, the abolition of slavery followed in 1834. This measure did not, however, put an end to the structural inequality between European settlers and the colonized peoples, either indigenous or forcibly brought there from abroad. For European settlers known as Boers or Afrikaners, the British abolition of slavery was an extra incentive to leave the Cape behind in search of new land and a space where they could set their own rules. Their 'Great Trek' into the interior of South Africa from 1836 onwards took them, their servants, and their enslaved further inland. There they founded the Boer Republics, Transvaal (1852) and Orange Free State (1854), after bloody confrontations with the indigenous African population.[11]

The discovery of diamonds and gold in these areas in the second half of the nineteenth century stimulated the desire on the part of the British to merge the two independent republics together with the coastal provinces (the Cape and Natal) into a South African federation under British rule. The first armed conflict (1880-1881) was won by the Boer Republics. Renewed frictions between the British and the Boers led to the South African War – also known as the (Anglo-)Boer War of 1899-1902 – which also involved South Africans of colour and quite a few volunteers supporting the Boers from abroad.[12] After the victory of the British, the Boer Republics were integrated into the Union of South Africa, which became a self-governing dominion within the British Empire. Political power in South Africa came into the hands of former Boer leaders. Yet, many Afrikaners pursued a South African Republic completely independent of the British Empire, and the former Boer Republics subsequently developed into a centre of Afrikaner nationalism with a strong anti-British sentiment.

The Dusseljee family considered themselves part of the Afrikaner White population. Both Lena's grandfathers had fought in the South African War

---

11   Research by the historian Fred Morton, most recently: 'Slavery in the South African Interior During the 19th Century', in: *Oxford Research Encyclopedia of African History* (April 2017), shows that with the Sand River Convention (1852) the northern Trek leader Andries Pretorius and the Cape representatives of the British Crown agreed that slavery and slave trade above the Vaal River were not allowed – but in practice slavery certainly continued until 1870.

12   Fransjohan Pretorius, *Kommandolewe tydens die Anglo-Boere Oorlog 1899-1902* (Kaapstad/ Johannesburg: Human & Rousseau, 1991) 266–271.

against the British. One of them had been interned as a prisoner of war on Bermuda, while his wife lost a child during her imprisonment in the concentration camp in Bloemfontein.[13] The collective and personal memories of the violent conflicts with the British had an effect on the attitude of Afrikaners in the run-up to the Second World War. Yet in 1939, under the leadership of Prime Minister and former Boer General Jan Smuts, the government decided to support the Allies in their fight against German National Socialism. The vast majority of the Afrikaner nationalists in the Orange Free State turned against participation on the British side. In fact, the radical, pro-German and antisemitic movements among the Nationalists – united in the *Ossewabrandwag* (Ox-wagon sentinels) since February 1939 – had their headquarters in Bloemfontein.[14] Close relatives of the Dusseljee family joined this political organisation.[15]

Lena's father, on the other hand, saw it as his duty to loyally support the government's decision, after he had previously taken the oath of allegiance to the British King as head of the British Commonwealth, which included South Africa. It is unclear whether he was involved in arrests of rebellious Nationalists who tried to sabotage the policy by blowing up electricity pylons and railways,[16] but with his loyalty to the legal authority Dusseljee came in for much scorn from many of his Afrikaner relatives, neighbours and friends. That disapproval affected not only himself, but also his wife and children. 'We were actually an established part of the Afrikaner community and there had been a lot of bad feeling towards us. How could we be such traitors (*Hoe kan ons so verraiers wees*)?!' Mrs. Valk-Dusseljee remembers more than half a century later. The result was 'that we placed ourselves somewhat outside the Nationalist community. My mom and dad were much more loyal to the United Party and General Smuts at the time'.[17] At the insistence of their mother, Lena and her two sisters continued their education not at and Afrikaans, but an English school.

Their church attendance also shifted: instead of going to the Afrikaner Dutch Reformed Church (*Nederduits Gereformeerde Kerk, NGK*), they went to

---

13   Conversation Barbara Henkes and Mrs. Valk-Dusseljee in Johannesburg, 9 July 2015 (hereafter: Conversation Henkes and Valk-Dusseljee). The British had set up a prisoner of war camp on Burt's island, Bermuda, as evidenced by a photograph of 18 May 1902 in the documentation of the South Africa House in Amsterdam.

14   Christoph Marx, *Oxwagon Sentinel: Radical Afrikaner Nationalism and the History of the 'Ossewabrandwag'* (Münster: LIT Verlag, 2008). In the following chapters 'Nationalist' will be capitalised when it refers specifically to the (Purified) National Party in South Africa.

15   Conversation Henkes and Valk-Dusseljee, 1 May 2008.

16   Brian Bunting, *The rise of the South African Reich* (n.p.: IDAF, 1986), 96.

17   Conversation Henkes and Valk-Dusseljee, 1 May 2008.

FIGURE 4.1
Lena Dusseljee (on the right) with her
two sisters, c. 1948.

an 'English' church on Sunday.[18] After completing her education, Lena became part of an English-speaking circle of friends in Pretoria and later in Johannesburg, and went to the 'English' Baptist church. Only with the arrival of Pim Valk in South Africa did Lena return to the Afrikaner community and its Dutch Reformed Church in Johannesburg.

In the Netherlands, Pim was ignorant of the mutual tensions between the White settler communities in South Africa regarding participation on the British side in the fight against German National Socialism. As far as he knew, South Africa had simply fought on the allied side with the Netherlands and Great Britain against the German enemy. In her letters Lena left this issue untouched, which allowed Pim to identify unhindered with the Afrikaner community in South Africa. Their correspondence shows how Pim's identification with an orthodox-Protestant Dutchness gradually expanded to a White, Protestant Afrikanerdom in South Africa. That process was fueled by the still current idea of *stamverwantschap* between the Dutch and the Afrikaners in South Africa. Both peoples were supposed to come from the same 'tribe' (*stam*), which had expanded itself further inland since the colonial conquests of the Dutch in the seventeenth century. The idea of *stamverwantschap* was supported by

18   Conversation Henkes and Valk-Dussljee, 1 May 2008.

references to genealogical, religious, linguistic and racial similarities that linked the Dutch in the Netherlands and Afrikaners in South Africa to each other in a transnational 'folk' community. That idea was articulated anew at the end of the nineteenth century, when the Afrikaner settlers came into conflict with the British.[19]

In the Netherlands the Boers were then 'rediscovered' as distant descendants of Dutch colonists from the seventeenth century. Their resistance to the mighty British empire appealed to nationalist sentiments and recalled the struggle of the fearless *Geuzen*, the Calvinist Dutch, who opposed Catholic Spanish rule in the Netherlands during the Eighty Years' War, or the Dutch Revolt (1568–1648).[20] Once more we can observe how tales of oppression and resistance from different places and times became entangled and led people to take action. Around 2,000 Dutch people left for the Boer Republics to fight and, if necessary, kill and die for the cause, although they had never met the Boers before. The passionately professed 'Boer love' among the Dutch calmed down after the British victory, although the image of *stamverwantschap* and its patriotic bonding between the Dutch and Afrikaners – as the Boers were soon called – survived for a long time, even to the present day.[21] Until the second half of the twentieth century, the narrative of the God-fearing, Protestant Afrikaner people who had opposed the morally corrupted, capitalist British superpower was a common thread in Dutch fiction and non-fictional stories.[22]

The fact that the same superpower had supported the Netherlands during the Second World War in the fight against Nazi Germany hardly changed that

---

19   Henkes, '*Stamverwantschap*'.

20   E.g. G.J. Schutte, *Nederland en de Afrikaners. Adhesie en aversie. Over stamverwantschap, Boerenvrienden, Hollanderhaat, Calvinisme en apartheid* (Franeker 1986) 176. Schutte emphasizes the religious element in this image, via which the Reformed saw the *Geuzen* as 'heroes of faith, who, relying on God, had taken on the struggle for freedom and justice'. See also Barbara Henkes, Caspar Dullemond and James Kennedy, 'Inleiding'(Introduction) in Dullemond, Henkes and Kennedy (red.), '*Maar we wisten ons door de Heer geroepen*'. *Kerk en apartheid in transnationaal perspectief* (Church and Apartheid in transnational perspective) (Hilversum: Verloren, 2017) 7–22.

21   Schutte, *Nederland en de Afrikaners* en B.J.H. de Graaff, *De mythe van de stamverwantschap. Nederland en de Afrikaners, 1902-1930* (Amsterdam 1993). Henkes, '*Stamverwantschap*'. For recent views on *stamverwantschap* between the White Dutch and Afrikaners in the political rhetoric of the Dutch populist *Partij voor de Vrijheid* (Party for Freedom, PVV), see the book by prominent party member Martin Bosma with the telling title 'minority in their own country': *Minderheid in eigen land – Hoe progressieve strijd ontaardt in genocide en ANC-apartheid* (Amsterdam, Bibliotheca Africana Formicae, 2015).

22   See for instance the popular and often reprinted *oeuvre* of the author Louwrens Pennings and the postwar reports by the Dutch authors Mary Pos and P.J. Risseeuw.

FIGURE 4.2
Cover of one of the many books on
the South African War by the popular
author Louwrens Penning, entitled
The War in South Africa (1900).
Caption: 'Fear God and keep your
powder dry'.

narrative in the short term – certainly not for Pim Valk's identification with the
Afrikaner community in South Africa.

With their regular correspondence an epistolary bond grew between Lena
and Pim: a mutual involvement that took shape on paper but was no less real
than if they had met in the flesh. Thanks to the global postal system they developed a commitment to the world of the other that became more and more familiar. This commitment ultimately contributed to Pim Valk's decision to leave
the Netherlands behind for an uncertain existence in South Africa. His letters
to Lena, together with his travelogues and other autobiographical notes and
memoirs, show with what kinds of images and ideas about a future life in
South Africa Pim set out on his journey. In addition to factual information,
these unique documents, combined with the oral and written memories of
both Mr. and Mrs. Valk, give access to the narratives by which Pim Valk identified himself with the Afrikaner community and the Nationalist Apartheid
regime.

After Pim's arrival, Lena on her part exchanged her English-speaking friends
and the Baptist church for the Afrikaans-speaking Dutch Reformed Church,
where Pim felt most at home. In that respect, she also experienced a form of
migration or return migration within her own country: back to the cultural and

political community her family had become alienated from. We shall follow how Pim Valk, in his letters from the Netherlands, began to identify himself with the White Afrikaner community in South Africa. From there we can trace how the 'race' category became a major element in his identifications with both Dutchness and South Africanness.

Foreign and yet so Familiar

Pen friendships were extremely popular in the postwar period, according to the overwhelming number of responses to requests for pen pals in the weekly magazines.[23] The practice also spread through personal mediation and advice, as in the case of Pim Valk and Lena Dusseljee, who helped their peers to start overseas correspondences.[24] After five years of wartime isolation, many yearned to broaden their horizons, while the possibilities for actually crossing borders were still limited in the time of postwar reconstruction.[25] Pim longed to see more of the world, and Lena also dreamed of 'traveling one day through the world'.[26] As long as this did not come about, the exchange of letters gave at least an impression of life 'overseas'. They stimulated each other's imagination with lyrical descriptions of sugar-sweet watermelons and flowering apple trees, shared experiences and sent each other photos and small gifts.

With the exotic, foreign stamps, the white, pink or blue airmail sheets, sometimes accompanied by small presents, pieces of South Africa fell onto Pim's Dutch doormat. In the other direction a newspaper clipping about the *Elfstedentocht*, (a long-distance skating event on natural ice past eleven historical cities in the province of Friesland), brought a dash of freezing Dutch cold to summery Bloemfontein.[27] The tangible contact with a distant, unknown world

---

23   From the postwar editions of the weekly magazine *De Spiegel* alone it is clear how great the need for pen friendships was. In the issue of 29 July 1946, the editors inform their readers that they can no longer pass on correspondence addresses from abroad. Readers are encouraged to contact 'a society for youth exchange' (*Vereeniging voor jeugdverkeer*) or the like. Nevertheless, in the edition of 3 May 1947 there is still mention of 100 addresses of South African girls between 15 and 22 years of age who want pen friends. From 1950, a new section is created, 'Correspondence club', with a list of hundreds of contacts for pen friendships around the world including South Africa.

24   Valk, 20 July 1947, 31 Aug. 1947, 13 Dec. 1947; and Dusseljee, 30 July 1947, 10 Sep. 1947, 24 Dec. 1947.

25   Cf. J.H. Elich, *Aan de ene kant, aan de andere kant. De emigratie van Nederlanders naar Australië 1946-1986* (Delft: Eburon, 1987) 94.

26   Dusseljee, 14 Dec. 1946. See also Valk's letter, 20 July 1947.

27   Valk, 9 Mar. 1947.

raised the status of the recipients. After Lena sent a leather wallet to Pim in June 1947, he wrote that others immediately envied him. 'It's something that is impossible to buy here'.[28] From her side, Lena reported how much jealousy arose amongst her friends when they saw the jewelry box that Pim had made for her.[29] Their correspondence was soon seasoned with a pinch of erotic tension. Lena wrote how Pim's portrait circulated among her friends, who wanted to know how old he was and what colour eyes he had. She wondered if he was 'really so innocent (*regtig so onskuldig*') as he had suggested: 'What about the church elder's daughter?'[30] A few months later Pim writes in so many words that he is afraid that Lena will start loving him: 'Because [...] if we were to love each other, you will never be allowed to go out with a boy, neither can I date a girl'. Lena answers that she could not at all say whether she loves him or not, and that she is not allowed to go out with boys (*seuns*) anyway while she is still at school.[31]

The urge to delve into each other's worlds was fuelled by curiosity, but in order to achieve an effective exchange common grounds were also needed. They both found these in many areas: the main thing was that they liked to express themselves on paper, and this might have been strengthened by a shared interest in (mostly Christian) literature and Bible study. In addition to their joint orientation to Christianity, their adolescence also contributed to a mutual involvement. They were in the same searching phase of life, in which they could share their enthusiasm and doubts about education, future work, love and faith. The significance of the Protestant faith as one of the cornerstones of their correspondence cannot be underestimated, certainly not in the Dutch and South African contexts of that time.[32] In the postwar Netherlands, the so-called pillarization (*verzuiling*) had been restored, which meant that Dutch society once again was organized along political-denominational lines.[33] Pim's letters show how he identified with an orthodox-Protestant culture and lifestyle. As a White Afrikaner from the Orange Free State, Lena too was anchored

---

28   Valk, 15 June 1947.

29   Dusseljee, 2 Oct. 1947.

30   Dusseljee, 8 June 1947.

31   Valk, 26 Oct. 1947 and Dusseljee, 9 Nov. 1947.

32   Pim and Lena sent each other bibles in Afrikaans and Dutch and wrote much about their religious reading. Lena for instance mentions several titles by the American Reverend Lloyd C. Douglas, while Pim highlights the books of the Dutch Protestant schoolmaster W.G.van der Hulst, the publications of the Protestant professor of psychology J. van der Watering with his study of puberty, and the Swiss orthodox-Protestant author of books on pastoral counseling Paul Tournier.

33   See Chap. 2, n.31 and 35 for more information about the so-called 'pillarization' of Dutch society.

FIGURE 4.3 Letters from Lena Dusseljee to Pim Valk, tied with a string, and the loosely
preserved letters from Piet Valk to Lena.

in a Protestant culture. It was no coincidence that Lena and Pim had found
each other through a Protestant medium: the weekly family magazine *De Spiegel* was part of a Dutch Protestant community. If a correspondence friendship
came about through a call in that magazine, both pen friends could assume
that they shared the same religious beliefs.

In addition, the similarities between the Dutch and Afrikaans language also
formed an important element that kept their correspondence going. The fact
that both were able to communicate with each other in their own language
was more than just a pleasant side effect. It also nurtured the idea of a shared
origin. For example, 'kitchen' (*keuken*) was a word in one of Pim's letters that
Lena could not understand. She wrote him that when her mother was also
mystified, her grandma had offered the solution: she could tell that *keuken* in
Afrikaans was a *kombuis* (galley).[34] Pim responded enthusiastically: 'You can
tell by the word *kombuis* that Jan van Riebeeck, who, as you know for sure,
founded the first colony at the Cape, was a true sailor. Because here in Holland

34   Dusseljee, 27 Nov. 1947.

they only speak of a *kombuis* on a ship, and in the houses they call it a kitchen'.[35] The linguistic similarities offered Pim and Lena a concrete handle by which to connect the Netherlands with South Africa through the colonial past. In their letters they mirrored each other. In Pim's case this was clear from the language he used: in November 1947 he switched to a form of Afrikaans that he often copied from Lena's letters. For example, when Lena wrote that she had decided not to worry about the high exam pressure and to see 'the bright side (*die blink-kant*) of the case',[36] Pim replied with that same Afrikaans phrase: 'I like it so much that you [...] are looking for a bright side'('*Ek vind dit so baie fijn, dat jij* [...] *'n blinkkant op soek*).[37]

Exploring a common language was not limited to specific words or phases. The base note was as important. In their letters they both present themselves as cheerful and practical spirits who, trusting in God's guidance, face the future. In addition to their Protestant faith, 'family' also became a shared, extended community in their correspondence. From the first letters and photos they were introduced to each other's families. 'I have to say that you and your family are already familiar to me and it feels as if I have known you all for years', Lena wrote in response to the first photos sent by Pim.[38] Pim never failed to send his warm greetings to her parents and sisters, or to wish that sick relatives got better soon. Birthdays, exam results, as well as national or Christian holidays in the Netherlands and South Africa became shared experiences. The other family members also joined in this process of community formation. For example, both mothers sent Christmas cards to each other and Pim was surprised by a gift from Lena's youngest sister, who drew a Dutch girl in clogs for his birthday. With their letters they initiated a development in which the circle of their own family, church and nation expanded and started to overlap with that of the other.

A Shared European Origin

The identifications that resulted from the correspondence between Pim and Lena were also driven by the narrative of *stamverwantschap* between the Dutch and the Afrikaners mentioned earlier. The military violence with which the British claimed the young, independent Boer Republics at the end of the

---

35   Valk, 8 Dec. 1946.
36   Dusseljee, 11 Aug. 1948.
37   Valk, 22 Aug. 1948.
38   Dusseljee, 14 Dec. 1946.

nineteenth century started a massive, international support for 'the Boers'. In the Netherlands this support was strengthened by an appeal to the *stamverwantschap* between the European Dutch and their descendants in the Boer Republics. Although the militant identification of the Dutch with the Afrikaners diminished after their defeat by the British, the idea of *stamverwantschap* remained alive.[39] This was especially true for the orthodox-protestant community in the Netherlands in which Pim Valk had been born and raised. Pim and Lena both lived in an environment where the idea of *stamverwantschap* based on a shared Dutch-European origin, White race and Christian culture was accompanied by positive images of each other's countries and 'people' (*volk*). Although they had started their correspondence from scratch, they also found the necessary indications in the Dutch colonial past, to connect experiences in their current lives and to identify with each other.

'I really like it when you ask a lot. About Holland, about my work, in short, about everything. I myself would like to know something more about life in South Africa', Pim wrote in his second letter. In her reaction Lena informed him that she would be 'very happy' (*baie bly*) with a book about Holland, so that she could find out more about Pim's country.[40] His magazines about Dutch farms and regional costumes were promptly answered with a photo album about the city of Bloemfontein.[41] The geography, history and politics of both countries were recurring themes in their letters. Pim illustrated his description of the division of the Netherlands into different provinces with a map,[42] while Lena informed him about the foundation of the two Boer Republics and 'the Bushmen (*die Boesmans*), who caused the pioneers a lot of distress and annoyance'.[43] Through their correspondence they stimulated interest in each other's whereabouts and experiences in the context of their national and local communities.

What they did or did not write about depended on their self-perceptions shaped by the ruling discourses within their social and political environments. Both Pim and Lena saw themselves as 'whites' of European origin.[44] From the very beginning that was a matter of course, tacitly confirmed with the exchange of the first photos. Being White was the norm about which nothing needed to be said. Both were familiar with the narrative in which a White

---

39   Henkes, '*Stamverwantschap*'.

40   Dusseljee, 14 Dec. 1946.

41   Dusseljee, 9 Mar. and 20 Apr. 1947.

42   Valk, 9 Feb. 1947.

43   Dusseljee, 2 July, 2 Oct. 1947, 10 and 24 Dec. 1947.

44   In a letter dated 2 Oct. 1947, Lena Dussljee mentions that ancestors of both her mother and father came from France.

European civilization was set against that of an 'uncivilized', 'dark' African continent. Stories and images about 'natives in the wild' circulating in school books and children's books, media and museums, church and family, moulded their perception of race and a racial order, both nationally and globally.[45] Thus, Lena wrote, in anticipation of the annual celebration of Heroes' Day (*Heldendag*) on 10 October 1947, about her ancestors who had entered the 'savage' interior of the country.[46] They had fought against 'wild barbarians, lions, animals etc. etc'. But in the end, they had succeeded in bringing civilization to the wilderness. This statement was followed by an explanation of the current 'native issue (*naturelle-vraagstuk*)': 'The kaffirs (*kaffers*) want to be on the same footing with the Whites. That can't happen, and if that happens I shall flee to another country where there are no kaffirs'.[47] Pim responded immediately, as a saviour in times of need: if Lena wanted to run away, she could come to Holland, 'because here there are no kaffirs'.[48] If he had ever seen people of African descent, these encounters were in all likelihood limited to printed pictures referring to the Protestant mission, posters announcing a performance of Black musicians or dancers, or a rare sighting in the streets of one of the nearby cities.

The same letter shows that the Netherlands also struggled with conflicts as a result of its colonial history. In it Pim announced that he had to be approved for military service because of his approaching conscription. It was the time of the Indonesian War of Independence (1945-1949) when the Netherlands – after the capitulation of Japan and the declaration of independence of the former Netherlands East Indies – refused to transfer sovereignty to the Indonesian indepence movement led by Sukarno. After Pim wrote he was looking forward to joining the troops in the East Indies and Lena responded in astonishment,[49] he realized that his statement required further explanation. In a subsequent letter he wrote: 'Here in Holland every able-bodied young man has to serve in the army, and for me that is the only way to go somewhere else. Do you understand,

---

45   Neederveen Pieterse, *White on Black*.

46   *Heldendag,* Heroes' Day or Kruger Day was a public holiday that from 1883 to 1899 was celebrated annually in the Boer Republics on 10 October, the date of the birth of the Boer leader and later President of the Republic of Transvaal, Paul Kruger (1825-1904). After the South African War and the Treaty of *Vereeniging* in 1902, it was no longer a public holiday although it was still celebrated in Afrikaner circles. A few years after the 1948 election victory of the National Party this holiday was re-introduced and observed from 1952 to 1993.

47   Dusseljee, 2 Oct. 1947. Indians, indicated by Lena as 'coolies' in the common terms of the time, also gave 'much trouble', according to her letters of 2 Oct., 10 and 24 Dec. 1947, and 9 May 1949.

48   Valk, 26 Oct. 1947.

49   Dusseljee, 9 Nov. 1947.

Lena? Because really I don't like to fight'. In the first place he wanted to broaden his horizon; in addition, he saw himself and the Dutch army playing a noble role in this disputed area. To elucidate this further, Pim relied on an approach to Dutch history that parallels Lena's version of South African history; he emphasized the civilizing, orderly influence of Europeans on the 'wild' indigenous population: 'In the East Indies you have [...] Javanese, Sundanese, etc. etc. In the sixteenth century those tribes always lived at war with each other, until the Dutch came and restored order (although I must confess that this was sometimes done rather brutally)'.[50]

He continued his exposé describing how under Dutch rule 'the tribes lived quietly until the Japanese arrived in 1942, who proclaimed and reinforced hatred of the Whites'. The result was that, after the defeat of Japan, 'a group of young Javanese thought they could rule the country themselves and that they no longer needed the Dutch'. These 'extremists', according to Pim Valk, 'who murdered the Chinese and set fire to the *dessas* (villages), no longer wanted to be under the authority of the Dutch'.[51] His summary of developments in the former Netherlands East Indies shows how the armed invasion of Indonesia was presented and perceived as a protective and 'recovering' action after the Japanese occupation. Pim's outspoken wish to 'bring civilization' to the Indonesian people was in line with the message conveyed by the Dutch government and supported by a large majority in Dutch society. The Indonesian population was regarded as an underdeveloped bundle of contradictions, which could only be protected from a violent revolutionary chaos if kept under Dutch leadership. The ultimate, though paradoxical, goals were to alleviate the mental, political and social needs of the people and at the same time to ensure that the Kingdom of the Netherlands continued to occupy the ranks of imperialist powers. This view also prevailed in the orthodox-Protestant (in terms of political parties, Anti-Revolutionary) community to which Pim belonged: 'In the East Indies not the chaos of the Republic but the rule of law', was the telling slogan with which the Protestant Anti-Revolutionary Party entered the national elections in 1948.[52]

Nonetheless, there were also voices among the Anti-Revolutionaries who argued for a transfer of power to the Indonesians.[53] The orthodox-Protestant Mission in particular emphasized that the legitimate pursuit of independence

---

50   Valk, 22 Nov. 1947

51   Valk, 22 Nov. 1947.

52   Doeko Bosscher, *Om de erfernis van Colijn. De ARP op de grens van twee werelden 1939-1952* (Alphen a/d Rijn: Kluwer, 1980) 265.

53   Herman Smit, *Gezag is gezag... Kanttekeningen bij de houding van de gereformeerden in de Indonesische kwestie* (Hilversum: Verloren, 2006).

FIGURE 4.4
Election poster of the *Anti-
Revolutionaire Partij* (ARP, 1948)
saying 'In the East Indies not the
chaos of the Republic but the rule
of law'.

should not be condemned by attributing the cause of the postwar violence
only to the communist-oriented Sukarno. These critics argued that 'the Dutch
people' were also guilty, because they had not been guided by 'the demands of
justice, selflessness and brotherly love'. This critical attitude opened up the
Mission to the accusation of supporting the revolution and having no eye for
the demands the Bible (with a capital B) made on the state.[54] Pim was aware of
this discussion, because he referred to 'others' who thought that the East Indies
should become independent. But he held on to a different opinion: 'If you read
the newspaper, the people who are liberated are very happy to be freed from the
extremists. And that is why I want to go to the East Indies, in order to rectify the
great injustice that is being done to the people'.[55] In her response, Lena wrote
that she thought it was 'very noble' (*baie edel*) that Pim was willing to 'liberate
those people'. But she was also concerned about the danger awaiting her pen

---

54   Bosscher, *Om de erfernis,* 238–239.
55   Valk, 22 Nov. 1947. He is referring to the Anti-Revolutionary daily *Trouw,* which had started
       as a mouthpiece of the orthodox-Protestant resistance, and after the liberation from Na-
       tional Socialism advocated the preservation of 'our' Netherlands East Indies under Dutch
       rule.

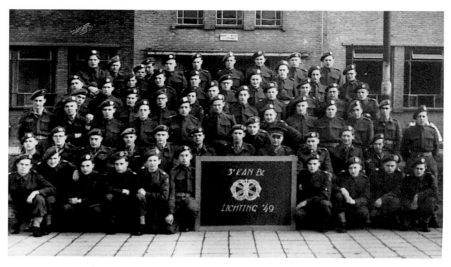

FIGURE 4.5　Pim de Valk (second last row, third from the right) with his group of conscripts in
Ede, called up in 1949.

friend there.[56] In subsequent letters Pim called on their common faith to reassure her (and probably also himself). After all, it was God who determined the moment he had to die. And what was more: Pim was convinced that, with death in mind, he was going to 'get closer to God'.[57]

Pim Valk was convinced that in the postwar Netherlands the sense of 'the love of God and His Service' tended to diminish. 'Right now', he urged Lena in October 1948, 'we must stand firm for our principles, to fight the false powers that force themselves upon us, such as communism, etc'.[58] The importance of maintaining Dutch authority was increasingly marked by the Cold War and the fight against communism.[59] Anti-communism was also used in South Africa to underpin the authority of a White, originally European minority and to justify the fight against African independence movements.[60] Ideas and visions

---

56　Dusseljee, 10 Dec. 1947.

57　Valk, 21 Dec. 1947 and 'Christmas' 1948.

58　Valk, 17 Oct. 1948.

59　Bosscher, *To Get the Erfernis*, 239.

60　In June 1950, the *Suppression of Communism Act* was passed, by which the Communist Party of South Africa (CPSA) was banned. This law led to the close collaboration of the illegal CPSA and the banned ANC. Cf. Stephen Clingman, *Bram Fischer. Afrikaner revolutionary* (Amherst: University of Massachusetts Press, 1998) Chap. 8; and Thomas J. Noer, *Cold War and Black Liberation: The United States and White Rule In Africa 1948-1968* (Colombia 1985).

such as Lena and Pim exchanged and encouraged in their epistolary universe were fueled by the 'master narrative of Whiteness': the narrative of a superior White, European civilizing mission common to both the Dutch and the Afrikaners.[61] This narrative was given an extra boost by an increasing fear of anti-religious communism. However, the Dutch government was forced by the international community to give up its pursuit to recolonize Indonesia. When the sovereignty of the Republic of Indonesia was sealed in August 1949, it was certain that soldier P. Valk and his group of conscripts were going to stay in the Netherlands.

Emigration Fever

From that moment onwards, the emigration theme gained a prominent place in the correspondence between Pim Valk and Lena Dusseljee. In February 1947, six months after the start of their correspondence, Lena had been the first to refer to a possible emigration: 'I am enclosing a newspaper clipping on immigration to South Africa. It says that there are a lot of Dutchmen amongst the immigrants'. Indeed, the promotion of the immigration of craftsmen from the Netherlands was announced in that paper,[62] despite the Dutch population policy that shortly after the war discouraged emigration.[63] 'Thank you also for your clipping on emigration. It was very interesting', Pim replied, dutifully rather than interested.[64]

Six months later, however, his interest in emigration was aroused. Then he asked Lena if there happened to be woodworkers in Bloemfontein, because he was considering settling in South Africa eventually. He was, still, non-committal: 'It will take a few years and then still: "Man proposes, but God disposes"'.[65] Soon, Pim was completely gripped by his approaching conscription and possible departure for Indonesia.

The emigration theme remained untouched until the autumn of 1949, when he reconsidered his prospects for the future. At the beginning of October 1949, after the Apartheid regime had come to power in May 1948, Pim wrote to Lena that he wanted to emigrate to South Africa after finishing his military service: 'But your country isn't so keen any longer on immigrants, unless they are skilled

---

61   Steyn, *Whiteness*. See also the introduction to this book.
62   '10.000 immigrante van jaar verwag. Nederlandse Vakmanne Sal ook Kom', unspecified
        newspaper dated 19 Feb. 1947, attached to a letter from Lena Dusseljee, 23 Feb. 1947.
63   Van Faassen, 'Min of meer misbaar', 34.
64   Valk, 9 Mar. 1947.
65   Valk, 31 Aug. 1947.

professionals. And I'm not very skilled yet. But I will let this plan sit for a while, because it still takes a few years before I get out of service'.[66] Lena responded enthusiastically and assured him that he would be 'most welcome' and would surely love the country very much. If he liked to have more information, he just had to ask, and she would look for it. 'So, if it's the Lord's will, I might see and talk to you in a few years'.[67]

Pim Valk was well-informed about the South African's immigration policies as they took shape in the first years after the election of Nationalist Prime Minister D.F. Malan in 1948. Malan and his National Party were wary of strengthening the more British-oriented population in South Africa through the arrival of immigrants from Great Britain and other Allied countries. Moreover, they were extremely apprehensive about the economic competition from European migrants, which might affect the less fortunate part of the White Afrikaner population. Only well-trained craftsmen were welcome, to fill a shortage in the South African labour market.[68] This was precisely what spoiled Pim's chances, since he had not followed any vocational training. Halfway through he had left a course in furniture making, shortly before joining the military. He was prepared to start somewhere 'at the bottom', he assured Lena, but even then he still needed a sponsor who wanted to stand surety for him. So, after he had been discharged from military service he hoped to be able to call on her father's contacts. Once again Lena assured him that she wanted to help him in every way.[69]

Twenty-year-old Valk was now touched by the 'emigration fever' that manifested itself in the Netherlands at the end of the 1940s.[70] In 1948 an annual survey revealed that more than 32 percent of the Dutch labour force seriously considered emigrating, while 17 percent toyed with the idea. Between 1946 and 1952 a total of 142,747 Dutch nationals were actually leaving, a number that by the end of 1955 had risen to around 245,103 (2.19 percent of the total Dutch population).[71] In Pim Valk's residence Breukelen the inclination to emigrate was also great. His eldest brother remembers how 'emigrating was a daily topic of conversation' in the village, and his sister talks about 'the time of migrations'

---

66   Valk, 9 Oct. 1949.
67   Dusseljee, 1 Nov. 1949.
68   Barbara Henkes, 'Shifting Identifications in Dutch-South African Migration Policies (1910–1961)', *South African Historical Journal*, 68:4 (2016) 641–669, at 660.
69   Valk, 13 Nov. 1949 and Dusseljee, 27 Nov. 1949.
70   Hofstede, *Thwarted Exodus*, 12–31.
71   J. Pen, 'De mirakels en de trend. Economische geschiedenis van de periode 1945-1963', in *Economisch Statistische Berichten*, Dec. 1980, cited in Van Faassen, 'Min of meer misbaar', 53. Given the context I assume that these numbers refer to the working population.

in the 1950s.[72] Pim felt the need to emigrate all the more because of the return of around 75,000 Dutch conscripts from Indonesia who would be looking for a job in civil society. 'All those young men have to find work, and there are hardly any jobs. So, there will be unemployment, also because Holland is overpopulated. We have already passed 10 million inhabitants', he explained to Lena in a letter dated 13 November 1949.

Like the Dutch government and many Dutch citizens at the time, he was convinced that the 'loss' of the Netherlands East Indies in combination with the growing population would inevitably lead to rising unemployment. Immediately after the war the government pursued a cautious emigration policy, to prevent her 'best sons' from leaving when they were desperately needed for rebuilding the ravaged country. From 1947 onward the Dutch government changed its course: postwar unemployment, the rising birth rate and the clear desire of many Dutch people to leave the war-ridden country led to the lifting of emigration restrictions.[73] In 1950, the Queen, as spokesperson for the government, announced that future structural unemployment could only be prevented by stimulating industrialization together with large-scale (overseas) emigration.[74] For the first time in Dutch history, an active emigration policy was developed as an instrument of employment and population planning. In 1949, 13,963 emigrants left the Netherlands, while in 1952 there were 48,690 in total, 4,500 of whom went to South Africa.[75]

Pim Valk did not put all his cards on one destination. At the beginning of 1950 he investigated the possibilities of going to South America. He found Lena by his side during this exploration, judging from her letters: 'Are you still going to South America? This is one of the places that I always wanted to see, also because of the Amazon. [...] If I get a chance one of these days, I will go there'.[76] With their correspondence they created an imaginary world in which everything was conceivable. However, reality proved intractable. Lena may have longed for long journeys, but for a young woman on her own the possibilities for realizing those desires were extremely limited, all the more so because

---

72   Conversation Henkes and Freek & CorrieValk (hereafter: conversation Henkes and F. & C. Valk), 19 May 2017.

73   Van Faassen, 'Min of meer misbaar'.

74   The Queen's Speech at the 1950 Opening of Parliament. https://www.parlement.com/id/ vjw7l4l9u2mt/troonrede_1950_volledige_tekst, retrieved 7 June 2019.

75   Hofstede, *Twarted Exodus*, 5, and A.P. du Plessis, *Die Nederlandse emigrasie na Suid-Afrika: sekere aspekte rakende voorbereiding tot aanpassing* (PhD University of Utrecht, 1956) 92–93.

76   Dusseljee, 11 Apr. 1950. Pim's letters between 9 Jan. and 5 May 1950 have not been preserved.

FIGURE 4.6
'Emigration is looking ahead'. 1950s
poster from the General Emigration
Center (*Algemene Emigratie
Centrale*) 1950s.

South African emigration policy was aimed at preserving the Afrikaner population for the White nation and strengthen the Afrikaner community within.[77]
Pim's plans for South America came to a dead end,[78] and he focussed on South
Africa again. However, the stimulus he received from the active emigration
policy of the Dutch government was offset by other forces that prevented him
from emigrating.

He mentions three obstacles that stopped him from leaving: his lack of professional education, his financial constraints, and his father and uncle who
could hardly spare him in their small furniture business. For his military service Pim had left the parental home and the woodwork, but in the meantime it

---

77   J.K. Loedolff, *Nederlandse immigrante. 'n sociologiese ondersoek van hul inskakeling in die
      gemeenskapslewe van Pretoria* (Kaapstad/Pretoria: Haum, 1960) 21.

78   Valk, 5 and 27 May 1950. In these years, emigration to South America, in particular group
      migration of Catholic and Protestant farmers to Brazil was promoted, though it remained
      limited and was not very successful. See H. Hack, "Dutch Group Settlement in Brazil", in:
      Research Group For European Migration Problems 7: 4 (1969) 9; Mari Smits, *Holambra: ge-
      schiedenis van een Nederlandse toekomstdroom in de Braziliaanse werkelijkheid, 1948 – 1988*
      (Nijmegen: Katholiek Documentatie Centrum, 1990) and other literature mentioned on
      https://holambra.nl/?page_id=567, accessed 15 July 2019.

had become clear that his father found it difficult to manage without him. Pim struggled with the question how far a son's obligation to his father should go: 'Should I sacrifice my happiness in life for him?' he asked Lena.[79] He was torn between his personal loyalty to his father and his eager desire to leave the parental home for good. Family ties played a paradoxical role in this phase of life, and despite all personal and social 'push factors' Pim saw no opportunity to move. Two months later, in a letter to Lena, he suggested another opportunity to change the course of their lives. After unburdening himself about an unhappy love affair, he mentioned the arrival of a group of South African nurses to remedy the shortage of a Dutch nursing staff. Wouldn't Lena feel like coming to work in Holland for a while after her training?[80]

This immigration to the Netherlands seemed at odds with the migration policies of both the Dutch and South African governments mentioned above. But in addition to stimulating the emigration of the male labour force, there was at the same time a pronounced shortage of care workers such as nurses and domestics in the Netherlands.[81] By then South Africa cooperated in the temporary emigration of nursing staff, in exchange for the Dutch encouraging the emigration of *stamverwante* Dutch migrants to South Africa. For Lena, this development offered the opportunity to put her *Wanderlust* into practice: 'If it is the Lord's will, it would be wonderful to make this happen, because I always wanted to visit foreign countries'. Such a move also offered her an opportunity to distance herself from an impossible love. Like Pim, Lena had experienced her first heartbreak.[82] The prospect of her coming to the Netherlands offered them both comfort in their shared grief for lost loves. For the time being it was something to look forward to, but first she had to finish her training as a nurse. The plans for Lena's passage were never elaborated further, unlike Pim's emigration plans. In his last letter of the year 1950, decorated with stickers of Santa Claus, Christmas bells and angels, he assured his pen friend that he still wanted to come to the Union.[83]

---

79   Valk, 6 Aug. 1950.
80   Valk, 22 Oct. 1950. After the war in the Netherlands there was a dire shortage of nursing staff in Netherlands. See also Annemarie Cottaar, *Zusters uit Suriname: naoorlogse belevenissen in de Nederlandse verpleging.* (Amsterdam: Meulenhoff, 2003) 14–24 on attracting especially Dutch-speaking (including Afrikaner and Flemish) trainee nurses in the 1950s.
81   Hilda Verwey-Jonker, 'Vrouwentekort', *Vrouwenbelangen* 15 (1950) 2, aangehaald in Henkes, *Heimat in Holland*, 11. See also Els Blok, *Loonarbeid van vrouwen 1945-1955* (Nijmegen: Uitgeverij SUN, 1978) 60–67.
82   Dusseljee, 15 Nov. 1950.
83   Valk, 24 Dec. 1950.

On the Way to the Promised Land

When his military service came to an end in March 1951, Pim Valk returned to Breukelen to help in his father's furniture workshop. He was back to square one, just like Lena, who in the same month wrote that she had stopped her training as a nurse in Pretoria and had returned to her parents in Bloemfontein. She was overworked and had to rest for half a year. For the first time, Pim then addressed her by the endearment '*Lieve*' instead of the more distant '*Beste*' Lena: 'Reading your letter almost broke my heart. Oh Lena, how can I express the pain it caused me now that you can no longer become a nurse. I know how much love you felt for this work'. That was the moment to declare his love to her, supported by God's guidance: 'I have come to feel that you are more to me than an ordinary pen pal, exactly because your disappointment has become my disappointment. The difficulty is that we are so far away from each other and we have never seen each other. An encounter can be a disappointment. [...] Yet I cannot emigrate to S.A., because I feel that I have a future here. Lena, how do you feel? Do you dare to write about this? I am convinced our correspondence has been guided by God'.[84]

Since she received his letter 'the sun is shining again', Lena wrote in her response to '*Lieve*' Pim.[85] It was clear to her that he was the man who understood her best and whom she had learned to love. But unfortunately, the sea lay between them. They could not change the fact 'that you are not here, or I am not there'.[86] Both wondered if their years of personal correspondence were enough for such an important decision about a common future. It took a while before Pim made the decision in November 1951: 'Lena, I don't know how to say it. I know you love me. I know I love you'. He interpreted this new development between them as a promise from God. Since great distances and lack of money did not matter to God, they must be able to come together not only on paper but also in real life. The unthinkable became conceivable and expressed in words: 'Lena, I want to ask you, can we accept this promise and trust in Him? May we build a future on that? My heart says yes'.[87] The same was true for Lena, as her answer shows.[88] The thin sheets of airmail paper offered them both a delicate but tangible handhold by which to keep going.

---

84   Valk, 24 June 1951.
85   Dusseljee, 14 July 1951.
86   Dusseljee, 2 Sep. and 1 Oct. 1951.
87   Valk, 14 Nov. 1951.
88   Dusseljee, 21 Nov. 1951.

Pim Valk's vision of the future underwent a radical change and the pace of his life was accelerating. He now not only had a concrete landmark (Lena and her family in South Africa) on which he could focus, but also an appealing (because romantic) narrative by which he was able to mobilize the necessary support to make his departure possible. It is remarkable that in the letters about his preparations he never even mentions the Netherlands South African association (*Nederlandsch Zuid-Afrikaanse Vereeniging*, NZAV), which actively propagated and supported the emigration to South Africa.[89] Instead, he went straight to the Utrecht Labour Office in December 1951, where he was told that in addition to a South African employer's statement and a housing declaration, a proof of 'creditworthiness' was needed. The solicitor A.F. de Savornin Lohman, who had met the young and energetic Valk at meetings of the Dutch 'Friends of Sailing' Association (*Vrienden van de Zeilvaart*), helped him to get an employer's statement from his friend P. Prins, owner of a large furniture factory in Pretoria.[90]

Pim asked Lena's parents for a housing statement.[91] In the meantime he began to save diligently for the passage. This cost around 800 guilders, while he only had 150 in the bank. According to the emigration desk of the Utrecht Labour Office, he was not eligible for government aid.[92] 'But this too is no obstacle to God', was Pim's familiar formula, which he was hanging on to.[93] In March, he received the necessary papers from Mr. Prins in Pretoria, who wrote in a friendly letter that he considered Pim to be a 'friend from Holland' and not an applicant, after the intercession by De Savornin Lohman.[94] The transnational network between the Dutch who had settled overseas and those in the home country, which plays such a crucial role in migration processes, was successfully activated in the case of Pim Valk.

In order to obtain the necessary travel money, Pim decided to place an appeal in the Reformed daily newspaper *Trouw* of 9 April 1952: 'Who is willing to

---

89   J.A.A. Hartland, *De geschiedenis van de Nederlandse emigratie tot de Tweede Wereldoorlog* (Den Haag: Departement van Sociale Zaken en Volksgezondheid, 1959) See also Henkes, 'Shifting Identities', 652–653.

90   Letter A.F. Savornin to Pim Valk, 12 Jan. 1952 by. (Private collection).

91   Valk to Mr. and Mrs. Dusseljee, 14 Jan. 1952 (Private collection).

92   Valk, 22 Dec. 1951. In an album by Pim Valk with photographs and autobiographical texts (hereafter: *Album*), he mentions that he did not qualify for a subsidy 'due to an error from the Employment office'. When asked, Valk cannot remember what error it was. See for the official policy on aid to emigrants 1949-1953: Hofstede, *Twarted Exodus*, 42–45.

93   Valk, 13 Jan. 1952.

94   Valk, 1 Mar. 1952. The original is preserved in Valk's *Album*.

lend f 900 to a young man who has been offered a good job in South Africa?'[95]
There were no responses, but a few weeks later a wealthy friend of his parents
was willing to lend him the money. This allowed him to pay for the trip and
meet the requirement of solvency.[96] With renewed determination, Pim em-
barked on an English course, immersed himself in informative reading about
South Africa, and was glued to the radio when there was a programme about
his intended destination.[97] 'It's so wonderful to feel the longing for the country
that I love so very much', he wrote Lena.[98] Four days later, he took his zeal to the
next level when paraphrasing the Afrikaner national anthem *The Voice of South
Africa* (*Die Stem van Suid-Afrika*): 'Yes, I know now the call of S.A. was too
strong for me to resist [...] I shall answer your calling/ I will offer what you ask/
I shall live, I shall die/ Yes, for you – South Africa (*Ek sal antwoord op jou roep-
stem/ Ek sal offer wat jij vra/ Ek sal lewe, ek sal sterwe/ Ja vir jou – Suid Afrika*)'.[99]
Five years earlier, he had mentioned to Lena that the anthem 'Die stem van
Suid-Afrika' was completely unknown to him.[100] Since then, Pim's sense of
commonality with his Afrikaner *stamverwanten* in South Africa had grown. His
passionate feelings for his South African pen friend increased through his identification with 'her people'. In Pim's experience, people, nation, race, religion,
church and family in the Netherlands and South Africa merged into one White,

95   In his *Album* Mr. Valk pasted the advertisement, with the comment that he got no
      response.
96   In a letter from 20 Apr. 1952 Pim writes that he asked for the loan. In his *Album* he recalls
      a loan of f 900 by 'Mr. vd Berge'. In his later memoirs *'n Terugblik op 'n lewe vol genade*
      (2010) Valk describes how he managed to place this amount of money in his savings
      account for just one day, so that he could prove that he had sufficient financial reserves –
      and then return the loan again. In addition, he was able to borrow 800 guilders for the
      journey from a Mr. Nagel, provided he would repay that amount within one year to nagel's
      son in South Africa.
97   The English course is mentioned several times in Pim's letters. In response to my ques-
      tionnaire, Mr. Valk wrote in 2006 that every Saturday afternoon at 2 o'clock English les-
      sons were presented on the radio by James Brotherhood. In the questionnaire he also
      mentions the book by the Dutch Reformed author Gerard H. Hoek, *Zuid-Afrika, land van
      mogelijkheden en contrasten* (South Africa, land of possibilities and contrasts) from 1948.
98   Valk, 16 Mar. 1952.
99   Valk, 20 Apr. 1952. Valk refers to the third verse: 'Op jou roep sê ons nooit nee nie, sê ons
      altyd, altyd ja: Om te lewe, om te sterwe – ja, ons kom Suid-Afrika'. *Die Stem van Suid-
      Afrika* had since 1928 been a popular anthem among Afrikaners in South Africa. In 1957 it
      officially replaced *God Save The Queen*. In 1997 the first four lines of the first verse and four
      English phrases, along with two verses of *Nkosi Sikelel' iAfrika* were merged into the offi-
      cial national anthem of South Africa. In a letter of 6 July 1952 Pim once more referred to
      'the calling voice' of South Africa to assure Lena that he would come to 'live and die for
      South Africa'.
100   Valk, 29 May 1947.

Christian, transnational – or better, Greater Dutch – community. In this way a life in South Africa became easy to imagine and worth pursuing.

The prospect of continuing his life in another country was accompanied by a change of perspective: the orientation towards Dutch society made way for South Africa.[101] The contact with his family and friends now revolved completely around his impending departure. Pim was lucky: where emigration plans of aspiring emigrants could evoke aloofness, rejection or feelings of betrayal from those who stayed behind, he experienced support and encouragement from his family and friends.[102] Even his father, who could hardly spare him in his business, made no objections. For his birthday in March 1952 his parents gave him a book about South Africa and an English dictionary. It was a special occasion, because it was probably the last time Pim celebrated his birthday in the Netherlands. On that same occasion one of his friends gave him a book of Afrikaner prose, while another friend had made a drawing with Pim in the Netherlands and Lena in South Africa connected through a church in the middle, because – as Pim wrote to Lena – 'the one thing that dominates our lives is the Bible, God's word'.[103]

Thanks to Pim's love of writing and his need to involve Lena in his preparations for the journey overseas, we can closely follow what steps he needed to take before he could leave the Netherlands. An emigration report was drawn up at the Labour Office, which was forwarded to the *Stichting Landverhuizing Nederland* (Netherlands Foundation of Emigration), which had to issue a statement of 'no objection'. As soon as it was established that he had no debts or criminal record, that statement was forwarded to the South African Immigrant Inspection Committee in The Hague.[104] When Pim Valk reported to the Committee on 21 May 1952, he found fifty people already waiting: single men and women as well as couples. If their children had been born in the former Netherlands East or West Indies, they, too, had come to The Hague to prove that they were White enough to qualify as of proper, European descent.[105] After a

---

101   See also Ellich, *Aan de ene kant, aan de andere kant,* 51–52.

102   See also Hylke Speerstra, *Het wrede paradijs. Het levensverhaal van de emigrant* (Amsterdam/Antwerpen 2008).

103   Valk. 28 Mar. 1952.

104   Valk, Easter 1952 and 22 May 1952, and Valk, *'n Terugblik.* See also: Archive of the Ministry of Foreign Affairs (hereafter: MvSZ), Directorate Emigration, No. 417: about the establishment and functioning of the South African Selection Committee, 1946-1947.

105   Henkes, 'Shifting identifications'. Other *Settler Societies* also had a history of a clear preference policy for White immigrants from Europe as shown by Lake and Reynolds, *Drawing the Global Colour Line* and for more recent developments e.g. Antje Ellermann, 'Discrimination in migration and citizenship', *Journal of Ethnic and Migration Studies,* 2019.

word of welcome from the head of the inspection committee, those present received the necessary forms to apply for a permit. Together with the certificate of solvency, a certificate of good conduct, an extract from the birth register, certificates, diplomas, and a medical certificate (all had to have been screened for tuberculosis), the entire package was forwarded to the Labour Department in Pretoria.[106] Then it could still take months before the much-desired permit arrived in the Netherlands.[107] That was agony, also for Pim and Lena.

Lena, on her part, fell somewhat silent after Pim had taken the initiative. She wrote less frequently. Occasionally doubt crept into Pim's letters, when he had not heard from her for weeks: 'I'm just a human being and I long so much for the support and strength that your letters give me'.[108] His plea to Lena to write shows the power of the written word, which made the absent person present. Lena in those days lived with her sister in Johannesburg and worked at the office of an insurance company. After a busy time at the office, she wrote in May 1952: 'Pim, I have to admit that there are days that I get very discouraged. [...] Then it looks as if time is so slow. But the Lord was always good to me. He always reminds me of that little point of light in the future'.[109] The uncertainty about Pim's arrival created room for doubts about a future with an unknown Dutchman who claimed her as his anchor and fiancée.

It was not only the waiting that burdened her mind, but also the political unrest in her country, where protests against Apartheid measures led to mass arrests in 1952. The opening of the Van Riebeeck festival on 6 April 1952 in Cape Town, celebrating the arrival of Jan van Riebeeck and the establishment of a 'White civilization' in South Africa three hundred years earlier, marked the start of the *Defiance Campaign against Unjust Laws*. This campaign was intended as a national, peaceful protest, organized by the African National Congress (ANC) and the South African Indian Congress against legal measures that promoted the unequal treatment and exclusion of 'non-Whites'.[110] In Johannesburg, where Lena Dusseljee lived in the spring of 1952, a protest meeting was also organized at the time. It made her and many others who enjoyed the

---

106   Blank form for 'Application for Permit to Enter the Union of South Africa or the Mandated Territory of South West Africa for Permanent Residence' (Private Collection; copy in possession of the author). Immigration still came under the South African Department of Labour at that time; in 1960 a Department for Immigration was created.

107   Archive of MvSZ, dir. Emigration, No 364, Map 1: Netherlands Embassy in Pretoria, Letter to the Government Commissioner for Emigration, B.W. Haveman, 25 July 1952, about 200 unanswered letters from Dutch aspiring emigrants.

108   Valk, 6 Apr. 1952.

109   Dusseljee, 25 May 1952.

110   Leslie Witz, *Apartheid's festival: Contesting South Africa's National Pasts* (Bloomington: Indiana University Press, 2003) 144–179.

FIGURE 4.7   Defiance Campaign, 1952 Johannesburg. Still from the documentary *The State Against Mandela and the Others* (2018).

privileges of Whiteness concerned about the future. A 'civil war' (*sivile war*) did not seem unthinkable to Lena, and a month later she still described the situation as 'precarious' (*haglik*). For the time being it did not look as if things would improve.[111] She seems to warn Pim about the rising tensions in South Africa. In addition, her statements can also be read as cautious attempts to reverse the direction of their movements. Given the circumstances, it might be a better idea if she came to the Netherlands.

   She did not write this in so many words and if she suggested it between the lines, Pim took no notice. He was too much preoccupied by the form-filling and other preparations necessary in the run-up to his emigration. From the Netherlands, Pim tried to follow the developments in South Africa, but did not allow political tensions to thwart his plans. In one of his letters to Lena he pictured himself in a drawing of a little man in a boat who was 'still' anchored on the Dutch shore.[112]

---

111   Dusseljee, 16 Apr. and 25 May 1952.
112   Valk, 13 July 1952.

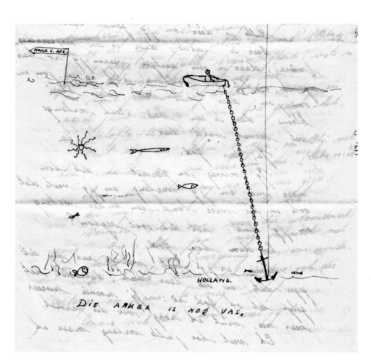

FIGURE 4.8 Drawing by Pim Valk in his letter to Lena of 13 July 1952.

The seriousness of the political situation and the profound inequality between Black and White in South Africa passed him by, judging from a humorously intended remark about his suntanned skin: 'I am afraid that I will be completely black when I come to you. You won't mind, will you?'[113] After two months of waiting, Pim began to show signs of despondency: 'Work here is scarce, my longing great; the permit has not yet arrived; not even a letter from you'. Would Lena be so kind as to go to the Union building in Pretoria to find out about the whereabouts of his papers? He himself had once again gone to The Hague, without result.[114] He continued the preparations for his departure, and made a wooden toolbox to transport his new saw, hammer and chisels to South Africa. Meanwhile, he assured both Lena and himself that it would not take long before his departure: '[It is] just like horses before the start of a race. They are champing at the bit, but they can't go yet. In just a short while the starting gun will go off for us, too'.[115]

---

113   Valk, 6 July 1952.
114   Valk, 27 July and 12 Aug. 1952.
115   Valk, 31 Aug. 1952.

At the end of August the moment had come: as soon as his permit had arrived, Pim Valk went to Amsterdam to arrange his passage. The Dutch emigrant ship *Zuiderkruis* (Southern Cross), which was set to sail on 28 October, was already fully booked. He went looking fervently for alternatives, all the more so because his permit was only valid until 11 February 1953. The *Grote Beer* (Big Dipper) offered a solution. This emigrant ship left on 27 November, but there was another possibility. Ships from the British Union Castle Line left every week, but he could only go 'at short notice'. This meant that he would only hear two or three days in advance if there was room for him. In that case he would be able to leave at the end of September, though at a higher cost. It was a difficult decision, but ultimately Valk chose the fastest option.[116]

The Dutch Reformed *'Dopper'* Church in South Africa

Before Pim Valk closed the front door of his parental house in Breukelen behind him, embraced his mother and shook hands with the other relatives and neighbors, he placed himself behind the harmonium. 'Hymn 280, verse 5, filled the house: "I know Whom I trust, although day and night may change; I know

FIGURE 4.9 Family portrait, taken before Pim Valk (third from the left) left for South Africa in September 1952.

116 Valk, 13, 14 and 15 Sept. 1952.

the Rock on which I build [...]'". This reassuring phrase is mentioned in Pim's travel account. He wrote how wonderful it was to 'let go' in this way. After one last glance in the living room, he got into the waiting rental car. 'There we go: Goodbye, Breukelen', says his travel account, entitled BREUKELEN – JOHANNESBURG.[117]

When he said goodbye to his relatives and his birthplace on 24 September 1952, Pim was 23 years old. Armed with a copper engagement ring and an intense faith in God, he began his journey to South Africa. What images of his destination did Pim Valk actually have, before he set foot on African soil? From his letters to Lena Dusseljee the image emerges of a man envisaging a 'White men's world'.[118] If Lena mentioned her Black countrymen, it was in terms of 'kaffirs' (*kaffers*). Whites from Europe had brought civilization to South Africa. In accordance with this view, Pim saw South Africa as an unambiguously White nation.[119] Within that nation he identified himself in advance with the Dutch Reformed, Afrikaans-speaking part of the population, as he was used to do with the Protestant community in the 'pillarized' Netherlands. He regarded the Afrikaners as his 'own' folk with whom after his arrival he sought and found affiliation in the broader context of a national community.

A similar image emerged from Dutch popular literature and history lessons. Young and old learned about the confrontations of the Dutch Captain Jan van Riebeeck and his crew with the Khoikhoi (*Hottentotten*) and the San (*Bosjesmannen*),[120] or about the hardships of the pioneers (*Voortrekkers*) and the heroic struggle of the Boers against the British. If Africans were present at all in these stories, they were assigned subordinate roles or appeared as villains.[121] The narratives of White European supremacy in South Africa and the entire African continent was decisive for the 'colonial gaze'[122] with which Pim Valk approached South Africa. That gaze is recognizable in Pim's enthusiastic descriptions of his first encounter with the African continent.

After a stopover in Lobito (Angola), Pim showed himself surprised in his report by 'a beautiful and wide asphalted street with spacious sidewalks'.

---

117   Pim Valk, BREUKELEN – JOHANNESBURG (n.d.), based on his journal entries.

118   See also Bill Schwartz, *The White Men's World*. (Oxford: Oxford University Press, 2011).

119   Henkes, 'Shifting Identifications'.

120   E.g., the comic book series about *De avonturen van kapitein Rob* (The Adventures of Captain Rob), drawn and conceived by Pieter Kuhn with a text by journalist Evert Werkman; in particular the episodes about *Jan van Riebeeck in Zuid-Afrika* (1952).

121   See for instance the often reprinted oeuvre of the Dutch Reformed author Louwrens Penning (1854-1927) with titles such as *De leeuw van Modderspruit* (The Lion of Modderspuit, 1900), of *De held van Spionkop* (The hero of Spionkop, 1901), *Onder de Vrijstaatsche vlag* (Under the banner of the Orange Free State, 1901).

122   Pratt, *Imperial Eyes*. See also the introduction to this book.

Everything looked 'just neat and tidy'. He also described the 'Negroes' as 'neat', 'even though they all walk barefoot'. He compared 'a black woman who cooked fish on a wood fire' with the activities of the boy scouts in the Netherlands'. He continued with a description of women walking 'quietly with a large pack on their heads or with a child in a cloth on their backs'. After he got back on the ship, everything was prepared for departure: 'The Negroes are ready at five o'clock. They are standing on the quay looking at the ship. Then, suddenly, a coin flies down. Three, four, ten dive for it. Again, something is thrown overboard. Cigarettes are also very welcome'. Pim and his fellow passengers found the scene of the 'struggling and wriggling mass of arms, legs and bodies' on the quay 'great fun' (*enig om te zien*). The European crewmembers and African clockworkers knew their role, and the passengers were happy to take part in this performance of White Europeanness, when looking down on the Africans receiving their leftovers. These observations made Pim Valk, as he wrote, even more 'curious about the racial issue in South Africa'.[123]

His emigration offered Pim Valk access to a privileged, White South Africa. There he complied, as a matter of course, with the established relationships under the Apartheid policy of the ruling National Party. An important role in that process was reserved for the Reformed Churches and the Protestant faith. Christianity, as practised in the Dutch Reformed *Dopper* Church, was a guiding element in Pim Valk's South African life. Already in the Netherlands he had committed himself to the Anti-Revolutionary notion that God had created the world in his own image and that man had to accept God's creation as given. Once in South Africa, Valk considered the unequal spaces and livelihoods imposed on those South Africans who were referred to as Black, Coloured, and Asiatic as ordered by God. That this racial order was man-made and enforced by political measures, and therefore thoroughly human, did not challenge Valk's view of Apartheid as a mission from God. Had the apostle Paul not proclaimed that God created man to inhabit the entire earth, and that He assigned each of them their own territory? To maintain that order, Valk and most fellow believers were convinced that it was necessary to isolate people of colour in separate townships and so-called 'homelands' (*thuislande*) or Bantustans. With this appeal to the Bible the far-reaching inequality was legitimized as a God-given necessity that he and others were not allowed to alter.

On arrival in Cape Town, however, Pim Valk had other things on his mind. Full of excitement, he scanned the people on the quay from the railing of the ship. Could he recognize 'his' girl from the photo in the crowd? Lena herself was not there, but her welcome telegram was waiting for him. Because he

---

123   Valk, BREUKELEN – JOHANNESBURG, 21–22. The same scene is described in Chap. 5.

unexpectedly managed to take an earlier train to Johannesburg, no one was waiting for him at the station after his long trek. Lena did not expect him until the next morning and was still at work. Pim found his way to Kensington, and bought a large bunch of flowers with his last money. Shortly afterwards he reported at the door of her *koshuis*. For the first time they looked each other in the eyes. The next day they took the train together to Pretoria, where Pim's future boss Prince picked them up from the station.[124]

From the first Sunday after his arrival, Pim Valk went looking for an orthodox-Protestant church where he could feel at home. After some wandering around Lena's English-speaking Baptist church in Troyeville and two Afrikaans-speaking, Dutch Reformed churches (*Nederduits Gereformeerde Kerke*, NGK), Pim and Lena found a spiritual home in the Reformed *Dopper* Church in Johannesburg East, near Lena's boarding house.[125] Pim was soon given the

FIGURE 4.10   The wedding of Pim Valk and Lena Dusseljee in 1954. From left to right: Lena's mother Mrs. Dusseljee; her father; Jan Flach, Pim Valk's best man, whom he knew from the Netherlands; Pim and Lena Valk; Lena's sister and bridesmaid Rita, and both witnesses: Mr. Nagel and Mrs. Nagel. Mr. Nagel had lent Pim the money for the passage to South Africa in 1952, provided he would repay it to his son in South Africa. At the time of the wedding Nagel and his wife were visiting their son.

124   Valk, BREUKELEN – JOHANNESBURG, 25–29.
125   The Reformed Church of South Africa or Dopperkerk is a Reformed-Calvinist church that was founded in 1859 by the Frisian immigrant Dirk Postma. Members of the church are called *Doppers*. It is one of the so-called three White 'sister' churches of South Africa,

opportunity to play the harmonium at some of the church services, and also as a deacon he soon became actively involved in church life. Eighteen months after Pim's arrival, Pastor Yssel married him and Lena; a year later their first child was baptised in the same church.[126] Once it became clear that the baby boy had a serious heart defect and could only survive after major heart surgery, the church was prepared to financially support the family so that Lena could travel and stay with their child who needed treatment by a specialist in the United States.[127] Despite this operation, their first-born died when he was only three. The support of their church community forever bound the Valk couple to this denomination and to Protestant nationalism that was part of it.

For the time being, the colour line in South Africa was not a theme in the exchanges with relatives in the Netherlands. The *Dopper* Church in South Africa had close contacts with the orthodox-Protestant Church to which the Valk family in Breukelen belonged. Despite the growing criticism of Apartheid in the Netherlands, especially after the fatal outcome of a peaceful demonstration in the township of Sharpeville in March 1960, the Dutch Reformed Churches continued to defend Apartheid policy in South Africa until the mid-1970s. Identification with Afrikaner believers from the White 'sister' churches in South Africa stood in the way of a critical attitude towards the racist exclusion of Black South Africans – even when they were fellow believers.[128]

This explains why neither Pim's sister Nel, nor his eldest brother Freek can remember any political discussions between them. Nel's decision to follow her brother Pim to South Africa in November 1960, shortly after 'Sharpeville', apparently did not lead to an exchange about the political tensions in South Africa. It took another twenty years before Pim's relatives in the Netherlands developed any critical notions about the political regime in South Africa, always carefully avoiding a discussion with their brother. Or, as Mr. Valk puts it in a letter to his eldest brother in 2014: 'If I write something about politics to Nel, she won't even respond to it. Well, we as a family were not that interested in

---

together with the Nederduits Gereformeerde Kerk (NG Kerk) and the Nederduits Hervormde Kerk (NH Kerk).

126 Valk, Questionnaire 2006; Valk, *'n Terugblik.*

127 Conversation Henkes and F. & C. Valk, 19 May 2017.

128 Erica Meijers, *Blanke broeders – zwarte vreemden. De Nederlandse Hervormde Kerk, de Gereformeerde Kerken in Nederland en de apartheid in Zuid-Afrika 1948-1972* (White brothers – Black strangers. The Dutch Reformed Churches in the Netherlands and apartheid in South-Africa) (Hilversum: Verloren, 2008), 353–397. Erica Meijers, 'Het zelf en de ander. De gereformeerde synode en de apartheid 1972-1978', in: Dick Boer et al. (red.), *Freedom! Oh Freedom! Opstellen voor Theo Witvliet.* (Zoetermeer: Uitgeverij Meinema, 2000) 97–110, at 104–105.

politics'.[129] Even since the Apartheid regime has been replaced by democracy for all South Africans, the relatives in the Netherlands still avoid the discussion with their brother about what – in his eyes – was and continues to be wrong under the 'Black' ANC government. They do not feel like breaking the silence they cherished all those years, despite their brother's ongoing criticism of the changes in South African society that is still struggling with the impact of its violent colonial past.[130]

In December 1961, more than half a century ago, Pim Valk had for the first time been confronted with sharp criticism of Apartheid policy when he visited the Netherlands with his wife and one-year-old daughter. The reunion with his relatives went without noticeable reservations, but he came into conflict with one of his former teachers and other acquaintances in Breukelen who were 'very anti-Apartheid'. Valk himself was convinced at the time that Apartheid was 'the right political system', as he stresses in his answers to my questionnaire, and he adds that 'obviously it [was] difficult to defend the system against your old teacher (or accept his position)'.[131] The critical discussions about Apartheid in the Netherlands did not reach his wife, also because these were held with acquintances from outside the family. Lena remembers that during their visits in the Netherlands 'we didn't talk about these things, or if they said anything, you ignored it. There was never an argument'.[132] According to her, members of the family respected each other's views and even more: her in-laws understood 'how difficult it was to live together' as Whites with Blacks, Coloureds and Asians. This understanding for the 'difficult' position of the privileged White population on the 'dark' continent also informed the attitude of the orthodox-Protestant Churches in the Netherlands until the end of the 1970s.[133]

Shortly after his return to South Africa Valk renounced his Dutch citizenship. He cannot remember whether the difficult exchanges about Apartheid in his hometown contributed to his opting for South African citizenship in 1962. But regardless of these confrontations in the Netherlands, his choice was undoubtedly strengthened by the euphoria in the nationalist Afrikaner community after the installation of the Republic of South Africa on 31 May 1961, which severed all ties with the British Commonwealth.

---

129   Valk, 6 July 2014.
130   Conversation Henkes and Mrs. Haak-Valk, 8 Nov. 2007 and 8 June 2012; Conversation Henkes and F. & C. Valk, 19 May 2017.
131   Questionnaire Valk, 2006.
132   Conversation Henkes and Valk-Dusseljee, 2008. Mrs. Valk-Dusseljee's statements on the attitude of her in-laws were confirmed in conversations with Pim's sister Nel and his eldest brother Freek, and the correspondence between them.
133   Meijers, *Blanke broeders*.

FIGURE 4.11
Our republic now, to keep South Africa white. A poster promoting a White Republic of South africa in the run-up to the referendum in October 1960 on the question whether the Union of South Africa should become a republic. The vote, which was restricted to Whites, was narrowly approved by 52.29% of the voters. The Republic of South Africa was founded on 31 May 1961.

While Pim and Lena were visiting the Netherlands in 1961, his sister stayed behind in South Africa. More than a year earlier she had arrived in Johannesburg and was welcomed by her brother and sister-in-law, who had encouraged her to come. The 26 year-old Nel wanted a breakaway after several years of office work. She initially intended to stay no longer than one year, but since she had completed the entire emigration process for her temporary stay and because she liked her life in Johannesburg, she decided to stay longer. Still, she would return to the Netherlands after three years, together with her mother who had visited her son and daughter in South Africa. Why she eventually returned, she could not say.[134]

Once in South Africa, Nel Valk got a job at the Anglo-Dutch Equipment office and after she got her driver's licence, she was able to move independently through the city on her motor scooter. In the Rhodes Women's Hostel she shared accommodation with other single women who were working or studying in the city. On Sundays she visited the Reformed *Dopper* Church together with her brother and his wife. Like so many people in South Africa, she moved between an English-speaking, internationally oriented environment and an Afrikaans-speaking, nationalist orthodox-Protestant community. In that community, she joined the Reformed Young People's Association with which she went out several times. She enjoyed these outings, judging from the photos and the captions formulated in Afrikaans in her scrapbooks. Neither in these books nor in the stories of her South African years is Apartheid an explicit theme, although the absence of Black, Coloured and Asian South Africans shows how segregated the Apartheid society was at the time. The only exception was a picture of three African children, with the caption 'Three little Niggers' (*Drie*

---

134   Conversation Henkes and Haak-Valk, 8 Nov. 2007; and a leaflet of the Dutch Emigration Service, The Hague without date with information about eligibility for a subsidised trip, in Haak's Scrapbook 1.

kleine nikkertjes), referring to the – well-known also in Dutch – countdown nursery rhyme *Ten Little Niggers* (1868).[135]

This absence also applies to the surviving correspondence between Pim, his mother, his sister Nel and his eldest brother Freek. After the criticism of racist Apartheid policy was picked up by the Dutch Reformed Churches in the Netherlands towards the end of the 1970s, the silence within the transnational kinship network remained. 'You could ignore it in the correspondence. It was a subject that we didn't spend much time on. [...] and it wasn't my big interest either', Pim's brother Freek remembers in 2017. His wife adds: 'we didn't know the details. Why would you create annoyances ... ?'[136] Family members in the Netherland were used to avoiding this political-moral issue in order to maintain their mutual bond, the more so because they were all busy building up their own family lives and careers. After her return to the Netherlands, Nel's silence was also fuelled by ambivalent feelings about her three-year stay in

FIGURE 4.12
Nel Valk in Johannesburg on her scooter, 1962.

---

135   Conversation Henkes and Haak-Valk, 5 June 2012 and Haak's photo albums.
136   Conversation Henkes and Mr. F. & C. Valk, 19 May 2017, in combination with their preserved correspondence with Pim Valk.

FIGURE 4.13   'Three little niggers'. Caption with a photo of the only Black South Africans in
               the album of Nel Valk, Johannesburg 1962.

South Africa. Positive stories about her stay in South Africa did not fit in with
the hot debates in the Netherlands about Apartheid that subsequently dominated the public domain. This may explain the significant silences in her narrative about the South African episode in her life.[137]

'A Life Full of Grace'

I met the then 73 year-old Nel Haak-Valk (1934) for the first time in 2007, on
the recommendation of her brother in South Africa. A year earlier, Mr. Valk
had responded to an announcement of my research in the monthly magazine *De Nederlandse Post in Zuid-Afrika* (The Dutch Post in South Africa),

---

137   Conversation Henkes and Haak-Valk, 8 Nov. 2007 and 8 June 2012.

with an appeal to those who had moved to South Africa.[138] For decades, the magazine offered a platform to Dutch migrants. In addition to information on developments in the country of origin and relevant regulations regarding pensions, visas and the retention of Dutch nationality, attention was paid to achievements of people of Dutch descent and other occasions where Dutch or formerly Dutch people in South Africa could gather to pay tribute to their Dutchness, such as the celebrations of the Dutch Queen's Birthday, the *Sinterklaas*-festivities on the 5th of December and other 'Dutch' moments in the year. In short: *De Nederlandse Post* expressed, encouraged and confirmed a sense of Dutchness among its subscribers. One could characterize its readership as a Dutch 'imagined community' in South Africa. More than ten years before Mr. Valk reacted to my appeal, he had already responded to an earlier invitation from the editor-in-chief to his readers to write about their emigration and integration into 'their new fatherland'.[139] This invitation provided material for a series going on for years, under the heading 'Immigrants'.

Valk attached his contribution to *The Nederlandse Post* of March 1995 to his first e-mail message to me, in which he wrote that he was 'still very happy with the privilege' that he had been able to come to South Africa with the *Bloemfontein Castle*. For the time being our contact was limited to the digital highway. Mr. Valk, it soon became clear, liked expressing himself, not only on paper but also online. He had already worked out his notes from his trip to South Africa in 1952 on the computer and he had just started to write his memoirs. If I was interested, I had to let him know, or in his own words 'If you have more questions or require information, I am fully prepared to be of service to you'.[140] It was the beginning of a long-term digital correspondence and several meetings in South Africa. In May 2008 I visited him and his wife Lena for the first time. They then lived in a retirement home in Randburg, a well-to-do district of Johannesburg. In the back garden, a miniature windmill made by Valk himself recalled his Dutch origins. On that occasion he handed me, with some hesitation, a shoe box full of chronologically arranged letters that Lena had written to him prior to his departure to South Africa. His wife followed his example and pulled out a plastic bag with letters that Pim had sent her at the

---

138   Valk, e-mail 8 July 2006. Barbara Henkes, 'Oproep', *Nederlandse Post in Zuid-Afrika,* May 2006.

139   W.S. van Ketel, 'Oproep aan immigranten', *Nederlandse Post van Zuid-Afrika*, May 1994.

140   Valk, e-mail 8 July 2006.

time. This is how I received an almost complete collection of the 190 letters they had exchanged between August 1946 and September 1952.[141]

Looking back on his life, Mr. Valk is grateful for his emigration to South Africa. Gratitude is also expressed in the title of his memoirs: *'n Terugblik op 'n lewe vol genade* (A retrospective look at a life full of grace). He completed this autobiographical text in 2010, more than sixteen years after the end of the Apartheid regime. He then sent copies to his family members in the Netherlands and South Africa.[142] Mr. Valk presents himself as a person blessed by God. And indeed, Apartheid South Africa had offered Valk, as a White Dutch South African, the opportunity to further develop his crafts-manship, to lead a good life with his wife and children as they accepted racial inequality as 'normality' in life. Despite the worldwide growing anti-Apart-heid movements and the political disputes and violence in South Africa, Pim Valk had never found reason to reconsider his stand in relation to the in-equalities along the colour line, either at work or in the church, nor in the domestic sphere. It stayed that way after Apartheid was brought to an end in 1994 and space was created for a critical evaluation of the racial policies pur-sued, also in the *Dopper* Church.[143]

From the various documents that Mr. Valk entrusted to me, and from our joint memory work, it becomes apparent how far he had absorbed the 'master narrative of Whiteness' – first in the postcolonial Netherlands and later in Apartheid South Africa. For example, under the heading 'Religious/moral', at the end of his memories, he takes stock of his life. He remembers how the orthodox-Protestant churches in the Netherlands were packed during war-time. However, as soon as the Second World War was over church attendance declined. He regards the 1960s as a time of 'wickedness' (*goddeloosheid*) in the Netherlands and Western Europe, and supposes the arrival of television to have contributed to this 'moral decline'.[144] Neither did the introduction of the welfare state with its social security benefit the religiousness of the Dutch population, according to Mr. Valk, in line with the position of conservative,

---

141   It comprises 83 letters from Lena and 107 letters by Pim (private collection of the author).

142   Valk, *'n Terugblik*.

143   Conversations Henkes and Valk-Dusseljee in 2008 and 2015; Conversation Henkes and F. & C. Valk, 19 May 2017; and conversations Henkes and Haak-Valk, 8 Nov. 2007 and 5 June 2012.

144   Valk, *'n Terugblik*, 217.

Protestant churches in and outside the Netherlands. Therefore, he expresses his satisfaction with his opting for the conservative, Christian Afrikanerdom that in the twentieth century maintained an orthodox approach to life and faith.

At the same time, Mr. Valk is concerned about contemporary developments in the Protestant churches in the Netherlands and South Africa. After the end of the Apartheid regime, 'enlightened' (*verligte*) Afrikaner professors and theologians advocated 'a full acceptance of those others (gays, Blacks, atheists, women, children)'.[145] For Mr. Valk, distinction and inequality – derived from race, gender, sexuality, age, or religion – still stemmed unabated from the order of creation given by God, which must be maintained. Four years later, he confirms this view again in a letter to his brother Freek and his sister-in-law: 'Apartheid is the greatest sin of humanity, so they say. I believe apartheid is part of creation. [...] Unfortunately you have developed races and underdeveloped races'.[146] A few years earlier he had shown a slightly more self-critical approach, when he stated that Blacks should have been 'uplifted': 'If we had trained them properly, we would now have craftsmanship instead of the scrapwork (*brouwwerk*) of someone who is a "builder" after three weeks of training. In that case there might have been coexistence, which is something else than the integration that is now being advocated'.[147] Racial segregation was still at the hart of Mr. Valk's outlook in life, but his legitimisation of racial inequality with reference to the Bible was now supplemented by a more paternalistic discourse, in which the development ('uplifting') of his African countrymen was possible – albeit within their 'own', racially defined group (a '*naastbestaan*').[148]

For Mr. Valk, distinction and inequality based on race was and remained an unchanging fact of life, based on his orthodox faith and his view of global society. Looking back on his youth in the Netherlands he recalls the takeover of power in the Netherlands by Nazi Germany as an attack on the God-given national community. He seemed not aware of the categorization, exclusion

---

145   Valk, '*n Terugblik*, 218, referring to an article in the *By* magazine, 8 May 2010.
146   Valk, e-mail to Henkes, 21 November 2014.
147   Valk, 2006.
148   Valk, questionnaire 2006. He writes in so many words: 'One problem was that it [Apartheid] was also defended from the Bible'. In a letter dated 24 July 2014, he added, in response to my question what he meant by that: 'We, the Afrikaner churches too, were firmly convinced that the existence of separate nations is simply part of creation. I am now, after 20 years of change, even more convinced'.

and persecution of Jews in the Netherlands – and this ignorance had not changed in the course of his life in South Africa. Mr. Valk approaches the Second World War primarily as a time in which the faith and morale of the Dutch population flourished under pressure from Nazi Germany. That idea ties in with the postwar narrative of 'the' Dutch, who had stood up as one man against the Nazi German repression. Since the acknowledgement that most Dutch people accommodated and many collaborated with the Nazis, the nationalist narrative of the brave Netherlands opposed to the brutal or Godless German enemy has changed.

The increasing awareness of the tragic fate of the deported Jews con- tributed to the replacing of the nationalist heroic narrative by a story about the collective failure of the Dutch, also amongst the orthodox-Protestants. From that time onwards, the war period has been approached as a time of moral decay: when, under pressure from National Socialist repression, few were able to offer protection to those fellow human beings who were perse- cuted for racist, religious or political reasons. That painful realization was to become a part of the collective memory in the Netherlands from the 1960s onwards. National Socialism and the Shoah became a touchstone against which political decision making and the government's use of violence were measured. This applied not only to confrontations between critical citizens and Dutch authorities, but also to political regimes abroad, such as the Apartheid regime in South Africa with its institutionalized inequality on a racial basis.

This shift of the dominant narrative about the Netherlands in wartime had bypassed Pim Valk and many other postwar Dutch emigrants. They or their parents had left the Netherlands with an image of the suffering and rebellious 'Dutch people' who had resisted 'the German enemy'. In their mind it was a history of national resistance and heroism. The failure of their compatriots to prevent the exclusion, persecution and murder of peo- ple who were supposed to undermine the consistency of a 'purely Aryan' community had escaped their attention. This ignorance made the compari- son between the Nazi and the Apartheid regimes, as used in the rhetoric of the anti-Apartheid Movement, incomprehensible and inexcusable to them. In the end, most Dutch migrants, like Mr. Valk, were unable to break free from the racist discourse to which they had committed themselves in the South African context. The *Dopper* church played a decisive role in this, al- though since 1994 a re-orientation has taken place within the Protestant communities. For Mr. Valk and many individual believers this reorientation went too far – in practice, therefore, it was hardly translated into an actual multiracial merging of believers. The inability to practise racial equality in post-Apartheid South Africa is certainly not limited to Afrikaner Reformed communities; it also applies to more liberal-minded Dutch migrants after their immersion in the South African Apartheid discourse, as the following chapter shows.

CHAPTER 5

'They are so Different from us'

Messages from a White Women's World

'Dear all', Wendela Beusekom-Scheffer (1928-2013) started the first letter to her parents and younger brothers in Amsterdam on 26 September 1952.[1] 'It may be a somewhat illegible letter, because we are rocking considerably and occasionally we are thrown in an unexpected direction, so that we can imagine ourselves in a ride at the fun fair all day'. During the sometimes turbulent passage from the Netherlands to South Africa, the pen provided some grip on the situation and the parental home acted as a landmark. Wendela right away wrote how she had managed to make her parents present – albeit virtually but also tangibly – in the intimacy of their comfortable first-class cabin: 'Our cabin is ever so pleasant, your photos and Corrie's flowers in a vase, and some books and candy on the shelf. When Bas saw your photo, he crawled over quickly and happily cried out Mmma, Mmma! In no time, grandfather and grandmother's face were covered with his little fingerprints'.[2]

One day earlier, Wendela, her husband Jan Peter and their one-year-old son Bas had been waved goodbye by friends and family from Central Station in Amsterdam. More than three years later, in January 1956, the Beusekom family, now with another son and a daughter, returned to the Netherlands. In the intervening years contact was maintained through a regular exchange of letters, photos and postal packages, in addition to a one-off visit by, successively, Wendela's parents and Jan Peter's mother in the last year of their stay.

Just as in the correspondence between Pim Valk and Lena Dusseljee, described in the previous chapter, South African Apartheid politics appeared only indirectly in the correspondence between Wendela Beusekom-Scheffer and her parents in Amsterdam. The mutual involvement of the relatives in the Netherlands and South Africa never came under pressure due to the racial exclusion policy of the Apartheid regime in South Africa. However, it is sometimes clear that her parents in the Netherlands had more questions about the propagated 'separate development' along the colour line than their daughter and son-in-law. In her review of their stay in South Africa, Mrs. Beusekom suggests that after their return to the Netherlands, partly encouraged by the

---

1   Synonyms were introduced for the protagonists in this chapter.
2   Letter Wendela Beusekom-Scheffer to her parents (hereafter Beusekom-Scheffer), 26 Sep. 1952.

© BARBARA HENKES, 2020 | DOI:10.1163/9789004401600_007

FIGURE 5.1
Wendela Beusekom-Scheffer and
baby Bas in the cabin on board the
Bloemfontein Castle.

worldwide condemnation of repressive Apartheid policy, she adopted a more
critical attitude. So how did the power of a dominant narrative about a White
civilization worked out in the lives of the young Beusekom family in South
Africa?

When asked about the reasons for their departure, Mrs. Beusekom emphasizes half a century later that there was no need to go. Her husband just wanted
'something else'. After graduating from university as a lawyer, he worked for
two years at the *Nederlandse Bank* in Amsterdam. The housing shortage at the
time meant that immediately after their marriage in 1950 they moved into the
upstairs floor of her parents' house, which had been converted into an independent apartment. Nine months later their son Bas was born in this spacious
villa in Amsterdam South. 'We lived very luxuriously, always cared for', she describes the situation at the time. Nevertheless, or precisely because of that, her
husband wanted to leave.[3] After an application to two banks abroad, he was

---

3   When Wendela's father offered to pay for the help in their South African household, she re-
    plied in a letter of 7 Mar. 1953 that they did not want to accept his assistance: 'That is our only

hired by the *Nederlandse Bank voor Zuid-Afrika* (Netherlands Bank of South Africa). 'If I am not mistaken, I thought it was all right', said Mrs. Beusekom.[4]

In the spring of 2006, she and I first met and spoke about the time she and her family spent in South Africa. Their emigration was limited to a few years, but this had not been decided in advance. The relatively short duration does not detract from the widow Beusekom's lively memories. These years had been formative, as she and Jan Peter stood on their own feet for the first time and were going to build a family household of their own. In addition, the contact with close friends they had met in South Africa, as well as the public debates about Apartheid in the Netherlands, kept the memories of their stay in South Africa alive. After our first rendezvous I received a package of 132 letters in which, with a single contribution from her husband Jan Peter, she reported almost weekly on her experiences overseas to her parents in the Netherlands.[5] The letters that her mother, sometimes supplemented by a paragraph or letter from her father, sent from Amsterdam to Pretoria with the same regularity have still not been found. However, traces of these letters are present in Wendela's writing when she responds to questions or messages from Amsterdam. The flow of letters from South Africa ends on 6 June 1955, shortly before Wendela's parents came to visit South Africa. They stayed for three months, after which Jan Peter's mother followed. In January 1956, Wendela and the children returned to the Netherlands by boat together with her mother-in-law.[6] Jan Peter had preceded them by plane because of a new job in his home country.

Although Mrs. Beusekom recalls that she thought it was 'all right' to leave for South Africa, her letters reveal a more ambivalent attitude. Saying goodbye to her parents was hard for her, and she sought comfort in the idea that their

---

satisfaction here, that we can take care of ourselves. J.P. especially finds this very pleasant, which I can imagine'.

4   Conversation Barbara Henkes and Mrs. W. Beusekom-Scheffer (hereafter: Conversation Henkes and Beusekom-Scheffer), 21 Mar. 2006.

5   The letters were handwritten in the period between 26 Sep. 1952 and 4 June 1955 and had an average length of four airmail sheets. The letters, photo albums and other material are now in the possession of Mrs. Beusekom-Scheffer's descendants (Private Collection Beusekom family; copies with the author). Twenty of these letters were written by Jan Peter. His contribution to this correspondence was mainly addressed to Wendela's father and often dealt with business matters: transferring money, financial support for the purchase of a car, or considerations about the next step in his career, with the exception of his detailed reports about the birth of the two youngest children when Wendela and the baby were still in the maternity clinic. For the rest Jan Peter left the description of 'the weekly events' to his wife.

6   Album Beusekom-Lanting, in which Jan Peter's mother reported on her trip to Cape Town starting on 2 Sep. 1955 and ending with her return journey together with her daughter-in-law and the grandchildren from Durban on 21 Jan. 1956.

emigration would be only temporary.[7] For the then 23-year-old Wendela it was obvious that she would follow her husband to the place where he wanted to develop his career. Neither was it an exceptional step: Jan Peter Beusekom had been born in the former Netherlands East Indies, where his father and previously also his grandfather had started their careers, later to continue their lives in the Netherlands. The same applied to some of Wendela's relatives.[8] 'Privileged mobility' along colonial lines was part of their well-to-do family history,[9] and their own postwar emigration from Europe to South Africa also fitted into that pattern: the Beusekom family belonged to a privileged White minority in the former Dutch colony. The departure of the Beusekoms, as well as that of many of their recently graduated friends, was also part of the sizeable postwar emigration movement that drew all layers of Dutch society in the direction of White settler societies, such as Canada, Australia, the United States, South Africa and New Zealand.[10]

Whitening at Sea

Thanks to the regular exchanges on paper, it is clear how Wendela Beusekom tested her impressions against the norms and values that she had imbibed from an early age. Other migrants and travellers also tried to organize their experiences by relating the unfamiliar to what was familiar to them. In that process, an image of 'our kind of people' and 'our culture' was constructed as a benchmark against which 'the Other' was assessed. This was soon accompanied by moral judgments: 'They are all apparently lower middle class, although there are some names from the German nobility in the passenger list, but they are more reminiscent of an operetta'. Wendela's characterization of her fellow passengers aboard the *Bloemfontein Castle* explains why she and

---

7   Beusekom-Scheffer, Oct. 14, 1952. Cf. her letter of 12 Nov. 1953 in which Wendela mentions J.P.'s plans to move to the US for a few years. Wendela adds: 'I think everything is fine and I will follow him with the children. In that way we at least get to see something of the world'.

8   Beusekom-Scheffer, 14 and 23 Oct. 1952, 18 June 1954, in which she referred to an uncle and aunt who had lived in Netherlands East Indies. During our conversation in 2006, Beusekom-Scheffer mentioned that her grandparents were also in the Netherlands East Indies for a short term.

9   See also: Caroline Knowles, 'Home and Away. Maps of Territorial and Personal Expansion 1860–97', *The European Journal of Women's Studies,* Vol. 7, 2000:263–280.

10   Van Faassen, 'Min of meer misbaar'.

her husband could not, at first sight, discover 'nice people' (*leuke mensen*) like themselves.[11]

'I had had such a sheltered upbringing, I had no idea of the outside world', says Mrs. Beusekom, looking back at her younger self.[12] Uncertainty in the midst of the unknown company is also evident from her report of the first 'party evening' on the ship, when she was confronted with passengers in rather varied clothes: an elderly couple appeared in tuxedo and evening gown, other ladies in cocktail dresses, and yet others in sports kit. She did not know what to think of this 'strange mishmash',[13] which was at odds with the dresscodes she was familiar with at home. Those codes offered her a handle to assess the social position of strangers and to position herself relative to them. In the end it was still a pleasant evening that ended with a wobbly dance in Jan Peter's arms on the ship's deck. It did not take long before she became used to the freedom to wear what she wanted without anyone paying attention to it: 'Very easy, anything goes', she wrote enthusiastically five days later to her parents.[14]

Gradually she adjusted her opinion about the other passengers. After a few days Wendela wrote that she enjoyed 'the different types of people you see on board'. By way of illustration she referred to 'an old Englishman, a sporty, sprightly type who has lived in Java for years' and 'a wholly South African lawyer', who spoke Dutch because his parents were from the Netherlands. Moreover, she and Jan Peter made the acquaintance of a 'very well-educated and pleasant' Dutch couple on their way to Durban. The other Dutch passengers, among whom incidentally also Pim Valk we have met in Chapter 4, were described as 'good people', albeit 'from a completely different milieu', so that conversations with them did not really get off the ground.

The Germans, also referred to as 'Krauts' or as people with 'very obnoxious manners', did not come out well in Wendela's letters. Unfortunately, she and Jan Peter were often mistaken for Germans, which meant that they met with cool and unfriendly treatment, 'until people knew better'.[15] In her disqualification of the German passengers the recent war resonated. In her eyes – and apparently also in those of many other people on board – 'the' Germans had

---

11   Beusekom-Scheffer, 26 Sep. 1952.

12   Conversation Henkes and Beusekom-Scheffer, 16 Apr. 2012. Also, in our conversation of 21 Mar. 2006 Beusekom-Scheffer presented herself as a particularly naive young woman.

13   Beusekom-Scheffer, 26 Sep. 1952. See also the popular etiquette book by Amy Groskamp-Ten Have, *Hoe hoort het eigenlijk?* (Amsterdam: Publishing House H.J.W. Becht, 1940) (4th ed.) 316, about 'dress on board '.

14   Beusekom-Scheffer, sent 15 Oct., referring to 1 Oct. 1952.

15   Beusekom-Scheffer, sent 15 Oct., referring to 3 and 7 Oct. 1952.

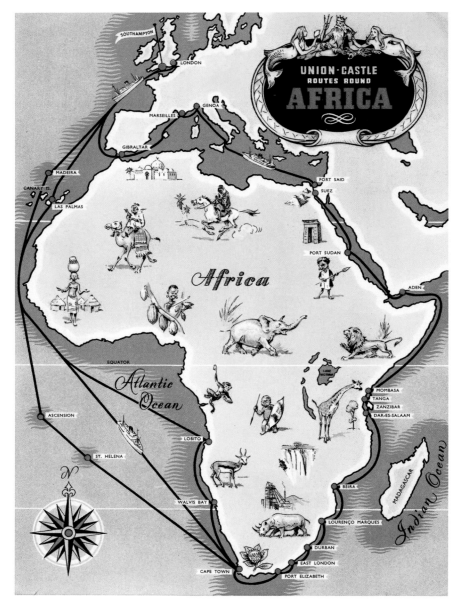

FIGURE 5.2   Map from a brochure of the *Union Castle line* showing a visual characterisation from a European perspective of the African continent (1950s).

lost their moral credibility. The contrast she experienced between 'bold' Dutch and 'annoying' or 'arrogant' Germans contributed to the growing significance of a shared Dutchness against the diminishing importance of class and social status among the Dutch passengers.

Wendela's assessment of the people around her had everything to do with her social and cultural background and the political discourse in the postwar Western world. She was part of a highly regarded kinship network in the Netherlands and came from a nation that was counted among the Allied victors. Both positions offered her a compass by which to determine her own place within the unknown company on board and make the story of the Other subordinate to that of her own.[16] Social inequality was central to the way in which she approached other passengers, but there was room for revision of her judgement: the gap that she initially experienced between herself and the other passengers narrowed during the journey, especially after the first encounter with 'Dark Africa', as she calls it in one of her letters.[17] At that time, the difference between Europeans made way for the apparently unbridgeable gap between White Europeans and Black Africans.

FIGURE 5.3   The port of Lobito in September 1952.

---

16   See James Baldwin, 'Stranger in the village', in: Idem, *Notes of a Native Son*. (Boston: Beacon Press, 1955).

17   Beusekom-Scheffer, sent 13 Oct., referring to 9 Oct. 1952.

She described to her parents how the ship entered the harbour of Lobito (Angola) at seven o'clock in the morning: 'on the quay was swarming with *zwartjes* (little blacks), who looked ridiculous in their worn clothes with bare feet that were grey with dust. The sight of this city, which is supposed to be one of Africa's most important ports, was certainly ugly and for Europeans (there are 2,000 mainly Portuguese) a nasty place to live'. Wendela stayed on board with the baby, while her husband and other passengers explored the area. According to her description, most returned 'disappointed' and complained that the town was 'dusty, warm and insignificant'. That didn't stop her from taking a stroll with Jan Peter later on. The result of their expedition was an ambivalent report, in which her dislike for 'the stink of rotting sardines' on the beach, where 'ragged, scratching, begging, laughing and screaming Black people' were moving about, became mixed up with admiration for their 'upright posture' and 'smooth' walk.[18] The mixture of aversion and exotic attraction in her story about the stopover in Lobito reveals the 'colonial gaze' with which she approached 'Africa' and its population in 1952. This gaze, which she already had before she ever set foot on the continent, was closely linked to the self-esteem of a superior, European, colonial power.[19]

From that moment onwards, Wendela Beusekom identified with the Europeans aboard the ship whom she set against the Black population on the African continent. Even the German passengers could count on some sympathy. When a large group of them disembarked in Walvis Bay, located in the former German colony of South West Africa (nowadays Namibia), she noted: 'I did not envy these people!'[20] Her distancing herself from the Germans because of the recent war made way for a rapprochement on the basis of a shared Europeanness. White supremacy was illustrated by her lively description of the departure from the port of Lobito: from the deck, the passengers and the crew were having fun throwing cigarettes, pennies, menu cards and other insignificant trifles to the 'smiling Negroes' on the quay. The excitement that arose among the Africans, who threw themselves 'childishly' eagerly on the ground to get hold of anything, 'was a scream', according to Wendela Beusekom, in line with Pim Valk's observations mentioned in the previous chapter.[21] When the ship sailed they were enthusiastically waved goodbye by the African dockworkers. 'Lobito' marked a turning point; it provided a repeated ritual by which the Europeans on the ship became a strongly united White body *vis-à-vis* Black Africans.

18   Beusekom-Scheffer, sent 13 Oct., referring to 9 Oct. 1952.
19   Pratt, *Imperial Eyes*. See also the Introduction to this book.
20   Beusekom-Scheffer, sent on 15 Oct., referring to 11 Oct. 1952. South West Africa was made
        a League of Nations mandate of the British-ruled Union of South Africa following Germany's losses in World War I.
21   Beusekom-Scheffer, sent on 15 Oct., referring to 9 Oct. 1952. See also Chap. 4, p. 150.

Compared to Lobito, Wendela described the arrival in Cape Town in very different terms: there, the wonderful Table Mountain – acclaimed in both brochures and in her letter – rose from the sea with a sun-drenched city at its feet. For many passengers, Cape Town marked the end of the journey. Strengthened by the enthusiastic stories of South African fellow travellers on board, this city had acquired a White, European aura that they found confirmed upon their arrival. There is not a word in Wendela Beusekom's report about African dockworkers on the quay who must have been there. Instead she mentions a man from the Thomas Cook travel agency, who had already completed the formalities around their luggage and made sure that they quickly passed through customs. They were met by a representative from the *Nederlandse Bank voor Zuid-Afrika*, who took them to the station by taxi and provided them with the necessary British pounds.[22] It all ran smoothly, as if they were in Europe instead of Africa.

FIGURE 5.4A   'The *voortrekkers*, on their way to Pretoria 1952', caption in a photo album of Wendela's parents.

---

22   Beusekom-Scheffer, sent on 15 Oct. about their arrival on 13 Oct. 1952. They were given £25.00 that equalled around 250 guilders at the time (903 euro's in 2019) according to Beusekom-Scheffer. After South Africa's 1961 departure from the Commonwealth, the British pound was replaced by the South African sand.

In Europe the narrative of South Africa as a White settler society with a European civilization was commonplace at the time. The South African government also promoted that perspective on their national history.[23] In April 1952, a few months before the departure of the Beusekom family, both the Netherlands and South Africa celebrated that 300 years earlier the Dutchman Jan van Riebeeck, his wife and his crew had set foot on Cape of Good Hope. Both nations presented Van Riebeeck's arrival as the beginning of a White, Christian civilization in South Africa, despite the protests of critical South Africans who opposed this celebration of White supremacy.[24] Heroic stories about the pioneering work of Van Riebeeck and the successful battles against 'primitive natives' during the subsequent Great Trek shaped the expectations with which Dutch emigrants left the Netherlands.[25] The caption under the photo of Wendela and Jan Peter with baby Bas on his shoulders, taken shortly before their departure, refers to this brave history: 'The *Voortrekkers*, on to Pretoria, 1952'.

FIGURE 5.4B
Cover reprint of L. Penning, Voortrekkersbloed (Voortrekker's blood) in the 'for freedom and justice' series (1965).

---

23   See also Schwarz, *The White Man's World*, 59 and Henkes, 'Stamverwantschap'.
24   Witz, *Apartheid's festival*.
25   See also Chap. 4, n. 110.

In the wake of the Great Trek, the Beusekoms were going to travel from Cape Province to Transvaal to settle there in the 'Boer' capital Pretoria. Incidentally, the narrative of the Great Trek was not only a heroic story about independent spirits of Dutch descent who developed the South African interior, but also a violent tale of bloody confrontations with 'unreliable' African tribes.[26] That story also affected the way in which Wendela Beusekom approached the people in her new environment.

A New World in Black and White

The reception in Cape Town might have offered a familiar, 'European' impression, but the presence of Blacks in the vicinity was new. In her report of the two-day train journey to their final destination, Pretoria, Wendela wrote that their first-class *Blue Train* compartment was cleaned by African staff. The proximity of Blacks made her 'uncomfortable'. The images and narratives portraying uncivilized people in 'dark Africa' were readily available in the cultural baggage with which the Beusekoms came to South Africa. In the inevitable contact with the colonial 'Other' Wendela became aware of her Whiteness, which she would rather have ignored as she used to do in the Netherlands.[27] So soon after their arrival she was not yet familiar with the social code of ignoring the presence of Black South Africans, which gave her an open eye for the sharpness of the colour line. In the train on the way to Pretoria she remarked that the separation between Black and White was carried out too far: 'Even now that we are here in the middle of the desert and occasionally stop at small hamlets, there are separate waiting rooms or *hokken* (hutches) for Blacks'.[28]

In order to explain and be able to tolerate the inequality along the colour line, Wendela Beusekom relied on narratives and images of a superior White civilization that had travelled with her from the Netherlands.[29] Two days after their arrival in Pretoria she saw the prevailing stereotype of 'the lazy Negro' confirmed in her observations of the 'masses of Negro workers', who worked opposite their hotel room on the construction of a new building: 'They are ever so lazy, stupid

---

26   See e.g. the *oeuvre* of the popular Dutch author Lourens Penning, in particular *Voortrek-kersbloed. De geschiedenis van de Grote Trek der Zuid-Afrikaanse Boeren en van de val van Koning Dingaan van Zoeloeland* (Pioneering blood. The history of the Great Trek of South African Boers and of the fall of King Dingaan of Zululand) (Zwolle: La Rivière & Voorho-eve, 1926). See also Chap. 4, n. 22 and 121.

27   Pratt, *Imperial Eyes.*

28   Beusekom-Scheffer, 15 Oct., referring to 14 Oct. 1952.

29   Nederveen Pieterse, *White on Black.*

and larky. Suddenly one of them will start clapping his hands, singing and dancing and the others stand around him, all grinning. But the Whites remain patient, urge them to start working again and just laugh along', she described the scene to her parents.[30] With the designation 'Negro workers' she introduced a similarity with the working class as she knew it in the Netherlands and Europe. This parallel is given more substance when she describes how the African construction workers cycle to work and are dressed 'just like Dutch workers'.

What Wendela thought about the position of the working class in Dutch society cannot be ascertained, but she was not inclined to link the subordinate position and great poverty of the Black South African workers to systematic discrimination. Instead, she ascribed the cause of their poverty to the inherent traits of 'the Africans': 'because they are lazy and dirty and love to sleep in the sun and to continuously chat and laugh with each other'.[31] Via this associative series of words, in which Negroes, workers, poverty, laziness, and filth became intertwined, Wendela Beusekom linked the distinction between poor and rich to the moral distinction between 'patient', responsible (White) overseers and undisciplined, lazy (Black) workers. She interpreted the unmistakable poverty among 'the Negroes' in terms of the liberal discourse of 'personal responsibility'. This made it possible for her, during her stay in South Africa, to accept both her own privileged position and the Apartheid policy in terms of 'the indigenous problem' (*het naturellen probleem*).[32]

Quickly and imperceptibly, she managed to accept life according to the racial divide as 'normal' or inevitable. After a visit to Burgers Park in Pretoria she wrote enthusiastically: 'This is for Whites (*vir Blankes*) only and there are the most beautiful flowers, palm trees, and a playground for children. It is remarkable how [...] plants that we also know in Holland grow much more exuberantly over here'.[33] She first mentions the most notable difference between the Pretorian park ('accessible only for Whites') and the famous Vondelpark in Amsterdam, which Wendela and her parents knew so well, but then she quickly jumps to the innocent floral splendour. With the lilac phloxes and red bougainvillea, she returns to a 'safe story'[34] about nature by which the forced absence of Blacks could be ignored. A few months later she wrote that she was still not used to the fact that 'you can walk anywhere in the parks and sit on the grass. I always expect gates and signs with all the prohibitions, which you will find everywhere in Holland'.[35] Thanks to her simultaneous seeing and looking

---

30   Beusekom-Scheffer, 17 Oct. 1952.
31   Beusekom-Scheffer, 17 Oct. 1952.
32   Beusekom-Scheffer, 30 Oct. 1952, 17 Apr. 1953, 4 Feb. 1955.
33   Beusekom-Scheffer, 17 Oct. 1952.
34   Johnson, 'Two Ways to Remember. See also the Introduction to this book
35   Beusekom-Scheffer, 12 Mar. 1953.

away from racial exclusion, she no longer noticed the signs with the inscription 'for Whites only'.[36]

When the Beusekom family lived in the Netherlands, their Dutchness was self-evident and the colour of their skin did not need to be considered. Whiteness was a matter of course for most Dutch, even though more and more Antillean-, Indonesian – and Surinamese-Dutch lent colour to the streetscape in the postwar Netherlands.[37] To this day, Dutchness for many is naturally White. For the South African authorities the Whiteness of the Dutch was less obvious: aspiring emigrants had to indicate in their documents whether or not they belonged to 'the White race'.[38] They were also quickly checked for skin colour during the mandatory visit to the South African emigration inspection service

FIGURE 5.5   Photographer: Ernest Cole, c. 1960.

---

36   J. Presser, 'Clio kijkt door het sleutelgat', in: *Uit het werk van J. Presser* (Amsterdam: Athenaeum-Polak & Van Gennep, 1969) 283–295, at 286. See also Mariam Dobson, 'Letters', in: Mariam Dobson (eds.), *Reading Primary Sources, The interpretation of texts from the nineteenth and twentieth-century history* (London/New York: Routledge, 2009) 57–73, at 62.

37   Guno Jones, *Tussen onderdanen, rijksgenoten en Nederlanders*, (Amsterdam: Rozenberg Publishers, 2007); Cottaar, *Zusters uit Suriname*.

38   On the application form for admittance to South Africa there was a question about *Ras'*(race) followed by the explication *nie nasionaliteit nie* (Not Nationality).

in The Hague – certainly if, like Jan Peter Beusekom, they had been born in the Netherlands East Indies.[39]

The Dutch knew that, like many other emigration destinations, South Africa was inhabited not only by Whites. Yet South Africa was perceived as a White man's world, even though the majority of the population showed various shades of Black.[40] The representation of a White South Africa was supported by the Apartheid policy, which sharply separated the worlds of 'White', 'Coloured', 'Asiatic' and 'Black'. On arrival, Dutch immigrants were given access to a 'White world': a space where White was the only colour that counted, and where people of Colour could only occupy subordinate positions.[41] As they moved into a world where Whiteness was the overall determining factor, Blackness was never far away. That explains how Wendela Beusekom, and many like her, were able to notice the inequality based on colour, and yet could simultaneously ignore or legitimize it.

The unequal relationship between a White minority and a Black majority, which had been enforced since South Africa was colonized, was made more and more absolute and institutionalised by the Apartheid regime.[42] This helped to activate the dormant representation of White supremacy that the Beusekoms had brought with them from the Netherlands. Wendela emphasized one element from the complex combination of images and narratives about the Black 'Other': the supposed violence of African males. In her letters, the initial emphasis on poverty, undisciplined behaviour and childishness soon gave way to fear and a manifest sense of being threatened when it came to Blacks. Two weeks after their arrival, she wrote about 'the great insecurity' casting a shadow on their life in South Africa: 'You can never go outside safely in your free time. In Holland there were sometimes people who told us about assaults on women in the dark, about thefts, etc. We didn't want to believe this, and we thought it

---

39   Henkes, conversations with several postwar Dutch emigrants who had gone to South Africa. See also Chap. 4, p. 145.

40   Schwarz, *The white man's world.*

41   Although the Mines and Work Acts of 1912 and 1926 already introduced a 'colour bar' for certain segments of the labour market, the existing dividing line between better paid positions for Whites and poorly paid positions for Blacks was made into general law by the Job Reservation Act of 1956.

42   Already at the beginning of the twentieth century, the foundations were laid for the later geopolitics of Apartheid with the introduction of the Native Land Act in 1913. This restricted the ownership of land by Africans to the 'native reserves' and, when in the 1930s the last remnants of the voting rights for Africans were undermined, race-segregated establishment in the cities was introduced. See e.g. Mark Mazower, *No Enchanted Palace, The End of Empire and the Ideological Origins of the United Nations* (Princeton, Princeton University Press, 2009) 50.

was just spite. In reality everything is much worse than we heard, and it gives us a locked-in feeling, even in a car you are not safe'.[43]

Nothing in Wendela's letters shows what that 'reality' consisted of. Neither these nor her memories contain references to robberies, rape, assault or threats that she or others in her immediate surroundings had actually experienced with the exeption of a burglary in the servant room.[44] Apparently the visible presence of Blacks was enough to replace the idea of 'just spite' with a sense of existential threat. 'I will never forget the first evening ...', Mrs. Beusekom starts her story more than fifty years later about her first evening walk in Pretoria: 'It was already dark and then there were all those Negroes sitting in the porches with *huge* sticks. [...] I thought that was just terrifying!'[45] The same 'dark figures in porches' with 'possibly evil intentions' are also mentioned in one of her first letters from Pretoria. The irony is that these Africans were hired to guard the property of their White, wealthy countrymen in the city and to guarantee safety. But that did not diminish Wendela's fear. Fear of violence from Black men was fuelled by South African newspapers, which were full of reports about 'one murder after another robbery'.[46] Her acute and intense feeling of insecurity was mainly evoked by stories about assault and rape of White women by Black men. Fear of the so-called 'Black Peril' was partly fuelled by White men's obsessive imagining of sexual competition by Black males.[47]

From the end of the nineteenth century, fear of the Black male body became inextricably linked to the need to channel female sexual desires and maintain social hierarchies – between European and African, White and Black, poor and rich, male and female.[48] Legal measures and social taboos on interracial 'mixing' were found necessary to prevent a weakening of the *Volksgemeenskap* (White people's community) and its colonial order. In 1927 the first *Immorality Act*, which criminalized sexual contacts outside marriage between (White) 'Europeans' and (Black) 'natives' was passed. Under Apartheid this prohibition was extended to the population classified as 'Coloured' or 'Asian'. The

---

43   Beusekom-Scheffer, 30 Oct. 1952.

44   Beusekom-Scheffer in a letter of 14 Sep. 1954, reports: 'Two sheets and the deposit booklet of Josefien's boyfriend were taken away. The police were alarmed and came to investigate but did nothing when it turned out to be the precious possessions of a *kaffermeid*'.

45   Conversation Henkes and Beusekom-Scheffer, 21 Mar. 2006, italics added to indicate emphasis during storytelling.

46   Beusekom-Scheffer, 17 Oct. 1952.

47   Cf. D.G.N. Cornwell, 'George Webb Hardy's 'The Black Peril and the social meaning of 'Black Peril' in early Twentieth-Century South Africa', *Journal of Southern African Studies* 22: 3 (1996), 441–453; also B.B. Brown, 'Facing the 'Black Peril': The Politics of Population Control in South Africa', *Journal of Southern African Studies* 13:3 (1987) 256–273.

48   Schwartz, *The White Men's World*, 172.

prohibition of interracial marriages (*Prohibition of Mixed Marriages Act,* 1949) and interracial intimacy (*Immorality Amendment Act,* 1950), in combination with narratives of the violent Black male body, reinforced the fears of 'the man of colour'. Wendela Beusekom was not insensitive to that. 'Having a daughter ... is a doubtful pleasure here', wrote the pregnant daughter to her parents in Amsterdam, fifteen days after arriving in Pretoria. Two weeks later she repeated this lamentation: 'Daughters are a *griezelig bezit* (an anxious possession) here because *Kaffers* (Kaffirs) are not only criminal but also sexually very, very abnormal. That is why women here are never very safe and why you can never leave daughters alone with the *boy* at home'.[49]

How deep the fear of the Black 'Other' had become during her stay in South Africa is also reflected in our conversations. Several times Mrs. Beusekom emphasized that it was 'all highly unsafe'. When asked about what made her life so unsafe at the time, she initially referred to thefts: 'We were rich compared to the Blacks, of course. The houses all had bars on the windows. But then they hooked through the bars of the open windows'. Not that this had ever happened to her, but she was warned immediately upon arrival and that made her 'terrified of the blacks', she wrote in one of her first letters from Pretoria.[50] The perceived dangers that dominate her stories about South Africa fit in seamlessly with current reports about theft and violence in post-Apartheid South Africa – also from her old friends, who stayed in South Africa and entrenched themselves with their riches behind increasingly higher walls and stronger electric wire.[51]

In addition, Mrs. Beusekom mentions two incidents in which the main issue was not so much the fear of theft as the fear of violence by Black men against White women. The first scene that comes to her mind took place during a picnic just outside Pretoria with Dutch friends: 'We sat there with some food near a little stream and then this Kaffir approached us'. One of her friends panicked and wanted to go back to the car immediately. 'Rather strange, actually. I didn't notice anything, I don't know if it was dangerous at all or not', is Mrs. Beusekom's evaluation afterwards.[52] The second incident took place around the house: 'I once sat on my *stoep* (doorstep) [...] when a Kaffir entered our premises. He

---

49   Beusekom-Scheffer, Oct. 30 and 11 Nov. 1952. In her letter she writes about the 'boy', using the Afrikaans and English word in South Africa for the Black male household staff.

50   Beusekom-Scheffer, 17 Oct. 1952.

51   Conversation Henkes and Beusekom-Scheffer, 21 Mar. 2006.

52   Conversation Henkes and Beusekom-Scheffer, 21 Mar. 2006, repeated during our conversation of 16 Apr. 2012. Also, in a letter from 19 Mar. 1953, in which she reports this meeting, Wendela thinks there was no reason for all the commotion: 'even if you never know with these nasty guys, especially on Sundays, when they are so often drunk'.

supposedly went to Lina, the Black resident help. But I didn't trust him. So, I quickly ran to my children in the back yard, collected them all and closed the door'.[53] During our second conversation she repeats this anecdote and adds that the man in question saw how scared she was. He had smiled reassuringly and said: 'Haha, the Missus is scared'. To my question whether that fear was justified, Mrs. Beusekom simply replied: 'No, no, absolutely not. But it is the Other anyway'.[54]

Wendela was sensitive to the verbal repertoire in her immediate surround-ings.[55] For example, the designation 'Negroes' in her letters gave way to 'Kaffirs' within two weeks of arriving in Pretoria. While remembering her life in South Africa, Mrs. Beusekom revives the past in the vocabulary of that time, ignoring current language taboos, until the moment she returns to the present. Then she comes back to her own words: 'Yes, I am talking about *Kaffers*, because ... that *is* the common term ... You *do* not say Negroes, you *do* not say Bantus ... that is very nice when you say Bantus. But people were talking about *Kaffers*. That *was* just an Afrikaner word, I think, for a Bantu'. This comment did not prevent her from continuing to use the term 'Kaffir' during our conversations. In addition to the use of past language, despite its present taboo-laden terms, her alternating of present and past tense shows how during the process of re-membering the distance between present and past fades, and the past comes alive in the present.[56]

Boers, British and Outlanders

More than the Black 'Other', it is the White 'Other' who figures in the letters of Wendela Beusekom. First of all, she and Jan Peter had to acquire an appropri-ate position in the White community, which, as it soon turned out, was strong-ly divided. Divisions among White Europeans, which seemed to disappear

---

53   Conversation Henkes and Beusekom-Scheffer, 21 Mar. 2006.
54   Conversation Henkes and Beusekom-Scheffer, 21 Mar. 2006. See also Elsbeth Locher-
      Scholten, '"So Close and Yet so Far": European Ambivalence towards Javanese Servants', in:
      Elsbeth Locher-Scholten, *Women and the Colonial State: Essays on Gender and Modernity
      in the Netherlands Indies 1900-1942* (Amsterdam: Amsterdam University Press, 2000) 86–
      119 at 116.
55   Her report of the crossing on the *Bloemfontein Castle* soon became peppered with English
      expressions, and this also happened with Afrikaner words and phrases soon after she
      settled in Pretoria.
56   Conversation Henkes and Beusekom-Scheffer, 21 Mar. 2006; I have used italics to articu-
      late her switches between the past and the present, as mentioned in the Introduction to
      this book.

when confronted with Black Africa during the crossing, returned in various forms and gradations after their settling in. The mutual tensions in the White community primarily concerned the English-speaking 'Brits' and the Afrikaans-speaking 'Boers' or Afrikaners. This division dated back to the time when the British took over colonial power, which ultimately had culminated in the dramatic South African War at the end of the nineteenth century. When, after the British victory, the Boer Republics formally merged with the Cape Colony and Natal into the Union of South Africa in 1910, the new government had to overcome the controversy between the two components of the young nation. In order to bring 'Brits' and 'Boers' closer together in the newly formed nation state, the joint mission to bring a European civilization to 'dark' South Africa was articulated.[57] Or, as the Prime Minister of the Union and former Boer Commander-in-Chief Louis Botha put it in 1911: 'to wipe out everything that stands in the way of the mutual rapprochement and reconciliation of the two White parts of our population, so that a young but promising nation can come about'.[58] The unification was realized at the expense of the political rights and economic livelihoods of the Black population. Racial segregation, unequal access to positions of power, and White supremacy became anchored in the new constitution. In this way a shared European identity was institutionalized, based on a racial order.[59] Nevertheless, the bitter memories of the South African War remained and were still alive during and after the Second World War.

Indeed, very different views remained about the design and future of the country. The Nationalists in the National Party wanted a purely White Republic of South Africa, which would separate itself from the British Empire and place its Black population in separate reserves, the so-called *thuislande* (homelands) or Bantustans. The Unionists in the South African Party (SAP), later United Party, (UP), on the other hand, saw better prospects in maintaining the relatively autonomous position as a self-governing dominion, which could count on the support of the powerful British Empire. They were convinced that a

---

57   The designation of Africa as a 'dark' continent refers not so much to the skin colour of the inhabitants as to the unfamiliarity of Europeans with the 'wild' nature and the 'primitive' population. The expression itself was popularized by H.M. Stanley, who published the story of his wanderings on the continent under the title *Through the Dark Continent* (1878), according to Angela Thompsell, 'Why Was Africa Called the Dark Continent?' https://www.thoughtco.com/why-africa-called-the-dark-continent-43310, retrieved 10 July 2019).

58   Louis Botha on the occasion of the establishment of the South African Party in 1911, cited by Peberdy, *Selecting Immigrants*, 37–38.

59   Dubow, *A Commonwealth of Knowledge*, 2.

united and prosperous South Africa needed cheap Black labour, which required a coexistence of White and Black, albeit in unequal positions. The distinction between adherents of these two main political groupings was and still is typified in terms of Afrikaners versus English or British, whereas in the end it was about conflicting political views.

The constant tensions within the White population in South Africa had flared up again at the outbreak of the First World War. At that time, a majority of the South African parliament voted for participation in the war on the Allied – and therefore also British – side. The occupation of the neighbouring German colony of South West Africa resulted in an armed uprising of Afrikaner nationalists, led by some veterans from the South African War. Not only did they regard the Germans, like the Dutch, as historical, cultural and biological kindred (*stamverwanten*), but the nationalists also saw the Germans as their allies in the fight against the British Empire from which they wanted to break free. The rebellion was repressed by the South African army, but it does indicate how sharp the contrasts were among White settlers in South Africa.[60]

The Second World War had once again sharpened the oppositions within White South Africa. While the country, led by Prime Minister and former Boer General Jan Smuts, went to war with the British on the side of the Allies, many Afrikaner Nationalists sympathized with the German National Socialists. Wendela and Jan Peter Beusekom, like Pim Valk in the previous chapter, had apparently missed the critical comments in Dutch newspapers regarding the Nationalist Afrikaners in response to the South African election battle in 1948. As long as General Smuts had remained South Africa's Prime Minister after the war, both countries were considered to be in the same camp. Three years later the National Party of D.F. Malan – and not Smuts' United Party – won the election in 1948, with slogans like '*Die Kaffer op sy plek en die Koelies uit die land*' (The Kaffir in his place and the Coolies expelled from the country). The Dutch media reacted with dismay. The memory of the fatal exclusion and persecution policy of the National Socialists was still alive, and the link between the proposed Apartheid policy and the 'racial delusion of the Nazis' was quickly established – reinforced by the antisemitism of prominent Nationalists.[61] Racism and antisemitism were central to the coverage of the National Party's narrow victory in the Dutch newspapers and weeklies. However, this outrage quickly evaporated, once the Dutch government endeavoured to restore good relations

---

60   Hermann Giliomee, *The Afrikaners. Biography of a people* (Cape Town: Tafelberg, 2003) 379–384.

61   *Vrij Nederland* of 5 June 1948, cited by De Graaff, 'De Nederlandse publieke opinie'.

between the two countries, in line with its active emigration policy in the 1950s.

After D.F. Malan took over, the postwar promotion of immigration from Europe, initiated under the leadership of Jan Smuts and his United Party, was immediately curbed. One of the main objectives of the Nationalists was to strengthen Afrikanerdom and its political culture, and to prevent the growth of its political opponents. 'Our (Afrikaner) people first' had been the creed of the National Party in 1948. Yet, within a few years the Nationalist government thought it wise to attract more European immigrants, even from the former Allied countries, to strengthen South Africa's economy and the White population as a whole.[62] For this purpose, the *stamverwantschap* between the Dutch and the Afrikaners was again emphasized, to which the Dutch government gladly responded. And with success: between 1950 and 1960 some 26,600 Dutch emigrants left for South Africa.[63]

Like most newcomers from Europe Wendela and Jan Peter Beusekom had little or no idea of the complex relationships between the British and Afrikaners within White South Africa at the time of their arrival. The space available to them to determine their position in South African society was partly dependent on the location where they settled down. The capital Pretoria was the heart of the former Boer Republic of Transvaal and a centre of the National Party, which manifested itself as unabatedly anti-British in the 1950s. How little the Beusekoms knew about the frictions within the White South African population becomes clear from Wendela's report of their visit to a colleague of Jan Peter's about a month after their arrival. He was a Dutchman, naturalized as South African, and Wendela called his wife 'an English South African'. By the time they met he had worked as an inspector at the Bank for ten years. From this couple the Beusekoms learned for the first time about the poisonous 'political hair-splitting' and even 'hatred' between the English and Afrikaners as a result of 'the Boer War'. The dubious position of the Afrikaner nationalists was underlined by a story about the reaction in Pretoria to the news of the capitulation of Nazi Germany in 1945: Jan Peter's colleague had witnessed how the University had raised a black flag half-mast by way of condolences.[64]

There were more reasons why Wendela and Jan Peter had little affinity with Afrikanerdom, which they identified with Afrikaner nationalism. Under the

---

62   Henkes, 'Shifting Identifications'.

63   Peberdy, *Selecting Migrants*, Appendix 2.

64   Beusekom-Scheffer, 30 Oct. 1952. The strong sympathy for Nazi Germany also dominated other 'centres of Afrikaner intelligentsia' such as Bloemfontein, Potchefstroom and Stellenbosch. See Gerrit Schutte, *Stamverwantschap onder druk. De betrekkingen tussen Nederland en Zuid-Afrika, 1940-1947* (Amsterdam: Zuid-Afrika Instituut, 2011) 86–94 and 104.

FIGURE 5.6   'Bas in front of the statue of Paul Kruger on the Church Square, in the
background the old building of the *Netherlandse Bank van Zuid-Afrika*'.
Pretoria c. 1955. Caption in photo album.

Malan government and its successors, the participation of the Afrikaner section
of the population was promoted in the civil service, education and other public
sectors. When postwar newcomers in South Africa wanted to make a career,
they were confronted with a preferential policy regarding Afrikaners.[65] This
applied to state-owned companies, but it also affected private companies. For
example, after two years Jan Peter's promotion was postponed for an additional six months due to 'the ratio of Dutch vs. South African personnel' (by which
Wendela Beusekom meant Afrikaner South African).[66] The *Nederlandse Bank
voor Zuid-Afrika* (1888–1969) had originally emerged from the Dutch pro-Boer
movement to support nationalist Afrikanerdom.[67] Yet, this institution was

---

65   Max du Preez, 'ANC could learn from Afrikaners', in: *The Mercury*, 3 July 2012.
66   Beusekom-Scheffer, 13 Apr. 1955. Their friend Rob Huisman – see Chap. 6 – had a similar
experience when he applied for a job at the South African Iron and Steel Industrial
Corporation Limited (Iscor), but according to Wendela was rejected as 'too continental':
'A Christian Afrikaner was of course preferred' (Beusekom-Scheffer, 10 Dec. 1952).
67   P.A. Geljon. *Een Nederlandse Overzeebank. De Nederlandsche Bank voor Zuid-Afrika, 1888–
1969* (Amsterdam: Boom uitgevers, 2017).

equally confronted with the government's aim to appoint more Afrikaners to positions previously held by Dutch employees. For those who wanted to make their career in South Africa naturalization could offer a solution.

The obstacles for Dutch staff members applied equally or even more to the British in Pretoria, according to Wendela's report of her encounters with an English couple. She came to the conclusion that Mr. Ford who worked at Barclays Bank and his wife, like she and Jan Peter, belonged to the 'hated *Uitlanders*'(Outlanders). This common bond facilitated their contact with 'the otherwise ever so stiff English'. At Barclays, the chances of building a career were even lower, 'just because they are English'. After the second election victory of D.F. Malan and his National Party in 1953 Mr. Ford feared that it would become 'worse for us all'.[68] In this regard, Wendela's Dutchness gave way to a shared 'foreignness', or rather 'outlanderness'. With the term *outlander* she refers to the non-Afrikaner fortune seekers in the gold fields of the Transvaal Boer Republic at the end of the nineteenth century, who after years of residence were denied citizenship by the then Transvaal government.[69] Although her comparison was flawed because Nationalist policy was aimed precisely at pressuring Dutch immigrants into getting South African citizenship in order to strengthen the Afrikaner ranks, she rightly identified a corresponding mechanism of inclusion and exclusion based on race and nationality. In her letters to the Netherlands, Wendela used the stigmatizing notion of *outlanders* as a badge of honour. With it, she emphasized their shared aversion to Afrikaner nationalism, thereby creating a new 'we-feeling' with other White immigrants in South Africa.

The long-standing rhetoric of the National Party against immigration contributed to the image of Afrikaners as an inward-looking community with an unwavering aversion to influences from 'outside'.[70] Jan Peter Beusekom wrote to his parents-in-law that most Afrikaners suffered from 'a kind of inferiority complex because the English and Dutch are doing so much better'.[71] The image of *stamverwantschap*, of a transnational community based on a common 'origin' and culture of Dutch and Afrikaners, was certainly not to be found in the perceptions of the Beusekoms, and they were not alone in that. In the Netherlands 'people really don't know anything about this place', Wendela wrote more than four months after arrival. Other Dutch migrants in Pretoria had responded with raised eyebrows to the recent publication of *Een Hollandse familie in zonnig Zuid-Afrika* (A Dutch family in sunny South Africa), written

---

68   Beusekom-Scheffer, 30 Apr. 1953.
69   Stanley Trapido, 'Imperialism, Settler Identities, and Colonial Capitalism: The Hundred-Year Origins of the 1899 South African War', in: R. Ross, A. Mager, & B. Nasson (eds.), *The Cambridge History of South Africa* Cambridge: Cambridge University Press, 2011) 66–101.
70   Henkes, 'Shifting Identities'.
71   Beusekom-Scheffer, 30 Nov 1952.

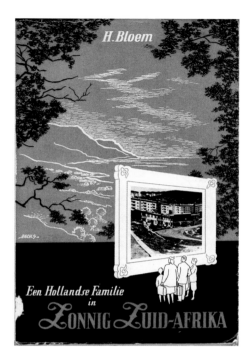

FIGURE 5.7
Cover of H. Bloem, *Een Hollandse familie*
in zonnig Zuid-Afrika (1949).

by H. Bloem. In his position as 'leader of the office of the *Nederlandsch Zuid-Afrikaansche Vereeniging*' (Netherlands South African Association) he was involved in promoting Dutch emigration to South Africa. The richly il-lustrated book was an easy read for aspiring migrants and 'for those who wanted to get to know the country better', as the cover text indicates.[72] In his propaganda for emigration to South Africa the author emphasized the commonality (in terms of *stamverwantschap*) of the Dutch and Afrikaners by pointing to the corresponding language and culture. According to Wendela Beusekom, the book contained 'pertinent untruths', but she gave no further explanation.[73] Wendela may have referred to Bloem's statement that 'all Dutch people' in South Africa had declared 'as one man' to support their fellow coun-trymen in Europe against Nazi Germany.

Nothing could be further from the truth: many Dutch conscripts in South Africa had evaded the call to report for their obligatory military service, supported by pro-German Afrikaner Nationalists.[74] This became known in the

---

72   H. Bloem, *Een Hollandse familie in zonnig Zuid-Afrika* (Amsterdam: J.H. de Bussy, 1949).

73   Beusekom-Scheffer, 29 Jan. 1953.

74   Peter Schumacher, *Voor het vaderland weg. Nederlandse dienstweigeraars in de Tweede Wereldoorlog* (Amsterdam: Van Gennep, 2007) Chap. VI–XVI.

Netherlands soon after the defeat of National Socialism, when reports were sent from the Dutch Legation in Pretoria about the many 'pro-German elements' among pre-war Dutch immigrants in South Africa. According to the Dutch envoy this was because the immigrants' vision of South Africa was all too often determined by the Dutch support for the Boer struggle for independence at the turn of the century. But times had changed, the envoy emphasized, referring to the alliance of South Africa and the Netherlands with the British against Nazi Germany. In the autumn of 1945 he stressed that it was high time that not only the Nationalist Afrikaners in South Africa became aware of this, but also the Dutch authorities which maintained ties with the South African government.[75]

Nevertheless, his unwelcome information about the political attitude of Dutch immigrants in South Africa who identified with the Afrikaner Nationalists, and their alignment with Nazi Germany, was soon forgotten. It would take another ten to twenty years before the affinity with Afrikaner Nationalism, so intensely supported by large groups of Dutch people only half a century earlier, gradually gave way to criticism and aversion amongst broad layers of Dutch society. But before that time came, the Dutch government did everything possible to restore relations between the two countries, as can be seen from their emigration policy in the 1950s. In line with the revised immigration policy of the Malan government in South Africa, the notion of *stamverwantschap* between the Dutch and the Afrikaners was again mobilized in Netherlands.

The Beusekoms, however, did not see this rapprochement between the two governments reflected in the everyday interactions between Afrikaners and Dutch immigrants in Pretoria. According to Wendela, the Dutch *kaasjes* (little cheeses) were just as much hated as the English *Rooinekken* (Rednecks). Jokingly, she suggests in a letter to her parents that she would call their son Bas 'cheese', so that it would have no negative connotation if he was later called by that name at school.[76] More than half a century after their return from South Africa, Mrs. Beusekom emphasizes that Afrikaners were 'not really Dutch at all' unless you compared them to the orthodox Protestants in the Dutch 'Bible belt'.[77] Nationality, class, denomination and the associated lifestyle and cultural

---

75   Report of 12 Nov. 1945 to the Minister for Foreign Affairs about 'Emigration from Dutch to South Africa ', cited in Henkes, 'Shifting Identification'.

76   Beusekom-Scheffer, 26 Nov. 1952, 12 Feb. 1953 and 29 Mar. 1954.

77   In the Netherlands this term refers to a narrow strip running from parts of Zealand and the South-Holland Islands, through the West-Betuwe and Veluwe, to the northern parts of the province Overijssel, containing a particularly high concentration of orthodox-Protestants.

taste were the aspects that determined the kind of Dutchness with which immigrants in South Africa could identify themselves. Both young Wendela
Beusekom and the older Mrs. Beusekom link orthodox Christianity to a 'narrowmindedness' and a lack of worldly orientation that she saw in both Nationalist Afrikaners and orthodox-Protestant Dutch.[78] By distancing herself from
this perceived narrow mindedness, Wendela moved closer to the internationally oriented British in South Africa or the more 'enlightened' South
Afrikaners.

Among the Dutch in Pretoria

The mutual reserve between Dutch newcomers and established Afrikaners in
Pretoria simultaneously arose from and strenghtened the immigrants' tendency to form their own social networks. Their Dutchness gained in significance as
soon as the immigrants had reached their destination. Previously settled compatriots assumed the position of 'cultural brokers',[79] who helped to bridge the
gap between the expectations of the newly arrived and everyday practices at
the receiving location. Many of them got involved with the newcomers –
whether from a sense of responsibility, self-interest or otherwise – and tried to
show them the way. The Dutch helped each other to find shelter in Dutch-run
hotels or guesthouses, or to find a job in Dutch-owned shops or companies,
and met with Dutch neighbours, colleagues and relatives in Dutch clubs, committees, or church associations. In this way various forms of Dutchness arose,
to which newcomers had to relate and to which they themselves contributed.

On his first day at the office, Jan Peter Beusekom learned from colleagues at
the *Nederlandse Bank voor Zuid-Afrika* that the *Hollandse Club* would not be
the right organization for him and his wife to join. They were 'a completely different kind of people', Wendela repeated to her parents. Just as in the Netherlands, new acquaintances – even though they came from the same country –
had to be carefully vetted, and relationships needed to be cautiously built
according to the economic, social and cultural capital these people had
brought with them. At the Bank they called the *Hollandse Club* the *cementvretersclub* ('cement-gobbling club'), because many of its members were builders who had left the Netherlands in the 1930s crisis and had become 'filthy rich'

---

78   Conversation Henkes and Beusekom-Scheffer, 21 Mar. 2006.

79   Cf. Sara de Jong, 'Cultural Brokers in Post-colonial Migration Regimes', Dhawan et al.
      (eds.), *Negotiating Normativity* (Cham: Springer International Publishing Switzerland,
      2016) 45–59.

in South Africa.[80] According to the gentlemen of the Bank, these were the *nouveaux riches*: the newly rich with a lot of economic capital, but without much cultural baggage. The Beusekoms would rather meet their 'own people' at the *Nederlandse Vereniging* (Netherlands Association) 'which aims at the cultural sustenance of the Dutch'. They soon joined in, but did not quite find what they had expected. According to Wendela their first bridge drive was 'very animated', although she was unable to discover 'nice Dutch people' on that occasion. Apart from a few exceptions, including the deputy director of the Bank, a professor, and the ambassador and his wife, they were mainly *intense burgerlieden* ('petty bourgeois') as she reported back home.[81]

The *Nederlandsche Bank* played an important role in accommodating its newly arrived employees and their families. In the first month after their arrival the Beusekoms were invited to Jan Peter's superiors and his close colleagues at home. They showed them the area, told them about the social and political relationships among Whites in Pretoria, and introduced them to other Dutch people. On their first Sunday afternoon, Mr. Bruins, deputy director of the Bank, picked up the Beusekom family in his car. He first drove them to the Union Building, from where they could see 'how vast and luxuriously Pretoria had been built'. The shabby townships, located at the edge of the city, where the Black population lived, remained outside their field of vision. Then the Cape Dutch style of the Governor General's house was admired, and they drove past the residence of Prime Minister Malan. The gathering ended with *een borreltje* (a drink) at the Bruins' home, before they were dropped off at their hotel. In spite of this tour of the highlights of the South African ruling power, Wendela afterwards called it 'a very Dutch afternoon', because she and Jan Peter had been 'interrogated' by the Bruins, undoubtely to determine in which 'pigeonhole' to place the newcomers: to whom they were related, who was in their circle of acquaintances, and which religious community they belonged to.[82]

Being Dutch was not an unequivocal category and always required careful scrutiny of similarities and differences. Mr. and Mrs. Bruins lifted a corner of their own veil by telling the Beusekom couple that they were related to the Van der Hoop family in Arnhem, who knew Jan Peter's family well. Family connections offered the possibility of mapping overlapping social networks; this also applied, for example, to student associations. Just like Jan Peter, Mr. Bruins had a degree from Leiden University. This Leiden connection gave an extra boost to their status, especially in the exchanges between the two men. Jan Peter was

---

80   Beusekom-Scheffer, 17 Oct. 1952.
81   Beusekom-Scheffer, 12 Nov. 1952; See also 23 Oct. 1952.
82   Beusekom-Scheffer, 23 Oct. 1952.

immediately added to the list of male guests for the annual celebrations of *Leidens Ontzet* (the local commemoration of the siege of this city during the Dutch Revolt, and its relief on 3 October 1574) that was organized amongst *Leienaars*, former students from Leiden University in South Africa. Because of the gender-segregated student life, the women did not participate in such festivities. They found each other by different means and criteria, often during coffee and tea parties at their homes.

In this way men and women were characteristically assigned different positions. While on the day of their arrival her husband went straight to his work, where he was introduced to his new colleagues at the Bank, Wendela stayed with the baby in their hotel. She could not leave Bas alone, except during the few moments when he was asleep. In a letter to her parents, Wendela wondered why she had not felt very well since her arrival: was it the change of climate, the high air, or perhaps her pregnancy or nerves? She had no idea.[83] In her explanations of her gloomy mood, she passed over her isolated position in their new and unknown surroundings, although she would indirectly address that theme when she mentioned other women with young children who 'had it not at all easy' and were 'locked in at home'.[84] After the Beusekom family had exchanged the Van Riebeeck hotel for the 'less expensive' hotel Irene, Wendela was doing better. This 'family pension', as she typified it in a letter to her parents, was run by two spruce Dutch women. Among the guests were quite a few Dutch people, and baby Bas acted as a magnet, creating multiple contacts with expectant mothers, parents and grandparents. They were occasionally willing to look after the baby, so that Wendela could go out alone or together with Jan Peter.[85]

For the Beusekoms the two-month stay at the Hotel Irene was a new phase in the transition from the Netherlands to South Africa. Like the passengers of the *Bloemfontein Castle*, the hotel guests met in a defined space with its own social dynamics, where the dining room had a central function. There, shortly

---

83   Beusekom-Scheffer, 17 Oct. 1952.
84   Beusekom-Scheffer, 23 and 30 Oct. 1952. It would take until the 1960s before specific problems for women emigrating with their husbands and children became recognised by the government. The emigration policy focused primarily on male breadwinners and their preparation for the labour market in the destination country. After it became clear that the success of emigration also depended on the women involved, Dutch policy makers started to pay attention to gender-specific problems in the emigration process. Marijke van Faassen, 'Vrouwen in den vreemde: emigratievoorlichting door het Nederlandse Vrouwen Comité' in: *Spiegel historiael: maandblad voor geschiedenis en archeologie*, 37: 7–8 (2002) 325–329.
85   Beusekom-Scheffer, 6 Nov. and 18 Dec. 1952.

after arrival, they experienced the obvious inequality between White (guest, owner) and Black (staff), which was further reinforced by rumours about the well-organised management having trouble with their undisciplined subordinates.[86] The guests saw each other at dinner time. Wendela mentions an elderly Dutch couple who had settled permanently in the hotel. Their daughter Margaret, who was expecting her first baby in January, was 'enchanted' by baby Bas and gave the pregnant Wendela useful tips about maternity clinics.[87] With 'Mrs. Huisman', as Wendela referred to the woman who was to become her close friend Margaret, and with her husband, the Beusekoms forged a lasting friendship.

A shared Dutch origin was not enough to evoke a sense of community in the new environment. The earlier reference to the Dutch 'cement-gobbling club' already pointed to the importance of cultural capital – expressed in various ways, such as the way people dress, talk or celebrate – for an equal-minded mutual contact. In Wendela's report of her first Christmas celebration with the Dutch Association in Pretoria, she emphasizes the differences rather than the similarities between those present. Once again, the deputy director of the Bank is mentioned as someone who made himself 'particularly useful' as the organizer of this Dutch get-together, even though his views on 'a domestic Dutch Christmas celebration were somewhat more conservative than ours'. On the stage there was a small Christmas tree with electric lights, and there was a children's choir. The presence of the ambassador and his wife gave extra glamour to the gathering.

With a few exceptions the room was filled, in the words of Wendela Beusekom, with 'Spiegel-type people', whom she describes in more detail as women with 'hair in greasy rolls and echoing singing voices'.[88] Here she refers to orthodox-Protestant circles in the Netherlands, where the illustrated family magazine De Spiegel was part of the household.[89] She contrasts this group of Dutch people with 'people like us', Remonstrants and liberal Protestants, in other words: 'the vrijbuiters ('freebooters')', as she typifies herself and her favourite company. Together with the Huisman couple they experienced this Christmas celebration as 'a religious exercise in an orthodox-Protestant church', especially when the devil was mentioned in the minister's speech. When they

---

86   Beusekom-Scheffer, 11 Nov. 1952.
87   Beusekom-Scheffer, 6 Nov 1952.
88   Beusekom-Scheffer, 23 Dec. 1952.
89   See also Chap. 4, p. 121.

found that due to the hustle and bustle they could not get to the snacks afterwards, they decided to leave quickly together with their liberal friends.[90]

Time and time again, Wendela's letters testify to the dividing lines within the Dutch immigrant community that reflected the different social-cultural and political allegiances in the so-called 'pillarized' Netherlands.[91] She had an unerring feeling for what the French sociologist Pierre Bourdieu has analysed in his famous work *La Distinction*: the value of external appearances – such as hairstyles, dress, choice of words and accent, but also home furnishings, tableware and table manners. 'Taste' was critical for the way in which people valued each other's social positions and interacted with each other.[92] From childhood Wendela Beusekom had learned to understand the meaning of these appearances, and to use these insights to promote the desired social intercourse. This skill was indispensable in her quest for a respected place in the new country of residence, and building up a network that made a return to the Netherlands possible.

However, what in the Netherlands was regarded as desirable manners with a matching performance was not necessarily the same in South Africa, not even within Dutch migrant communities. Wendela's reaction to a postal package from her parents shows how much ideas about an 'appropriate' appearance in South Africa could change through the institutionalized, racial distinctions. In reaction to receiving a colourful sweater, Wendela first wrote that it did not suit her. Then she added that such a thing was not worn by Whites 'because with its colourful stripes it really is *Kafferdracht* (clothing for Kaffirs').[93] Wearing 'flashy colourful patterns' would blur the distinction between the 'civilized' population of European origin and the 'primitive' African population. In her new surroundings she had to re-examine which codes applied to which occasion, in order to be able to signal common grounds or distinctions. Her husband too, as the letters show, had to re-examine with whom and how he could best connect himself to make a career as a Dutchman in South Africa – and what role his wife, his relatives in the Netherlands, the chess board, the whisky bottle or the tennis racket could play in the process.

---

90   Beusekom-Scheffer, 23 Dec. 1952.

91   For more information about the so-called 'pillarization' of Dutch society and how the concept is used to describe both the pre-war and postwar relationships between different cultural-political groups in the country: Chap. 2 and Chap. 4.

92   Pierre Bourdieu, *Distinction: A Social Critique of the Judgment of Taste*, trans. (Boston: 1984. Harvard University Press, 1984; orig. 1979).

93   Beusekom-Scheffer, 14 Apr. 1954.

Blank Baasskap (White Rule)

Already at an early stage Wendela wrote to her parents in the Netherlands how sorry she was that among the nice Dutch people she met 'no one ever says that they are happy over here'. There was always something: if it wasn't the insecurity, it was the climate, the high costs of living, the parochialism, or the uncouth nature of the White Afrikaners, in short: 'a whole laundry list'.[94] It is an intriguing list, especially because amongst these negatives the so-called 'racial problem' is missing, or only indirectly mentioned with a reference to insecurity. Shortly after their arrival, in response to a question from Amsterdam, Wendela had written that 'the racial problem does indeed *seem* to be the greatest, besides that of drought and erosion'.[95] Her use of *seem* might indicate that she herself had not yet experienced much of a 'racial problem' as such, although her report about the train journey tells a different story.

Soon, however, it becomes clear that she did experience 'race' as an overriding problem. With the national elections in April 1953, just as in 1948, race was a prominent theme in the election campaign. The Beusekoms followed the vehement election struggle fought mainly between the United Party and the National Party. If the Nationalists remained in power, they would first drive all *naturellen* ('natives') into the sea, followed by 'all English-speaking people', Wendela quoted a radical student who found the Nationalist regime under Malan 'still too weak'. She added: 'When you think that most of these Nationalists are ridiculously resentful Boers, who simply cannot be reasoned with, because "the Lord has ordained it this way!!", you shiver, and you get visions of dictatorial governments, which we have more than enough of in this world'.[96]

Moreover, the elections had 'uncovered a few examples of corruption' at which 'our good Dutch ears were flapping'. She sighed wistfully to her parents: 'How wonderfully good and kind a country you live in'. According to Wendela, the election result was 'a deep disappointment for English-speaking South Africans, natives and foreigners', bringing uncertainty about the future.[97] It is striking that at this point she put White, English-speaking inhabitants of South Africa, Black Africans, and 'outlanders' or foreigners in the same category, and that she had replaced the term *Kaffers* with the English 'natives'. This indicates that she oriented herself on the political discourse of the United Party. Although she never mentioned that the Black majority of the population was

---

94   Beusekom-Scheffer, 6 Nov. 1952.
95   Beusekom-Scheffer, 17 Oct. 1952, Italics added by the author.
96   Beusekom-Scheffer, 17 Apr. 1953.
97   Beusekom-Scheffer,17 Apr. 1953. Elections took place on 15 Apr. 1953.

excluded from the elections,[98] her aversion to the Afrikaner Nationalists was partly derived from their attitude towards *het naturellenprobleem* ('the native problem'), as she called it by the Afrikaner term. The re-election of Malan in 1953 was 'a disaster' if this issue was to be addressed, Wendela Beusekom wrote, without further explanation.[99]

A week later, following the example of his wife, Jan Peter expressed his worries about the election results. He hoped 'that it will not go in the dictatorial direction here [as] in South America'. In addition to corruption and the lack of free school choice,[100] he mentioned the 'Apartheid implemented in legislation'. It was difficult for him to take a position on this: 'I believe that it is fundamentally wrong, but for practical reasons one must simply just take the necessary measures to keep the Kaffirs down. Finally, a weak policy (Indonesia, India, Kenya) has turned out to be disastrous.'[101] His ambivalent attitude shows strong similarities with that of the United Party in South Africa. In 1948, under the leadership of Jan Smuts, this party had lost the elections by a hair's breadth. In that election the 'racial issue' had also played a prominent role.

The United Party and the National Party presented divergent policies regarding the position of the Black population. Smuts' party took a pragmatic approach: it was of the opinion that the South African economy could not do without Black (cheap) workers. For this reason the UP argued for more space for the Black population to be able to settle in urban areas where they could get plenty of work. Although the UP felt that White supremacy should be maintained, it was in favour of a gradual reform of the political system in order to give the Black population more of a voice. In contrast to this pragmatic, but equally paternalistic approach to race relations, the National Party led by D.F. Malan and his successors argued for a principled, strictly implemented dividing

---

98   Due to legislation relating to franchise requirements, very few people of Coloured and Asian descent were allowed to vote in this election; Africans had been banned altogether since the late 1930s, with a limited number of Africans meeting electoral qualifications voting for four white MPs 'of their own' separately.

99   Beusekom-Scheffer, 17 Apr. 1953.

100   If Afrikaans (or Dutch) was spoken in the household, the children could only get free education in public Afrikaner schools, while children from an English-speaking household were allowed free education at an English/a British school. If Dutch parents in the Transvaal wanted English-speaking education for their children, only private schools offered an alternative. Dutch liberals such as the Beusekoms were very critical of the Afrikaner approach of nationalist schooling.

101   Jan Peter Beusekom, 24 Apr. 1953, referring to the recent struggles for independence in these three countries.

line between the 'races' with a complete marginalization of Black South Africans and unlimited White rule.[102]

Despite these divergent approaches to how the White *baasskap* could best be guaranteed, both parties shared the principle of White supremacy and a European civilizing mission. This also applied to the vast majority of self-declared 'liberal' circles, among which the Beusekoms counted themselves.[103] Under Apartheid their environment was radically separated from that of the Black South Africans through contact bans, curfews, separate entrances, segregated townships or locations and the so-called 'homelands' (*thuislande*) for the African population. But in practice Africans remained indispensable as cheap labour in the service of Whites, both in corporations and government institutions and in private households.[104] White and Black inevitably saw much of, and remained dependent on, each other. At the same time this proximity was difficult, especially since the 'White civilization' narrative repeatedly emphasized the danger of 'Black' contamination, theft and violence. This paradox between distance and proximity was especially true for the relationships within the household, where different variations of race, class, and gender came together, illustrating the complicated social patterns of the colonial divide.[105] How did Wendela Beusekom handle the many contradictions that resulted from the presence of Black domestic staff in and around her house?

In the second half of the twentieth century, domestic staff in South Africa was by definition Black. Apparently this was not sufficiently clear to those left behind in the Netherlands, because after six months Wendela emphasized in one of her letters to her parents that it was not advisable for 'a Dutch girl' to come to South Africa as domestic help: 'The housekeeping is simply *Kafferwerk* (work for Kaffirs)!'[106] A comparison between her mother's White housekeeper

---

102   Henkes, 'Shifting Identifications'. See also Giliomee, *The Afrikaners*, 475–482.

103   E.g. Mazower, *No Enchanted Palace*, Introduction.

104   Limited schooling and the Job Reservation Acts made it impossible for Black workers to make a career.

105   On this confrontation in the Netherlands East Indies see Locher-Scholten, *Women and the Colonial State*.

106   Beusekom-Scheffer, 12 Mar. 1953. This racial divide within the household must have been strengthened since World War Two. Conversations with children of Dutch immigrants who had settled before 1940 refer to white Dutch domestic staff working in their family's households, which is confirmed by the publications of Cecillie Swaisland, *Servants and Gentlewomen to the Golden land. The Emigration of Single Women from Britain to Southern Africa, 1820-1993* (1993) and of Ena Jansen in her *Soos familie* (Like family). Stedelike huiswerkers in Suid-Afrikaanse tekste (Pretoria: Protea Boekhuis, 2015) 108–112, where she refers to documents of the *Nederlands Zuid-Afrikaanse Vereniging* (*NZAV*), founded in 1881 – that stimulated emigration to South Africa.

in Amsterdam and their Black *Kaffermeid* was definitely out of place. It did not often happen that Wendela corrected her mother in her letters, but on this matter she did.[107] The position of domestic staff in Dutch households was equally marked by inequality and by fears, on the part of employers, of infectious diseases or theft by their subordinates. However, since the nineteenth century there had been a trend referred to as the *beschavingsarbeid* (civilization work) by the well-to-do through education, welfare work and the like, aimed at the 'uplifting' of the working class.[108] This could be achieved within a wealthy household, too, by ensuring that young women from the working class became familiar with the values and skills of the established bourgeoisie. The expectation was that, if the servants learned to speak *Algemeen Beschaafd Nederlands* (the Queen's Dutch, so to speak) and to appreciate art and music, their 'level of civilization' and that of their future family – and by extension that of their class and the entire nation – would be raised. Conversely, there was also a desire among domestic workers to familiarize themselves with these values and thereby increase their social standing and chances of upward mobility.[109]

In the Netherlands East Indies, where Jan Peter was born in 1927, a specific kind of 'civilizing mission' had begun at the turn of the century as well. The so-called *ethische politiek* (ethical colonial policy) intended to fulfil the 'moral obligation' of the metropolitan state towards the native population. This colonial policy was voiced in a rhetoric of 'the family': Indonesian children under tutelage of the West, with strong paternalistic overtones.[110] If and how Jan Peter's mother translated this colonial civilization mission into the domestic sphere during her stay in the East Indies cannot be traced. She did in any case try to do so during her visit to South Africa, as Mrs. Beusekom remembers and ridicules later on. In Pretoria, Wendela did not have any 'civilizing' ambitions. She, and those with whom she could identify, viewed South Africa before the arrival of European settlers as a *Terra nullius*: an undeveloped area, inhabited by primitive and violent 'tribal' Blacks. They had to be kept in line by Whites,

---

107   Beusekom-Scheffer, 23 June 1954.
108   Ali de Regt, *Arbeidersgezinnen en beschavingsarbeid: ontwikkelingen in Nederland 1870-1940; een historisch-sociologische studie* (Meppel: Boom, 1984).
109   Barbara Henkes and Hanneke Oosterhof, *Kaatje ben je boven? Leven en werken van Nederlandse dienstbodes* (Nijmegen: SUN, 1985).
110   Locher-Scholten, 'So Close and Yet so Far'. This ethical colonial policy was seen as contributing to the 'moral reform' of the Indonesians by introducing them to a capitalist, bureaucratic and Christian 'modernity'. When ethical politics were found to stimulate self-awareness, which contributed to the establishment of an Indonesian national movement, the Dutch authorities turned their back on it with the ultimate consequence of the War of Recolonization of 1945-1949.

voluntarily or involuntarily, especially when the struggle for independence, and hence 'black chaos and violence', began to spread on the African continent.[111] The idea of 'uplifting', with which both Wendela and Jan Peter had been brought up in the Netherlands and the Netherlands East Indies, quickly made way for oppression under Apartheid, especially when Africans threatened to take their fate into their own hands.

A Servant Hutch in the Garden

Wendela Beusekom's concern was to find the 'right' balance between physical proximity and necessary distance from her household staff. As soon as she and her family exchanged the hotel for a flat, she was confronted with a 'boy': John's work was included in the rent. He came every morning from 8–9 am to sweep the floor and sand the bathtub. Later, for three mornings a week, 'the maid' Christien was hired for the laundry, ironing, polishing silver, brushing shoes, cleaning vegetables and potatoes and washing the dishes.[112] With the Black staff the fear of contamination and theft also entered the house. They had only just moved into their flat on Schoemanstreet, when Wendela saw how 'the boy' crouched on his heels near Bas, and the child 'all the time wanted to grab his hair'. She writes to her parents that she did not know 'how soon I had to wash his hands'.[113]

Jan Peter, too, wanted none of it: '[Bas] sometimes strokes his hideous frizzy head, which gives us goose bumps', he wrote to his in-laws.[114] At another moment, Wendela saw how Christien wanted to open the door to the bathroom with her hands full of clean-washed cups for brushing teeth. She kept one of the cups in her mouth, as she otherwise couldn't open the door: 'It was Bas' cup, and I didn't know how long to wash it to restore the idea of "clean". I now understand why [doctor] van Doorn finds the maids such a danger for children's diseases'.[115] However, it was about much more than fear of infectious diseases through the African staff; it was mainly fear of mixing the White and Black worlds that came so close within the household. As with theft and

---

111   E.g. the many writings by the British journalist L.E. Neame, including his passionate defence of the Apartheid policy published shortly before the 1953 elections: *White man's Africa: the problem of a white nation in a black continent.* (Cape Town: Stewart, 1952).
112   Beusekom-Scheffer, 20 June 1953. For the time being, Wendela herself took care of the intimate tasks of making the beds and preparing the food.
113   Beusekom-Scheffer, 15 Jan. 1953.
114   Jan Willem Beusekom, 13 July 1953.
115   Beusekom-Scheffer, 10 June 1954.

violence, the fear of infections was about a complex mix of real risks because of deep poverty and poor health care, and the imaginary risk when the distance between Black and White was about to fade away.

Fear of infectious diseases could be fought with a regular medical check of the domestic staff. Together with her Dutch friend Margaret Huisman, Wendela decided to have their maidservants screened, but in practice this turned out to be extremely difficult to achieve.[116] The necessary connections had to be mobilized, because 'as an ordinary person it is impossible to have your maid screened as a control measure', wrote the indignant young mother.[117] Previously, she had already indicated that the White Afrikaners 'were absolutely insufficiently aware of the danger posed by all those nannies etc'.[118] The hospitals offered 'no care at all' to their Black patients, according to Wendela, who apparently did not realize that hardly any money was made available for health care for the largest group of ailing people among the South African population.[119] Her observations show not only the failing health care for Black South Africans, but also the consequences for White households that depended on the work of healthy domestic staff.

Precisely because of their dependence on Black domestic staff, White housewives were immediately confronted with the consequences of Apartheid policy in their everyday lives. The wife of a Dutch diplomat, for example, told Wendela about an incident in which she had had to cancel her guests at the last minute. Her cook had unexpectedly been arrested and imprisoned because he did not have 'a valid pass' with him. She meant the so-called *dompas* or reference book, which curtailed the freedom of movement of the population in order to enforce the spatial segregation of Whites and Blacks or Colourdes in South Africa. Pass laws were not new in South Africa, but with the introduction of the Native Laws Amendment Act of July 1952, the measures were tightened up. All Blacks over the age of sixteen were obliged to carry their pass at all times outside their so-called homelands or assigned locations.[120]

---

116   Beusekom-Scheffer, 8 Sep. 1954.

117   Beusekom-Scheffer, 17 Jan. 1955 (although it says 1954).

118   Beusekom-Scheffer, 23 June 1954

119   Beusekom-Scheffer, 8 Sep. 1954. See also: Melody Brown and Anne Stanton, 'Governance of the public health sector during Apartheid: the case of South Africa', in: *Journal of Governance and Regulation* 5: 1 (2016) 23–30.

120   http://www.sahistory.org.za/topic/segregationist-legislation-timeline-1950-1959, Aug. 2013. In *The swerfjare of Popping Nongena* (Cape Town: Table Mountain, 1978) – translated in 1980 as *The Long Journey of Poppie Nongena* – the South African author Elsa Joubert presents a probing literary impression of the everyday consequences of these racial measures.

This pass, which had to be extended every month or sometimes every few weeks, contained detailed information about the owner of the pass, as well as the name and address of the employer, who had to be classified as White. When, for instance, the household staff went shopping or took the employers' children to school, 'the maid' or 'the boy' needed an extra temporary employer's statement, defined by Wendela as 'a scrap of paper' by which 'the Mr. or Mrs. must always declare that their boy, named so and so, needs to go there or there'. She typified this whole thing as 'pretty idiotic and troublesome' and observed that innocent staff were locked up when the papers were not in order. However, she primarily sympathized with the *malheur* of the unfortunate hostess.[121]

When the Beusekom family moved from a flat to a house with a garden eighteen months after arriving in Pretoria, Christien came with them and was then hired for day and night. Wendela wrote to her parents that a 'servant's hutch' at the back of the garden without electricity offered Christien a place to live.[122] In response to her mother's questions, she answered that Christien's husband '(if she has one!)'[123] and her children lived in Lady Salborne, a township on the outskirts of Pretoria.[124] Christien's children 'naturally' would not be able to live with their mother in the garden of the Beusekom family, and a determined Wendela continued: 'No way. It is a raw deal for her, but it is not possible'. As an explanation, she added: 'Kaffirs never live in the city or near the Whites. There are various so-called locations around the city where no White person is allowed and where they live. This is the case everywhere. [...] By the way, I think this situation is allright [...]. They are so different from us'.[125] The poor accessibility of the locations or townships on the outskirts of Pretoria and the long

---

121   Beusekom-Scheffer, 4 Dec. 1952.

122   This description of the 'servant's hutch' does not alter the observation of the South African sociologist Jacklyn Cock in *Maids and Madams. A study in the Politics of Exploitation*. (Johannesburg: Ravan Press, 2001) (first print 1980), 62–63 There she points out that the domestic staff could see this 'room of their own' as a considerable advance. Her findings were based on research on the position of Black domestic staff in the Eastern Cape at the end of the 1970s.

123   The addition 'if she has one' suggests that Wendela Beusekom is inclined to interpret the possible absence of the father of the children in terms of a 'loose' morality instead of realising that the Apartheid system enforced separation between family members.

124   The township Lady Salborne was located about 16 km northwest of the city centre of Pretoria. For more information on its history see C.K. Kgari-Masondom, *A Superstitious respect for the soil? Environmental history, social identity and land ownership – a case study of forced removals from Lady Selbourne and their ramifications, c. 1905 to 1977.* (PhD Stellenbosch. University of Stellenbosch. 2008) 127–149.

125   Beusekom-Scheffer, 7 Apr. 1954.

FIGURE 5.8   Lina, the domestic worker in the Beusekom household with the eldest son Bas,
Pretoria, c. 1955.

working days ensured that Christien and her colleagues could see their children at most once a week, while looking after the children of their White employers every day. Christien was denied a regular family life, and with her so many other African women, men and their children under Apartheid – also because the men often stayed in hostels elsewhere near their work.[126]

Asked about her domestic staff in South Africa, Mrs. Beusekom talks about the children of her last resident maid Lina, who were raised by their grandmother in her 'homeland'. Because the children 'could not be with her', she explains to me, immediately adding a retrospective judgment: 'Yes, it was actually a terrible regime, you know. I only realized that much later: how they separated those families there. That is simply unimaginable'.[127] Her statement raises the uncomfortable question of what it means to 'know' and at the same time 'not to know'; the question if something remains implicit because it is self-evident or because it is not negotiable.[128] At the time, Wendela Beusekom was

126   See also Cock, *Maids and Madams*, and Jansen, *Soos Familie*, 231–232 and Chap. 6, p. 212.

127   Conversation Henkes and Beusekom-Scheffer, 21 Mar. 2006.

128   In *The White Man's World*, 184 ff, Schwartz interprets the impossibility of facing the reality of racial power (and impotence) as psychological repression or ideological mystification. James Baldwin, *The fire next time* (New York, Dial Press, 1963) calls it 'innocence': a deadly,

unable or unwilling to face the racial repression of the Apartheid regime. Or better: she noticed it but felt more comfortable ignoring what she noticed of structural inequalities along the colour line. Such an attitude, as Zerubavel underlines, 'is usually a product of social norms of attention designed to separate what we consider conventionally "noteworthy"'.[129] Not until many years after her return to the Netherlands did Mrs. Beusekom acknowledge and articulate the dramatic effects of Apartheid on the family life of Africans in South Africa – and with it on the domestic staff who worked for her. In that respect she was not an ignorant spectator, but an 'implicated subject' in the racial order, as Michael Rothberg calls the position of an individual in situations that surpass their agency as individual subjects.[130]

Unless it benefited the 'poor Whites' – the uneducated Afrikaners who went to the city and found it hard to get to work there – in the South African context the idea of 'raising' the poor Blacks was inconceivable. This also applied to the Beusekom household. An attempt by Wendela's mother-in-law to introduce such an emancipatory effort in their home during her stay in Pretoria is ridiculed. Mrs. Beusekom smiles pityingly when she remembers how Jan Peter's mother asked Lina to listen to classical music on the radio with her: '[My mother-in-law] was always very ethical. She would say: "Come, Lina, you must listen. Here you have the umpteenth symphony of Beethoven". Well, those people ... they never have, they don't feel any connection with that, I think. But she would try to uplift Lina (laughs) [...] [My mother-in-law] was one of these very well-bred girls, slightly socialist, but not really. We always said "armchair socialist"'.[131] Mrs. Beusekom's memory of her mother-in-law's somewhat naive, paternalistic, but nevertheless genuine attempts to introduce the domestic worker to cultural heritage from Europe reflects how resolutely the dividing line between Black and White was drawn in the Apartheid discourse. Next to her mother-in-law's colonial civilizing mission in terms of education and guidance of the indigenous population by White superiors, Wendela at the time placed the image of Black domestic staff as essentially 'different' and therefore beyond education and emancipation.

During her stay in South Africa the elder Mrs. Beusekom did not have to adapt to the White world in which her son and daughter-in-law participated. But Wendela's assessment of her mother-in-law's actions afterwards shows how deeply the narrative of White supremacy with its 'own' civilization, which

---

self-destructive pathology that feeds the racial traumas of the nation (in his case the US). See also Wekker, *White Innocence*. and the Introduction to this book, n. 25.

129   Zerubavel, *The Elephant in the Room*, 23. See also the Introduction, n. 40 and Chap.1.
130   See the Introduction to this book.
131   Conversation Henkes and Beusekom-Scheffer, 21 Mar. 2006.

the Black population of South Africa could never match, had become entrenched in the few years that she lived in Pretoria. Her liberal Dutchness, with
its aversion to rabid racism that was fuelled by Afrikaner nationalism, by no
means implied a critical reflection on her own privileged position and White
supremacist thinking.

Stay or Return?

As became clear from her letters shortly after their departure from the Netherlands, the prospect of soon returning home offered relief during difficult moments when Wendela missed her parents, friends, or the home country. Within
a month, she informed her parents that she and Jan Peter had planned 'to try
for three years to really like it here, to get to know people and to participate
enthusiastically in everything'. Then they would take it from there. If they were
to become 'as sour' as many other Dutch immigrants, they would explore the
possibilities in the Netherlands or elsewhere, 'because I'm sure that the experience J.P. gains here at the Bank is not thrown away'.[132] Within six months she
wrote that it might become a difficult decision, because after a while she and J.P
'moved more easily' and the climate was wonderful for children, 'especially
boys'.[133] However, shortly after the 1953 elections Jan Peter foresaw that his
preference would eventually turn to the Netherlands, because he was 'opposed
to the whole political thing. [...] You always have to be careful not to tread on
people's toes and be kind to Nationalists as well as to the other party, seeking
compromises all the time in order to stay friends with everyone, while you
know that you always remain the hated outlanders in the eyes of the Nationalists'.[134] The burden he experienced from the 'political hassle' came primarily
from the Nationalists, although the Unionists were also involved. Racial politics
are conspicious by the absence in this critical account of this political joust.

In the autumn of 1954, more than two years after their arrival, Wendela made it
clear that, despite the 'unsympathetic' relationships among the White population, she was increasingly appreciating life in Pretoria. By that time, she began to
dread a return to 'the Dutch climate', the cramped housing and the life 'without
help' that awaited her if they returned to the Netherlands. However, she and Jan
Peter did not want to be like many other Dutch migrants who always complained
about 'this rotten politically stupid land' with the bad school system, and still

---

132   Beusekom-Scheffer, 6 Nov. 1952.
133   Beusekom-Scheffer, 17 May 1953.
134   Jan Peter Beusekom, 17 May 1953.

stayed.[135] Although they rejected this 'complaining' attitude – after all, personal responsibility was at the forefront of their liberal worldview – Wendela feared that she might regret leaving her comfortable existence in 'sunny' South Africa. After careful consideration, 'because with small children it is ideal here',[136] Wendela and Jan Peter finally decided in November 1954 *eventually* to go back to Holland.[137] With the emphasis on 'eventually', Wendela still left her options open, but the forces that drove her and the family back to the Netherlands were strong: in addition to good schools for the children, Jan Peter's career opportunities were just as important. After two years it became clear that 'the banking business' in South Africa was less interesting than in Europe.[138] Their kinship network in the Netherlands was mobilised and an uncle came up with an attractive job for a jurist outside the banking sector. Jan Peter wrote to his father-in-law that, after consulting with Wendela, he wanted to take him up on this proposal. The prospects in the Netherlands outweighed the 'bright future' that South Africa offered them.[139]

Wendela's own reaction shows that she had to choke down her reluctance to leaving South Africa behind. The positions had reversed: while Jan Peter initially enjoyed his new work, his wife felt lonely and out of place. As time went on he got tired of his work, while she felt more and more at home in a comfortable house with a garden and a resident maidservant near a close circle of friends. She had become accustomed to the daily interactions with the Black domestic staff and the freedom of movement the staff gave her. Although Wendela had initially sworn that she would never entrust the children to the concerns of 'those irresponsible girls',[140] after the birth of her second child she soon changed her mind. Christien and her successors regularly took care of son Bas, who otherwise would become jealous as soon as his mother gave attention to his newborn brother.[141] And when Christien went out shopping with the children, Wendela could finally write to her parents without being disturbed by a crying baby or a whining toddler. Yes, 'a golden time' had arrived since they moved to Bereastraat, where Christien joined them as a resident domestic servant. Wendela had 'a life that is totally unthinkable for young housewives in Holland', she wrote to her parents.[142]

'If anyone had told me two years ago that I would find it miserable to return from here to Holland, I would have declared them outright crazy. But at the moment the sadness of leaving everything here is predominant and therefore

---

135   Letters Beusekom-Scheffer, c. 21 Sep. (no date) and 12 Nov. 1954.
136   Beusekom-Scheffer, c. 21 Sep. 1954.
137   Beusekom-Scheffer, 12 Nov. 1952, underlined in the original.
138   Beusekom-Scheffer, 21 Sep. and 12 Nov. 1954.
139   Jan Peter to his father-in-law, 29 Mar. 1955.
140   Beusekom-Scheffer, 12 Feb. 1953
141   Beusekom-Scheffer, 20 June 1953.
142   Beusekom-Scheffer, 19 Mar. 1954.

FIGURE 5.9 Photographer: Tony McGrath.

I am the one who always finds arguments to [...] stay', she wrote on 1 April 1955. Apart from the burdensome return journey with two of her three children in nappies, she was upset about the prospect of a household in our *kouwe kikker-land* (cold little country), with little sunshine and without resident domestics. In the Netherlands she would have to do everything herself again, or be supported at best by 'a help that you should address as "mrs." and "please" etc'. Also, after-school care was going to be hard for her in the Netherlands, where the children often stayed inside, due to the climate. She did not want to think about the possibility that she and the rest of her family were going to end up 'in some flat in the city'.[143] Wendela counted her South African blessings.

For his part, Jan Peter was 'very enthusiastic' about the new job offered to him. A 'Dutch' upbringing for the children was high on their priority list, certainly after all the horror stories about a harsh and inadequate school system in South Africa. In addition, Wendela consoled herself with the idea of 'returning to the warm bosom of the family', but this was immediately followed by yet another reservation: 'One of the main arguments for me against returning is the world situation'. She expected that in South Africa they would be protected from the 'East-West conflict' that might develop into a bloody war.[144] Unrest because of the tensions between the 'capitalist West' and the 'communist East' played a role in postwar emigration from the Netherlands and other European countries; that fear also applied to a possible return in the 1950s. Yet it is remarkable that Wendela Beusekom believed that the African continent

---

143   Beusekom-Scheffer,1 Apr. 1955.
144   Beusekom-Scheffer, 1 Apr. 1955.

would remain free from violence, all the more so because the South African government was eager to portray critics of the Apartheid policy and other freedom fighters on the African continent as communist terrorists.[145] In her view, Europe apparently was more at risk. Nevertheless, they would return to Western Europe in January 1956, where Jan Peter accepted a new job in the Netherlands and the children went to a Dutch school.

The White Civilisation Narrative

The regular correspondence between the Beusekoms in South Africa and her parents, other relatives and friends in the Netherlands provided Wendela and Jan Peter in Pretoria with both a breeding ground for and a guarantee of Dutchness. This also applied to other immigrants of Dutch origin who had come to South Africa. Through transnational correspondence they imagined, maintained and strengthened a transnational family; in addition, they developed a social network in Pretoria. The content of Wendela's letters shows how she and Jan Peter repeatedly emphasized their Dutchness and Europeanness, depending on the situation and the company they were in. At one time Dutchness was identified with 'foreignness', bringing them closer to the British and right opposite nationalist Afrikanerdom; at another time, when they linked Dutch orthodox-Protestants to nationalist Afrikaners, the Beusekom couple emphasised their liberal Dutchness.

In addition, there was one constant: Dutchness was White, and Whiteness had to be carefully 'guarded' by keeping the right distance from Black South Africans. After their arrival, the Beusekoms tried to fathom the relationships within the 'White world' that connected South Africa with the Netherlands and Europe. They sought and found affiliation with a group of internationally oriented, highly educated, well-bred Dutch people – for example, sharing former membership of the student corps, or being able to exchange colonial experiences of a youth in the netherlands East Indies. When exploring shared features within the local migrant community, the transnational correspondence with family and friends in the Netherlands fulfilled a function in identifying and mobilizing such connections in South Africa.[146] In addition, the 'We' sentiment felt by the Beusekoms and their new friends in South Africa was reinforced by opposing 'Other' Dutch immigrants who belonged to a different class or denomination.

---

145   In 1950 the Malan government passed the *Suppression of Communism Act*, prohibiting all communist (or alleged communist) activities, including organisation of the South African Communist Party (SACP).

146   As is apparent from the answers in Wendela and Jan Peter Beusekom's letters to the (still untraced or lost) mail from Amsterdam.

The position that Wendela and Jan Peter Beusekom-Scheffer occupied in White Pretoria had consequences for their dealings with the Black population. The right combination of distance and proximity, in particular with regard to their own household staff, was of great importance. Neither the correspondence with the Netherlands nor Dutch etiquette books, such as the famous *Hoe hoort het eigenlijk* by Amy Grosskamp-ten Have, could advise them on this. The protectively raised and rather insecure Wendela felt herself dependent on the information provided by other Whites in Pretoria. That information – with stories about infectious diseases, theft or (sexual) violence – would only reinforce her fear of the Black 'Other'. In a short time, racial inequality was accepted as a matter of course in the lives of the Beusekoms in Pretoria.

A critical public debate about the Apartheid policies in South Africa had not yet started in the Netherlands in the 1950s. The letters that Wendela and her husband sent to her parents show no signs of discomfort between the relatives in the Netherlands and South Africa about racial exclusion. These debates only started later, after the global anti-Apartheid Movement managed to mobilize critical voices and actions against the Apartheid regime.[147] By then, the Beusekom family had been back in the Netherlands for quite some time. The condemnation of the South African Apartheid regime became an international issue that the Dutch media and government could no longer ignore.[148] The discourse of *stamverwantschap* and associated identification with White Afrikanerdom was replaced by a discourse of international solidarity with the repressed Black majority in South Africa. Thanks to this cultural-political shift, Mrs. Beusekom revised her approach to the Black 'Other', although the narrative of White supremacy continued to shine through in our memory work about the years she spent in South Africa. This is evident from the vocabulary with which she talks about her South African experiences, and also from the perspective she chooses to narrate her stories. The narrative of White supremacy and the repression this involved was hard to escape, even more so as it was already part of the cultural baggage with which Dutch migrants came to South Africa.

While the Beusekoms – using their kinship network – returned to the Netherlands without losing any economic or cultural capital, their close friends, the Huismans, stayed in South Africa. Mrs. Beusekom put me on the track of their transnational history, which also connects the Netherlands and South Africa. This will be explored in more detail in the next chapter, on the basis of the film material their cousin from the Netherlands shot in South Africa.

---

147   Thörn, *Anti-Apartheid*.
148   Stefan de Boer, *Van Sharpeville tot Soweto. Nederlands regeringsbeleid ten aanzien van apartheid, 1960–1977* (Den Haag: Sdu Publishers, 1999).

CHAPTER 6

'I never set out to Wage War Against my Family'

Cinematic Explorations of Whiteness

'Do you know my cousin?' Geert Huisman asks me in April 2008, while we enjoy a glass of South African wine and thin slices of biltong, served by his wife Elsa.[1] Within half an hour of my arrival at their home in Pretoria he refers to his cousin in the Netherlands, Maarten Rens.[2] Both are grandsons of prominent Dutch economist Jaap Grotenhuis, who in 1949 left the Netherlands with his wife to settle in South Africa, together with some 1,754 Dutch emigrants that same year. One of their three daughters and her husband followed a few years later. Her children grew up in Pretoria, while the children of the other two daughters reached their maturity in the Netherlands. Geert and Maarten knew each other from regular family reunions in the Netherlands, before Maarten – after finishing high school – visited his relatives in South Africa for the first time in 1967. He then attended the Film Academy in Amsterdam and worked as a freelance documentary maker.

Maarten travelled to South Africa for the second time in 1981, on his own initiative, to make a film about his family in the land of Apartheid. Geert Huisman: 'We thought it was going to be a pleasant movie, but he actually used us. In that film he gave a very distorted picture of our family and how we lived. "The nice thing about Africa", the title was, or something like that'. Three months later Maarten tells me: 'I named that movie "I've been there"'.[3] The label on the film canister he brings from the attic where unedited film and audio recordings are stored reads *You should have been there*. This title refers to the

---

1   This chapter is a revised version of Barbara Henkes (2013) Negotiating the '(Ab)normality' of (Anti-)Apartheid: Transnational Relations within a Dutch-South African Family, South African Historical Journal, 65:4, 526–554. © South African Historical Journal reprinted by permission of Taylor & Francis Ltd., http://www.tandfonline.com on behalf of South African Historical Journal. The members of the Grotenhuis family (later: Huisman-Grotenhuis and Rens-Grotenhuis families) who lived or still live in South Africa have been given pseudonyms; the relatives in the Netherlands figure under their real names.

2   Conversation Barbara Henkes and Geert and Elsa Huisman (hereafter: Conversation Henkes and Huismans), 22 Apr. 2008.

3   Conversation Barbara Henkes and Maarten Rens (hereafter: Conversation Henkes and Rens), 27 July 2008. See: International Institute of Social History (IISG), Amsterdam, the African Skies Foundation video collection (1982-1994) (hereafter: Collection African Skies) nr. 13e: *Ik ben er geweest / I was there*, 1981, tape 161. This rough cut from 1982 never developed into a finished production. The footage and sound material is kept by the filmmaker (hereafter: private collection M. Rens).

© BARBARA HENKES, 2020 | DOI:10.1163/9789004401600_008

FIGURE 6.1 Maarten Rens with his daughter and Sienna.

standard argument that people 'must have been there', before they had the right to express criticism of the Apartheid regime. Maarten Rens was there in 1981, with his one-year old daughter, the buggy, and his super-8 camera and sound equipment.

Family as a Gateway to a 'Strange' World

It was the time when criticism of racial exclusion and violently enforced Apartheid policies had grown into a global Anti-Apartheid Movement.[4] In the Netherlands, too, the Anti-Apartheid Movement was by that time firmly anchored in society; a political development that rarely remained without consequences for the kinship networks connecting the Netherlands and South Africa.[5] Before leaving for South Africa in November 1981 Maarten Rens had not yet been involved in the *Anti-Apartheidsbeweging Nederland* (Netherlands Anti-Apartheid

---

4 Thörn, *Anti-Apartheid*.
5 The political scientist Adrian Guelke offers a critical historiographical analysis of the place of Apartheid in a global context with his *Rethinking the Rise and Fall of Apartheid. South Africa and World Politics* (New York: Palgrave, 2005). See also S. de Boer, 'Nederland en de apartheidskwestie, 1948-1990', in: M. Kuitenbrouwer en M. Leenders (eds.), *Geschiedenis van de mensenrechten. Bouwstenen voor een interdisciplinaire benadering.* (Hilversum: Verloren, 1996) 259–280.

Movement, AABN), though his views on the situation in South Africa were informed by the critical debates on Apartheid that had started since the end of
the 1950s. The idea for the documentary, according to the filmmaker, came
about when he asked himself: 'What happens when you portray people in a
strange political situation, and show the result without comment, without any
explanation of what you see?'[6]

His relatives in South Africa offered him access to that 'strange' world. A single phone call was enough for a warm welcome from his aunt and uncle in
Pretoria. They thought it a nice idea that their nephew wanted to make a 'family movie' without any political axe to grind, as they had understood it.[7] The
presence of his young daughter undoubtedly contributed to an informal 'family feeling'. Images of their daily life in South Africa could strengthen the personal ties with the family in the Netherlands, at a time when the connections
between the two countries were under pressure.[8] The visit of their filmmaking
nephew gave his relatives the chance to show another, more positive representation of South African society in order to counterbalance all the negative
reports. With his camera Maarten took on the role of cultural broker between
the two worlds.[9] As a professional filmmaker he wanted to document the daily
routines and lifestyle of Dutch migrants and their descendants in South Africa,
and show the results to interested parties in the Netherlands and perhaps beyond.[10] That way he might bridge the divide between the Netherlands and
South Africa, but could also emphasize the distance. When Rens states that he
conceived the plan to create a portrait of 'people in a strange political situation', it is clear that he took difference as his point of departure.[11] The distinction between 'us' (in the Netherlands) and 'them' (in South Africa) was a fore-
gone conclusion for him, centred on the controversial issue of Apartheid.

The baggage with which Rens arrived in November 1981 contained not only
his film and sound equipment, but also a hefty dose of scepticism. He wanted
to add an original and personal contribution to the then highly polarized and

---

6   Conversation Henkes and Rens, 27 July 2008.

7   On a preserved soundtrack we hear how Uncle Rob introduces his nephew as a filmmaker,
      'who travels over the world with a super-8 camera' and is now preparing a movie about
      South Africa: 'Not at all political, but in order to film our ordinary lives here on the spot'
      (private collection M. Rens).

8   De Boer, 'Nederland en de Apartheidskwestie', 275–278.

9   Cf. De Jong, 'Cultural Brokers'.

10   Rens left on his own initiative, without any prior agreements with broadcasters or other
      agencies.

11   K. Hastrup, 'Anthropological Visions, some notes on visual and textual authority', in: I.
      Crawford and D. Turton (eds.), *Film as ethnography* (Manchester/New York: Manchester
      University Press, 1992), 14 and 19.

morally charged debates about South Africa in the Netherlands by 'only registering, without any comment', as he emphasized in our first conversation.[12] That meant: no omniscient narrator who introduces the images and explains their meanings, much less a raised finger, pointing to what was right or wrong; good or bad. However, under no circumstances can filmmakers limit themselves to a blank 'registration' of reality. Before the camera was even turned on, Maarten's position as a relative from the Netherlands already had an impact on what was or was not asked and registered. His choice for the camera position, for the moments in which he zoomed in or gave an overview and many other seemingly technical decisions affected the message of the film too. And then the editing still had to be done: forging the various images into one storyline. These elements, and the reception of the end result, led to his relatives' uneasy feeling that they had been 'used', or rather abused.

The cast does not consist of random people in South Africa, but of close relatives: a more or less intimate unity in all its diversity. It was precisely this focus that provided a context in which everyday negotiations with Apartheid policies at different levels could be investigated and visualised. The rough cut of the film stars Uncle Rob Huisman (1920), Aunt Margaret Huisman-Grotenhuis (1925) and their adult children Geert (1953), Loes (1954), Martha (1957) and Sylvia (1959). Siena (c. 1963), the resident maidservant of his uncle and aunt's household, is also given a prominent role, along with two colleagues at Sylvia's work, Precious and Luasi (both c. 1960). The interview with Hugo, a foreman at Geert's work, was not included in the rough cut; the film images of this encounter have not been preserved, but the sound has.[13] The filmmaker, who is at the same time the cameraman and (most of the time) interviewer, remains invisible throughout, though he is strongly present through the questions he asks. In the recordings from 1987 Maarten's cousin Sylvia stars together with Barbara Masekela (1941), a prominent activist of the African National Congress (ANC) in exile. The language used in all the footage is either Dutch or English. Between themselves his relatives speak mostly Dutch, elsewhere, and also in their performances before the camera, they mostly speak English.[14] Barbara Masekela, Siena, Luasi and Precious speak English. Only on one rare

---

12   Conversation Henkes and Rens, 27 July 2008. With this statement he places himself in the
      tradition of the 'direct cinema' that has flourished in the Netherlands since the 1970s, es-
      pecially in the VPRO public broadcasting company. See: B. Hogenkamp, H. Hosman, H. de
      Wit (eds.), *Direct Cinema, maar soepel en met mate* (Hilversum: Nederlands Instituut voor
      Beeld en Geluid/VPRO, 2006) 13–88.
13   The last names of Hugo, Siena, and Precious are not mentioned and could not be traced.
14   From the unedited footage it becomes clear that the filmmaker has asked his cousins to
      speak English for the camera, while the family members speak Dutch among themselves.

occasion do we hear Afrikaans; other African languages have not penetrated the recordings.

The film opens with a brief scene in the garden at the edge of the private pool. The day has just begun: the filmmaker's young daughter is skipping around. Aunt Margaret and her three adult daughters, all in light summer dresses, discussing what they have already done and what they intend to do that day. Dutch is their medium, sometimes coloured by an English accent. Breakfast, 'toast, sliced thin', has been digested and their conversation is about swimming and gardening. The location as well as the clothes, the topics and the casual way they are discussed show how the intersection of gender, class, and race qualifies their position. Father and son Huisman are absent, but the first cut brings the viewer face to face with Uncle Rob, a successful business-man. Seated on a bench beside his wife, he poses as a *pater familias,* when he states that South Africa is a 'great' country to raise one's children. He stresses its attractions by referring to 'the average of 285 sunny days a year' and the 'many more opportunities' South Africa can offer in comparison to Europe.[15] His words are reinforced by his confident tone and self-conscious posture that ra-diates both male authority and White power. Whatever his conscious beliefs about the situation in South Africa, he has inherited the legacy of White men who have in the words of James Baldwin 'made the modern world' and have never been 'strangers', regardless of their geographical location in the world.[16]

In the same setting Aunt Margaret, housewife and a former Montessori teacher, speaks about the upbringing of their children. They each had their specific tasks or responsibilities in the household, as for instance cleaning the swimming pool. Referring to the comments by others who wondered 'why don't you make the Blacks do the job?', she explains that she feels this is not fair, as their Black staff never uses the swimming pool. When Maarten asks her why they do not, she says: 'Because they just don't ... they can't even swim ... as yet ...' The last addition is significant. 'As yet' seems to refer to a future where everyone, White, Black or whatever colour could learn how to swim and share a swimming pool.[17] The scene is revealing: it not only shows how minor daily routines were leavened with race issues, but it also shows his aunt ignoring the

---

Rens cannot remember the reason for this, although he may have envisaged distributing his documentary abroad.

15   After the economic boom in the 1960s, Europe, including the Netherlands in the 1970s, was confronted with a recession, while South Africa was expanding.

16   Baldwin, *Strangers in the Village.*

17   Although the Reservation of Separate Amenities Act (1953) applied to public, not to pri-vate swimming pools, it meant just the same that there were hardly any facilities for Blacks to learn to swim. Cf. S. Clingmans, *Bram Fischer,* 221.

FIGURE 6.2
Video still: the Huisman couple, Pretoria
1981.

very limited possibilities for South African Blacks to learn to swim. With her reference to a future change, however, she presents a 'liberal' or 'evolutionary' version of a narrative of Whiteness.[18] This version assumes that Blacks would eventually achieve the level of White, European civilization, as symbolised by the swimming pool. Mrs. Huisman articulates what we also might call a paternalist narrative about the progress of Blacks under the guidance of Whites. The image of the private swimming pool, with which the rough cut of film starts, functions as a marker of Whiteness.

The 'Other' in the Household

The filmmaker leaves this issue and moves on to explore the position of the resident domestic in his uncle and aunt's household. Dressed in a white apron with a white cloth around her head, Siena is ironing in the scullery, when Maarten asks her why she works for 'White people'. Her father said she had to find a job: 'to help him with the money', she explains. Rens makes a naive and vain attempt to elicit a statement from her about unequal relationships between Blacks and Whites: 'He did not tell you it was a bit strange?' 'No', she answers concisely. Nothing is strange about this situation, on the contrary: Black women working in White households belonged to everyday 'normality' in South Africa. The filmmaker tries a different approach. He knows she has a baby and asks her where it is. 'She's at home'. Home was located in one of the townships of Pretoria. Since her arrival in the Huisman household, Siena has not seen her child very often. 'It's too far'. When Maarten Rens remarks that

---

18   Steyn, *'Whiteness'*.

that is too bad, she smiles uncomfortably while confirming: 'Yes'. Her answers are limited to the very essentials, after which she continues her work in silence. True to his premise, the filmmaker gave no further explanation about Siena's limited choice: like so many African mothers she needed to earn money as a resident domestic servant. In this position she and her colleagues often cared for the children of their employers, while their own children 'on location' were raised by others. Whereas for the White part of the nation, 'home' and 'family' were based in one place, Black families were torn apart by the institutionalized racial divide. 'Home' was often far away from work. For Siena this was not an issue to be discussed, and certainly not during this recording in her employers' house.

Rens did his best to create a 'contact zone'[19] and to communicate with Siena on a basis of equality, but he ignored the fact that there was no basis for equality in these circumstances. When he asks her why she calls him and other men in the house 'master', she at first does not understand what he is talking about. 'Master? Yes'. 'Why do you call us master?' Maarten tries again. Siena shakes her head, smiles and says finally: 'Because I do not know your name'. The complex mix of intimacy and distance, and of wealth and poverty, so characteristic of domestic service – even more complicated by the formal segregation and informal proximity of Whites and Blacks in a prosperous household under Apartheid – made a 'candid' conversation with the housemaid an impossible undertaking. By talking about himself in terms of 'us', Maarten Rens unintentionally emphasized his position as 'the Other', and more specifically as a member of the employer's family. But precisely because this is exposed on film, Siena becomes a telling witness of Apartheid and of the well-intentioned filmmaker's own Whiteness. This is nowhere more painfully obvious than when he asks her if she 'would like to be White'. When she replies with an uncomfortable smile and a 'yes', she rubs her hand across her cheek as if to scour away the colour that has been inscribed on her skin. Asked why she wants to be White, she answers: 'White people is always nice'. It may have been that Siena thought this was the only tactful reply, though her body language also reflects the working of a racial order in postcolonial societies, as critical intellectuals such as Franz Fanon and Edward Said have pointed out. They show convincingly how racial discourse was taken inside the Self, not only by White colonisers but also by the Black colonized.[20]

---

19   Pratt, *Imperial Eyes*.
20   Catherine Hall, *Civilising Subjects. Metropole and Colony in the English Imagination 1830–1867* (Chicago/London: University of Chicago Press, 2002) 14–15.

FIGURE 6.3
Video still: Sienna ironing in the
scullery, Pretoria 1981.

The contrasts between both sides of the racial divide in and around the
household are further explored when Maarten and his camera follow his cousin Martha. She and her husband have just started their own household and she
introduces him to a 'garden party', a gathering of about twenty women interested in garden design. They are welcomed in Afrikaans by the hostess, who is
'very worried', because her garden 'is not in good shape'. The facilitator reas-
sured her: 'Look how beautiful and very well kept the garden is!' After the ladies have been filmed with coffee and cake, there is a transition to Martha's
own garden, where she points to the roses and bottle brushes that are suffering
from the summer heat. 'So it doesn't look too good at this stage'. By focussing
on his cousin's and other White women's problems with their gardens, the
filmmaker has created a contrast between the carefree prosperity of a White
minority and the poverty of a Black majority in South Africa, even though the
latter remained out of sight. However, prosperity was not at all as carefree as it
seemed, Martha emphasizes, when it came to her domestic staff: 'It sounds
fantastic, having help for two or three days a week. But on the other hand: a lot
of private life disappears, because you can't always exactly do what you feel like
and just relax. If I relax, I wonder what she is thinking: "she is lazy" or "the
house is untidy", and that she'll tell all her friends: "the madam is very untidy,
and the house is always upside down". [...] So, it is not always as nice as they say
it actually is'.

Martha apparently feels the need to defend her lifestyle before the camera
of her filming cousin from the Netherlands. She seems to identify him with an
unspecified 'they': those who believe she is leading a life of luxury thanks to
the efforts of Black domestic workers. Once 'the madam', as she calls herself in
the third person, has explained the burden of this invasion of her privacy, she
indicates that she feels 'obliged' to employ Black domestic staff. It then also
becomes clear that the work of her domestic is not limited to the two or three

FIGURE 6.4
Video still: garden party, Pretoria
1981.

days previously mentioned: 'If I didn't ... they wouldn't have any money and they didn't have anything to buy food ... so you are helping them indirectly. I don't need her four days a week, but you can't get a job for the other two days, so... I just keep her on. So, I'm doing her a good turn and she is doing me a good turn'. Martha positions herself in opposition to two types of 'Others': firstly against critics outside South Africa (more particularly in the Netherlands) with insufficient insight into the needs of the Black population, and secondly against this same Black population that – despite its dependence on her and other Whites – may oppose the unequal distribution of South African resources between Blacks and Whites. Her performance in front of her cousin's camera illustrates the more widely held view of a natural and unbridgeable gap between Whiteness and Blackness. Later she will express this essentialist narrative of difference and inequality more explicitly.

Apartheid at Work

Maarten Rens followed some members of the family to the work floor. At the time of his visit in 1981 his cousin Geert worked as a site engineer for a construction company. On site he proudly explains to Maarten and his camera that they are building 'one of the most modern railway stations in South Africa'. The scale of the project strengthens his self-presentation as a responsible man-of-progress who is in charge, in order to advance his country in the modern world. The construction of the station was closely related to the racial divide under Apartheid: every day some 60,000 Black workers were going to use the station, bridging the distance between their work and residence. With his work, Geert contributes to the geopolitical infrastructure that should enable the rapid 'supply and drainage', as he puts it, of cheap labour from the homelands and townships to the city of Pretoria. During his explanation the camera pans over the building site and focuses on Black construction workers in action, dressed in blue overalls and wearing variously coloured helmets. Geert himself is dressed in a light shirt and khaki pants; together with his white construction helmet his appearance demonstrates how the dresscode emphasize White supremacy.

Geert Huisman mentions the people involved: apart from himself and another site engineer there are three White 'foremen' and two Black 'gang bosses' who supervise about 120 Black workers. When asked if they were 'good workers', Geert says: 'They are very... well I don't know how to put it, you know, you still have to teach them how to do everything, and gradually they get to know, like the two gang bosses, they are very good. Because of the tremendous boom we are experiencing in South Africa, the construction industry has shot up and there is a lot of new employment. And of course, they are raw material, you have to teach them'. The indication 'raw' for the Black workers was not meant as a moral category. Nevertheless, it refers to the opposition between cultivated and uncultivated that is part of a racial discourse,[21] and to what is called the 'master narrative of Whiteness': the collection of diverse stories that give meaning to the world around us in terms of racial inequality and White supremacy.[22] Just like his mother, Geert presents an evolutionary and paternalist version of a narrative of Whiteness that connects progress and modernity with White supervision and projects racial equality into the future.

Interestingly, the rough cut of the film does not include the interview with Hugo that was found among the sound recordings.[23] He was one of the three White foremen on the building site. Talking to the filmmaker, Hugo does not beat about the bush: 'What I can't understand is ... I'm a White man in this country, this is my country, I'm born here. And the Blacks are helping, working next to us, bringing this country up to where it is today, but they got no privileges. Why don't they get equal pay? [...] I didn't ask to be White and I don't think they have asked to be Black. So, I shouldn't discriminate against them. Look: if they stay this way and [in] the culture they are used to, it is because they don't get a decent wage. If you give them equal pay, they can raise their own standards...'[24] The foreman clearly sees no reason at all for the privileged position of White workers and expresses his disgust about the deprived

---

21   Cf. J. Neederveen Pietersen, 'Savages, Animals, Heathens, Races', in: Idem, *White on Black*, 30–51; Steyn, *Whiteness*, 7–11.

22   Steyn, *Whiteness*, 3–43. See also the Introduction to this book.

23   Film and soundtracks were independently recorded and stored; the film track could not be retrieved.

24   Private collection M. Rens, soundtrack interview 'Hugo'.

position of his Black colleagues. He reverses the argument that was used in 1924 for a series of government measures to disadvantage Blacks in order to guarantee a 'civilised' standard of living for their White colleagues.[25] In retrospect, Maarten Rens thinks that he did not include this interview in his rough cut because it was 'too political'.[26] The statements of the foreman indeed constitute a break in style with the other material, because of his outspoken criticism of Apartheid and its racial discourse, and also because the direct connection with Rens's relatives was missing. However, the filmmaker could have re-established a link to the family by confronting his cousin with Hugo's statements, or by initiating a discussion between the two men.

Such an approach was used at the Nedbank office where Maarten's cousin Sylvia worked. She was a staff consultant at Nedbank, which until 1971 was known as the *Nederlandse Bank voor Zuid-Afrika* (Netherlands Bank of South Africa).[27] There is a change of approach here: Sylvia, according to Maarten at her own request, took on the role of interviewer.[28] Instead of the filmmaker, it was his cousin who determined the course of the conversation with two Black female bank employees whose appointment she had promoted. In their conversations, too, the issue of the racial divide was raised. However, this time the narrative that ensued was not *about* Blacks, but in dialogue *with* Blacks. Everyone involved spoke for herself and had a name and a face.

Sylvia starts the interview with a reference to the Black Advancement Programme of the Nedbank, which aimed at hiring more Black employees and

---

25   Prime Minister's Circular No. 5 of 1924, cited by Guelke, *Rethinking*, 73. The Civilized Labour Policy (*Beskaafde Arbeidsbeleid*) was implemented after the two main opposition parties – Hertzog's National Party and Cresswell's Labour Party – won the 1924 elections. Its aim was to uplift the White working class (typically poor Afrikaners) to a 'civilized' standard of living by reserving the better-paid jobs and positions for Whites only, and leaving the 'dirty', subordinate, lower-paid jobs to Black workers (who were considered 'uncivilized' anyway).

26   Conversation Henkes and Rens, 16 Jan. 2009. It may also be possible that this critical voice did not match the image the filmmaker wanted to show of the acceptance of Apartheid as part of 'normal', White life.

27   Until 1971 Nedbank was known under the name *De Nederlandsche Bank voor Zuid-Afrika*. See: Geljon, P.A. *Een Nederlandse Overzeebank: De Nederlandsche Bank voor Zuid-Afrika 1888-1969*. Amsterdam: Boom, 2017 and G. Verhoef, 'Nedbank: The Continental Approach to Banking in South Africa', in: F.S. Jones ed., *Financial Enterprise in South Africa* (London: Macmillan, 1992) 80–114.

28   Conversation Henkes and Rens, 7 Dec. 2008. As a staff consultant, Sylvia was not the manager of the two Black employees. Yet their positions were not equal, which is a factor in what was and what was not said.

training them for higher positions.[29] 'We started with some adverts in the paper and one of the applicants was Luasi Mapanze, who is sitting here'. Asked about her motivation Luasi recounts how she was looking for a job after she finished school: 'Most of the companies I phoned said they were full already, or the placement agents said they don't have work for Blacks. Nedbank was the only company that responded'. When asked how she liked the work so far, Luasi says: 'It tends to be a bit boring now and then, most of it is quite clerical, but I am learning quite a lot'. 'And how do you feel about mixing with the other people, how do you feel you have been received by other people in the branch, in your work?', Sylvia asks neutrally, avoiding any mention of the Whiteness of 'the other people'. 'Well...', with an apologetic smile Luasi hesitates. '...I am really the only Black in the places I am working [...] So it is a bit... it is a different environment really. But the people are very nice. Most of them are quite nice, but we've got different cultures, different environments. So, they are very nice, I can't really complain'.

Without going further into this ambiguous response, Sylvia turns to the other bank employee: 'And Precious, how do you feel? If you were White, do you think your work would be different?'[30] It is a question that can only be answered in the affirmative. Precious gives an explanation in which she, too, uses a cheerful smile to soften her painful findings: 'I should think so, yes, because most of the people who come at the reception are surprised seeing a Black receptionist and a lot of them don't want to talk to me [smile], but I do talk to them, to make them feel at home [smile]. I greet them even when they don't greet me'. With her constant smile Precious seems to smooth over her uncomfortable statements. Next, Sylvia, who is familiar with Precious's career, asks her why she gave up her job as a teacher to become a receptionist at the bank. 'I liked teaching and I liked the little ones. The children were very interesting, but there wasn't enough money. So, I looked for a better job'. In a few sentences she makes clear how racial segregation and inequality in the Apartheid years worked, both in the labour market and in education: qualified work in education for Black children was paid much less than work as a receptionist at a White institution such as the Nedbank.

---

29   Such programmes were established in the 1970s under strong international pressure. Cf. Guelke, *Rethinking*, 198–201.

30   In the rough cut only Luasi Mapanze is introduced with her last name. Precious's last name is not mentioned, though this may be due to the editing.

FIGURE 6.5A&B&C   Video stills: Luasi and Precious interviewed by Sylvia.

Contact Zones

After the inequality between Black and White at work has been touched upon casually, the conversation between the three women then focuses on the impact of Apartheid in the private sphere, although soon enough it becomes clear how the public and private spheres are inextricably intertwined. When Sylvia asks what Precious and Luasi think about marrying 'a White man',[31] Luasi initially emphasizes the importance of preserving one's 'own' culture: 'There is this thing about preserving our culture. And ... you know, if I'd marry a White man, I would have Coloured children, you see. They wouldn't have peace. I think I would try to avoid it really'. Precious agrees: 'Me too, I wouldn't like to live with a White man...because of our customs'. Their statements were

---

31   Homosexuality obviously did not cross her mind, or she did not think of referring to it, as it was taboo at the time.

shaped by the 'narrative of difference' about irreconcilable dividing lines be-tween White and Black or Coloured cultures. How difficult it was to escape the construction of differences based on 'race' – also outside South Africa – is shown as soon as Sylvia refers to her personal experiences when she studied in Paris at the Sorbonne a few years before.[32] There she shared a residence with students from Ghana who had told her they'd rather not get involved with White families because of the 'cultural differences'. At that moment in their conversation, however, Precious confronts her with a crucial difference be-tween the situation in South Africa and Europe: 'It [interracial contact] hap-pens overseas, but it is very rare you see it happen here in South Africa, 'cause people who are doing that are taken to jail, such things, so I try to avoid it'. Lu-asi adds: 'It won't happen here because there is a law. I mean: Whites are not supposed to marry Blacks'.

While Precious and Luasi initially went along with the narrative of an es-sential 'cultural divide' between Blacks and Whites, they now point to the legal constructions of inequality on racial grounds, which prevented any rapproche-ment between the 'races' and made 'mixed' marriages in South Africa utterly impossible. 'Because of Apartheid they would have to leave the country', Luasi concludes. Sylvia at that point feels the need to negate the institutionalised racial inequality and the dramatic consequences of Apartheid, when she suggests that it is 'just as much from the Black side' that the racial divide is maintained. Luasi once more tries to explain: 'Because I was born in South Af-rica, I would never think of getting married to a White man. Maybe in another country, because you meet there, you get used to each other and such things. But here...'. During their recorded conversation an essential ('cultural') divide between Blacks and Whites is both confirmed and debated. Openings are of-fered by Sylvia, and taken up by Luasi and Precious, for a discussion about the impact of Apartheid – in contrast to the earlier conversation between the film-maker and Siena. This might have been due to the freer environment offered by the terrace of Nedbank as opposed to the vicinity of the employers' house, but also to a more equal communication between the three young women due to their corresponding ages and gender, the better education of the interview-ees, and their shared (though very different) positions as employees of the same bank.

---

32   In his classic *Peau noire, masques blancs* (1952) the psychiatrist and writer Frantz Fanon exposed the phenomenon that the colonized Blacks approach themselves and their envi-ronment through the eyes of the dominant White colonial. H.K. Bhaba, 'Foreword: re-membering Fanon. Self, Psyche and the Colonial Condition' in the English reprinted translation *Black Skin, White Masks*, vii-xxvi.

Precious and Luasi are well aware of their unequal chances and positions, but they carefully try not to offend Sylvia when they point to the politically constructed and legally enforced divide along the colour line that inevitably leads to cultural differences (besides many other inequalities). In contrast to the failed conversation between Maarten and Siena, this meeting shows how the three women managed to create a 'contact zone' as defined by Mary Louise Pratt in terms of a social space where actors with different cultural backgrounds meet, collide and struggle with each other, in a context of highly asymmetrical power relations.[33]

Luasi and Precious found themselves in structurally unequal positions that made it impossible for them speak with full frankness, although they carefully tried to explore the possibilities of this exchange. Sylvia, too, made an effort to bridge the racial divide. Her approach to the colour line differed greatly from her sister Martha's. When the filmmaker asks Martha if she also counts Blacks amongst her circle of friends and acquaintances, she replies 'My husband plays hockey with a Coloured, [...] but there is a big difference between a Coloured and a Black'. No further consideration is given to her statement about this 'big difference', which reproduced the usual categories and hierarchies that were institutionalised under Apartheid. Martha, that much is clear, keeps her distance from people of colour and certainly Blacks: 'I find them... they all look exactly the same. I mean: with the Whites you have different colour hair, you've got different colour eyes and complexion, where all their eyes are dark brown or black and their hair is all exactly the same, so there is not that physical attraction as you have with the Whites'.

It is a well-known theme in the 'master narrative of Whiteness' that Whites recognize each other as distinct individuals, while Blacks are approached as an amorphous mass without clearly recognizable, let alone attractive facial features. The distance created by unequal power relations was soon accompanied by a lack of interest in the individual, and the effort to recognise the Other as an individual easily disappeared. Blacks became not only interchangeable, but also unrecognizable and therefore uncontrollable and frightening. When Martha, as a White married woman, mentioned the absence of physical attraction, race, gender and sexuality unwittingly intersect in her narrative. Her dislike of the black body was consistent with a long-standing theme of the so-called 'Black Peril' (*swart gevaar*) amongst Whites in South Africa: the threat of sexual abuse by Black men that might 'contaminate the White race'.[34] This existing fear was strengthened by the possibility of 'Black rule', which was no longer

---

33   Pratt, *Imperial Eyes.*
34   Although 'Black Peril' is defined as 'the threatened rape of white women by black men', many authors suggest that the rape threat was essentially a rationalization of White men's

unthinkable, since decolonisation on the African continent was well under way. Martha's anxiety was intensified by the events in Rhodesia, where shortly before, in 1980, the White minority regime was forced to give way to a Black majority government. Immediately after this transfer of power – symbolized in the country's new African name Zimbabwe – many Whites left the country. 'I would not like to leave South Africa', Martha emphasizes, 'I want to stay here all my life. But when things become dangerous, if... and a big IF ... no one knows what is going to happen... But you can feel that there is a change [...] It is frightening when you think: maybe one day I will have to leave my beloved country and where do you go to?'[35]

Martha's worries about her personal future in a continent where since the 1950s African independence movements had changed colonial power relations, were in sharp contrast with the confidence expressed in the film by her sister Loes and her Dutch husband Kees about their future in South Africa. They had met in the Netherlands, where Loes trained as a nurse. After their marriage in 1980 they settled in the city of Leeuwarden, until Uncle Rob promised the newly married couple financial support and plenty of opportunities in South Africa. Not long after Maarten shot his film, they migrated to Pretoria with the prospect of setting up a garden centre.[36] From the interview with the upcoming entrepreneurs, on the still bare site of their planned garden centre and the plot where they would build their own house, it appears that they looked to the future with confidence. Their child 'is going to have a lot of space and a lot of opportunities', insists Loes, then in the last months of her pregnancy. Like Uncle Rob, she and her husband emphasize the favourable conditions in South Africa, without mentioning any of the political confrontations or the growing international isolation of the country. The critical debates on Apartheid in the Netherlands seem to have passed them by altogether, although they both kept their Dutch nationality, their house in the Netherlands, and their Dutch bank account.[37]

---

fear of sexual competition from Black men. Cf. Cornwell, 'George Webb Hardy's The Black Peril' and Brown, 'Facing the "Black Peril"'. See also Chap. 5, n. 46.

35 It seems as if her phraseology echoes the title of Alan Paton's famous novel on the dramatic effects of race segregation in South Africa, Cry, the Beloved Country (New York and London: Charles Scribner's Sons and Jonathan Cape 1948).

36 Kees and Loes mention her father's promises during a family gathering on 21 Aug. 2008 in Amsterdam, as did Rob Huisman himself in the footage of the family film from 1981. After their arrival in South Africa the planned garden centre did not work out and it took them quite a while to get their life going there.

37 When I asked them – during a family gathering in August 2008 in Amsterdam – about critical discussions in the Netherlands before their migration to South Africa in 1982, their answer was evasive.

Hope and fear for the future in South Africa is the theme with which Maarten Rens ends the rough cut of his documentary. Sylvia has the last word: she highlights the complexity of South African society, with its many different political and cultural communities that could not be reduced to racial categories: 'We don't only have the Black people: we have about eight different tribes of Black people who don't get on and have different ideas: some want revolution, some want peace'. The Black population of South Africa, Sylvia concludes, was not one people, and neither were the Whites. Her emphasis on the different 'tribes', in combination with the choice between 'revolution' or 'peace', implicitly refers to a recurring element of the Apartheid discourse: the narrative about Blacks murdering each other without the 'civilizing' presence of Whites. It is a narrative that ignores the South African war, initiated by 'Brits' and Afrikaner 'Boers' who killed each other in large numbers, as it also ignores the two World Wars that so recently raged through 'white civilization' in Europe. Sylvia, however, does not restrict herself to the internal conflicts within the Black population. She also mentions the animosity within the White population, although she frames this in 'cultural' or 'ethnic', and not political, terms: 'We have the Afrikaans and English-speaking people that don't get on; we have the Germans, the Dutch and the English. So, in South Africa it is a very complex situation. If you haven't been in South Africa and spoken to the Black people, to the White people, to British and Afrikaners, you can't understand the problem'.

This consideration brings her to the theme from which Maarten derived the title for his unfinished documentary *I've been there*: 'That is why I don't feel served by the criticism from overseas [...] If people come here and see it and criticize constructively, there is no harm in it. But so many people in Europe criticize before they even know what is actually happening here'. Although she asks for understanding of the complexities with which the people – and especially the White population – of her country were dealing, she is not insensitive to external criticism: 'So many people in Europe [...] have read stories in the newspaper which sometimes are blown up tremendously. And of course, then we have the opposite in South Africa: we are not aware of it enough, and in Europe they are over-aware of it, so... There should be a happy medium and I don't think that has been found'. In this way she addresses both an epistemological and a moral problem: who has the most valid knowledge and who, on that basis, has the right to speak?

Partly due to her previous residence in Europe – where she not only studied and lived with Black students from Africa, but also faced criticism of Apartheid – Sylvia signalled a different perspective from which the situation in her country could be approached. This led her to the question about '[the] truth' and the impossibility of reconciling all sides and points of view. Apparently, she was alive to the criticism on the racist conditions in her country. It seems that Sylvia, of all her close relatives in South Africa, was the most aware of the necessity or desirability of changing the racial order as it existed under Apartheid. At the same time, it becomes clear that she had no idea of the direction these changes might take and how they could be accomplished: 'I don't think the people realize the difficulty of the problems in South Africa. You can't give Black people rule when they are not capable of it, yet'. Just like her mother and her brother, Sylvia, too, refers to future changes in the subordinate positions of the Black population, but 'as yet' under White supervision. The recording ends with Sylvia concluding: 'And if it was not us Whites, it would have been other Whites that would have come and exploited the situation'. It is an impotent platitude, but it is also an acknowledgment of a historical situation in which a White minority, which she herself belongs to, enriched itself at the expense of a Black majority.

And then there is silence. Clouds are gathering over the terrace and the film-maker waits, just like Sylvia, who finally asks in Dutch: 'More questions ...?' No more questions, but a rumbling of approaching thunder.

A Tense Family Reunion

Back in Amsterdam Maarten Rens made a rough cut of his 'family film' entitled *I've been there*. It was shown during a family reunion in August 1982 at his mother's house. Apart from he himself, his mother, his two sisters and their partners, there were his aunt and uncle from South Africa, as well as their daughter Loes and her husband Kees, and two cousins from The Hague. When I asked Maarten to make a drawing of the setting in which the screening took place, he suddenly remembered that he had been filming at that occasion, too.[38] This happened on the advice of the chief editor of one of the Dutch public broadcasting companies, who showed interest in the film after he had viewed the rough cut. However, he thought the film was lacking a more general framework within which the actions and statements of the various actors could be placed and understood.[39] Rens wanted to create such a framework during the family reunion, by initiating and filming a discussion about Apartheid following the screening. Unfortunately, these recordings failed for technical reasons, which explains why *I've been there* was never finished. Maarten

---

38   Conversation Henkes and Rens, 7 Dec. 2008.
39   Conversation Henkes and Rens, 16 Jan. 2008 on his contacts with Roelof Kiers of the VPRO-television.

remembers how his Uncle Rob initially responded enthusiastically to the images: he was clearly proud of the performance of his son Geert on the site of his
dynamic construction works. He was also pleased with the contributions of his
three daughters, and his own performance together with his wife. The questions with which their nephew had confronted the maidservant were less
appreciated – the family rightly felt he had put her in an awkward position –
but all in all they thought their nephew had done a good job.[40]

However, the family reunion soon turned sour. At first, Uncle Rob apparently saw nothing offensive: he recognized the everyday normality of their
successful lives in South Africa. That was different for his relatives in the Netherlands. For some, the film gave rise to critical questions about the political
situation, which might indeed provide the necessary framework for the final
editing of the film. Maarten remembers that one of his sisters or her partner
made a remark along the lines of 'Well, now we have an idea of how you live
there, but ... the United Nations is rather critical about South Africa ...'[41] His
uncle waved away the remark by disqualifying the UN as a 'trashy organization'
in which each country, even the smallest, had an equal vote. The discussion
escalated, whereupon the hostess felt compelled to side with her sister and
brother-in-law from South Africa. She told her son Maarten that his attitude
was not appropriate, certainly not after the hospitality he had enjoyed in Pretoria. The family reunion ended with a dinner, but the atmosphere was thoroughly spoiled.[42] What at first glance was experienced as a 'safe' film story
turned out to be quite 'risky' for the family.

The idea of the family as a 'safe', border-transcending unit unexpectedly
came under considerable pressure. The main oppositions arose from the different political cultures in which the relatives lived, and also from the different
political discourses on Apartheid in the Netherlands and in South Africa. As
long as cheerful anecdotes about a shared past, nice food and good wine made
it possible to ignore those differences, the family members could continue to
enjoy each other's company. However, the second generation had less of a
shared history and felt the need to examine and confront these different
worlds. This did not mean that there was one 'Dutch' voice and one 'South
African' voice – as the footage itself shows. The relatives in South Africa had

---

40   According to Loes during a family gathering in Amsterdam, 21 Aug. 2008, together with
      the filmmaker's mother Mrs. Rens-Grotenhuis, her daughter Margo, her sister Margaret
      Huisman-Grotenhuis, her daughter Loes and son-in-law Kees.

41   This remark refers to the discussions within the Security Council and to the arms em-
      bargo the United Nations had required in 1977 after the bloody suppression of the Soweto
      uprising. Cf. Guelke, *Rethinking*, 194–195.

42   Conversation Henkes and Rens, 27 July 2008, a statement that was repeated almost verba-
      tim during our conversation six months later, on 7 Dec. 2008.

different narratives of Whiteness and different approaches to Apartheid than did the relatives in the Netherlands. But whatever position was taken, the thorny issue of Apartheid, which previously had been carefully avoided during family reunions and more generally within the kinship network, was now put openly on the table. It was particularly Uncle Rob who had problems in coping with such a confrontation. In this charged moment he was forced to recognize the benefits of his Whiteness independently of his own abilities, which not only meant a painful blow to his authority but also a loss of innocence.[43]

Sometime later Rob Huisman undertook an unfortunate attempt to take the edge off the matter, when he surprised all nephews and nieces in the Netherlands with a gift of money from the inheritance of their grandparents.[44] Maarten's sister Margo remembers that she, her brother and other sister, as well as their cousins in The Hague, decided to transfer the money to Radio Freedom, the radio station of the banned ANC.[45] 'I thought, being informed is always good. But I did not feel like giving it to the ANC itself', she recalls in 2008 during a family reunion in Amsterdam. 'Can you imagine', her cousin Loes from South Africa responds, 'the ANC was to us as a group of terrorists, those were the *Baddies*. That was how you were indoctrinated in school. And suddenly your family in the Netherlands are going to sponsor that organisation, so to us that was …' 'Yes, that's what I could understand and I found it troublesome', is Margo's quick reaction.[46] Like her mother during the film viewing in 1982, she now figures as a 'kinkeeper', who watches over the communication and feels responsible for a harmonious atmosphere during the family gathering.[47] For although Apartheid belonged to the past, the memories of that past were still present and formed a potential minefield within their kinship network.

From both sides efforts are made to bring the different positions together. '[T]hat's what I find so strange: I've been part of it and I was never aware of

---

43   Hall, *Civilising Subjects*, 5–6.

44   Their grandfather in South Africa died in 1974, followed by their grandmother in 1982. Rob Huisman, their son-in law, was probably their executor.

45   In the summer of 1982, the AABN organised a campaign in support of the ANC radio station, Radio Freedom, which broadcasted from various countries in Southern Africa. The campaign went on for many years. In the archives of the AABN no names of former Dutch donors can be found. See also P. de Cock, *Radio Freedom: de stem van het verzet* (Amsterdam: AABN, 1987) and the *Internationaal Instituut voor Sociale Geschiedenis* (IISG), Amsterdam: ARCH03259, Archief Omroep voor Radio Freedom, 1982-1996.

46   Exchanges during the family gathering, Amsterdam 21 Aug. 2008, and a conversation between Barbara Henkes and Margo Rens, 22 Oct. 2008. According to Margo Rens the amount was six times 500 guilders; a considerable sum of money at the time.

47   Leach and Braithwaite, 'A Binding Tie'. See also the Introduction of this book.

FIGURE 6.6
Call for financial support of Radio
Freedom, 1982.

what was going on. Now, when I see those documentaries about the oppression in those days, I wonder how it is possible that I [could ignore it] ...', confesses Loes fifteen years after the end of Apartheid. This is immediately followed by an attempt to explain: 'But it was kept away, we were so protected. And do not forget: our TV only came ... at the time that I had left [my parents'] home. I mean it was never discussed. You had no exposure to anything ...' '... which was weird for us, to see that you did not know', Margo responds.[48] During this dialogue both of them ignore the fact that Loes had lived in the Netherlands for years and surely must have come across some of the criticism of the Apartheid regime in South Africa that circulated so widely in Dutch society at the time. Lack of information, or 'propaganda', is often mentioned to explain either acceptance of or support for the repressive Apartheid policies. It is a way to emphasize one's own ignorance or 'White innocence' when it comes to personal responsibilities in accepting and perpetuating injustices based on racial discrimination.[49]

48   Conversation during the Grotenhuis–Huisman/Rens family reunion, 21 Aug. 2008.
49   Alison Bailey, 'White Talk' as a Barrier to Understanding the Problem with Whiteness', in: George Yancy (ed.), *What Is It Like To Be a White Problem?* (Lanham, MD: Lexington Books,

In South Africa at the time, where any criticism of Apartheid was equated with revolution and terror and where there was censorship, a critical debate on the impact of the policies of Apartheid was certainly not encouraged. There was some hard-won space for criticism as shown by the activities of writers such as Nadine Gordimer, clergymen such as Beyers Naudé, or MPs such as Helen Suzman. Criticism of Apartheid in South Africa was a risky affair for anyone, but information was indeed available, especially for the Huismans who regularly visited the Netherlands. Apparently that information could then simply be ignored or blocked by most members of the Huisman family. Perhaps 'compartmentalized' is a better term to indicate how disturbing information about violence and repression could be simultaneously present and absent in the minds of many living in South Africa.[50] Nevertheless, without the rhetoric of blame, which is – as Edward Said stipulated – 'neither intellectually nor morally sufficient', the question of individual and collective responsibilities remains.[51]

This very issue was indeed discussed in a conversation between Sylvia Huisman and the ANC activist Barbara Masekela, initiated by Maarten Rens in December 1987. It was during the festival 'Culture in Another South Africa (CASA)' in Amsterdam,[52] more than five years after Rens filmed in Pretoria. In the meantime, he had changed his approach to South African society and Apartheid: in 1981 he used his lens and microphone to explore the 'normality' of Apartheid in the lives of his relatives, but since then he had focussed on the 'abnormality' of Apartheid by documenting the Anti-Apartheid Movement and the struggle of the ANC in Southern Africa. In 1987 he tried to bring those two approaches together by inviting his cousin Sylvia to interview and be interviewed by ANC activists during the CASA festival.

2015). See also Melissa Steyn '"White Talk": White South Africans and the Management of Diasporic Whiteness' in Alfred J. Lopez (ed.), *Postcolonial Whiteness: A Critical Reader on Race and Empire* (New York: State University of New York Press, 2005).

50   P.A.L. Bijl, *Emerging memory: photographs of colonial atrocity in Dutch cultural remembrance* (D.Phil. thesis, University of Utrecht, 2011) Chap. 3, referring to E. Goffman, *Frame analysis: an essay on the organization of experience* (Cambridge: Harvard University Press, 1974). Stoler introduced the term aphasia for this phenomenon in her article 'Colonial Aphasia'.

51   Edward Said, 'Always on Top', *London Review of Books*, 25, 6 (20 Mar. 2003) 3–6.

52   The CASA conference was organised by the AABN and held from 12 to 19 Dec. 1987. The documentary was a co-production of the video unit of the ANC (Lusaka) and the video collective of the AABN (Amsterdam). Besides the documentary the footage of the interviews has also been preserved and made accessible through the catalogue of the African Skies Foundation in Amsterdam, since 2015 hosted by the IISG.

FIGURE 6.7
Announcement of the manifesta-
tion *Culture in Another South Africa,*
Amsterdam 1987.

You must have been – or gone away from – there

At the CASA festival some 250 South African artists and ANC activists came together: they gave concerts, put on plays, and held discussions with each other
and the public about the need for an international boycott of the Apartheid
regime in order to achieve a democratic, non-racial South Africa. For the documentary *Before Dawn. Culture in Another South Africa* (1988) Maarten Rens
filmed several interviews, in some of which his cousin Sylvia was involved both
as interviewer and interviewee.[53] Two years before she had come to the Netherlands to work at a bank in The Hague 'to gain new experiences' and to broad-
en her horizons.[54] In a sense, this occasion offered a follow-up to the role she
played in Maarten's previous recordings of her family's daily life in South Africa, although the context was fundamentally different. Again, Sylvia was challenged to reflect both on the relationship between Blacks and Whites under
Apartheid and on her own position as a White woman from South African. The

---

53   In the credits Sylvia appears under the pseudonym Sylvia Fischer, in view of possible re-
     percussions on her return to South Africa.
54   Statement by Sylvia in the interview with the Dutch-South African psychiatrist Bevin
     Hoek at the CASA conference. Collection African Skies: tape 103.

FIGURE 6.8A&B   Video stills Barbara Masakela en Sylvia Huisman at CASA, Amsterdam 1981.

unedited tapes of the interviews show how, first a little uncomfortably, but gradually more confidently, she asks questions and looks for answers to questions submitted to her, including those put by Barbara Masekela.[55]

At the time, Sylvia Huisman experienced the festival in Amsterdam as a revelation: 'I've been speaking with a lot of people, finding out about the things that I haven't been able to find out in South Africa. [...] From within South Africa it is very difficult to understand what is going on: you just live, from day to day and you see things, but you don't really understand them. By being here I have been able to understand things that are happening in South Africa', she tells Barbara Masekela. 'Does that mean that it is necessary to leave South Africa in order to be able to discover what was really going on?', a friendly but critical Masekela asks her. Sylvia acknowledges that it should be possible to learn more in South Africa itself, but in her view this process is hindered by lack of debate: 'People don't communicate. People are scared, especially the White people in South Africa, they are scared just to sit down and talk'.[56] In the context of the CASA festival, centring around the structural violence against people of Colour in South Africa, it is remarkable that Sylvia stresses the fears of 'especially the White people'. But that does not alter her observation: indeed, Whites had their fears, too, although of a different kind, as her sister Martha had said some years before in the interview with Maarten. Their fears were partly evoked and certainly strengthened by the repressive measures of the Apartheid regime, and at the same time they legitimised these measures.

Sylvia's statement makes clear how racial repression kept all layers of society in its grip. In Amsterdam she found herself surrounded by Black, Brown and

55   In addition, she spoke with the poet Willy Kgositsile, the journalist Ruth Bengu from Johannesburg, the musician Isaac S. Ntsamai, and an actor of the Bopha! theatre group. Collection Archives African Skies, No 7. Culture in Another South Africa (CASA), 1987.

56   Collection African Skies, no. 7: Tape 118, Section 4.

White South Africans, many of whom had fled the country – either because they could no longer tolerate the Apartheid policy and its related forms of repression, or because their lives were in danger. In retrospect it is fascinating to see how, thanks to the role the filmmaker has given to her, Sylvia entered into conversation with these South Africans. When she speaks enthusiastically about the new information and perspectives she has gained during the conference, Barbara Masekela warns her: 'It is very nice in a festival like this, where you have progressive people who have already overcome racial antagonisms and so on, but [...] there will always be a situation where there are Black people who, because they have suffered so much, will not have the same kind of warmth and willingness to communicate, to break down barriers – who are very, very angry. [...] It means that you still have to work for acceptance with the bulk of South-African Blacks'. She also asks Sylvia if she realises that the necessary changes in South Africa would be at the expense of her own privileged position.

Sylvia – who considered herself and her family 'liberals' (in contrast to the Nationalists who were in power) – had no direct answer to that question, though she remarks that it is too easy to say 'I'm liberal'. Those words had to be translated into action: 'more should be done for schools, housing, that sort of thing'. Segregation must be broken down, according to Sylvia, 'because if you aren't equal at school and you aren't training together [...], you don't understand each other'. Just like six years before, during the interview with Precious and Luasi, Sylvia emphasizes the necessity of abolishing the 'petty' Apartheid of everyday segregation. No reference is made to the 'grand' Apartheid that pushed Black South Africans into the margins of the poor 'Bantustans' and deprived them of their human rights. She expected that bringing Blacks and Whites together would lead to mutual understanding. However, according to Barbara Masekela and many others present at the CASA festival, understanding was not enough to overcome the structural inequalities along the colour line. Health care, housing and other social services would come under great pressure if they had to be shared with the Black and Coloured population in the future: 'Do you think White people will accept this? Or do you think they will fight against it?'[57]

Masekela, who acts as the representative of the politically articulate, non-racial opposition, soon realizes that Sylvia was not involved in the Anti-Apartheid Movement that had organised the CASA-festival. Sylvia was a newcomer in the political arena, unfamiliar with the politicised Anti-Apartheid discourse. She was receptive to the new information, arguments and ideas that were put forward in Amsterdam, although her perspective was still tinged by a 'liberal' version of the narrative of Whiteness with which she was raised: the

---

57   Collection African Skies, nr. 7: Tape 118, Section 4.

idea of Whites 'uplifting' the South African Blacks. With her question whether 'White people' would be willing to share prosperity with their Black countrymen, Masekela approaches Sylvia as a representative of the White community. Her question refers to the fear of change among many Whites in South Africa. A fear that was not unrealistic, Masekela emphasizes, 'when you consider the atrocities committed over the centuries against Blacks, like the massacres [...] the hunger in such a rich country and the deliberate underdevelopment of certain sectors of our community'. Sylvia agrees that fear plays a major role: 'a fear of the Blacks turning against them, and a fear of being punished for what they have done in the past'. The question of what can be done to combat that fear brings Sylvia back to the importance of exchanging views openly and without prejudice. However, the willingness to listen to each other does not come automatically. As long as not all South Africans had the opportunity to fully participate in a democratically and multiracially organized society, there could not be mutual exchange on an equal basis, her interlocutor stresses.[58]

The final documentary shows just a small excerpt from the unedited tapes of the conversation between the two women. At the end of the film Sylvia appears, when the ANC-activist in exile Page Boikanyo asks her if she is not afraid of being arrested when she goes to visit her family in South Africa, now that she has become involved in the Anti-Apartheid Movement.[59] Sylvia answers: 'I thought about it, but not seriously. [...] If what I am doing is treason, then I'm in the wrong country with the wrong government'.[60] With this recording the role of Sylvia and his South African relatives in Maarten Rens's cinematic oeuvre came to an end. What the introduction to the political culture and non-racial narratives of 'another South Africa' brought about in Sylvia's mindset, and how she looks back on this, cannot be explored further here.[61] It is known that she continued to live in the Netherlands until – after the end of the Apartheid regime – she went back to live in South Africa together with her South-African husband and their three children. In 2004 she and her family left South Africa again for a new life in Australia. Rob Huisman died in 2002. Apart from the children of Loes and Kees, the rest of the Huisman family and their

---

58   In the final documentary *Before Dawn. Culture in Another South Africa* (1988) only a single excerpt from the conversation between the two women is included.

59   For security reasons Page Boikanyo is identified as Page in the credits. After the end of Apartheid Boikanyo worked for the Ministry of Labour in South Africa. Thanks go to Fons Geerlings, who informed me about his identity.

60   Collection African Skies, no. 7: Tape 118, Section 4: Fragment from the exchange between Page, Sylvia and Klaas de Jonge are integrated in Maarten Rens' documentary *Before Dawn. Culture in Another South Africa*.

61   Sylvia has not responded to my attempts to make contact.

descendants remained in the now democratized, yet extremely complicated post-Apartheid South Africa.

Once in a while the relatives from South Africa visit the Netherlands. In April 2009 Maarten Rens received an unexpected visit from his cousin Geert and his wife Elsa. Cheerful photos show a social gathering of the two cousins. On that occasion they talked about the time when – in the 1980s – they were each operating on different sides of the border with Angola: Maarten as a film-maker for the Anti-Apartheid Movement, and Geert as an engineer for the South African army. At that time Rens was faced with the horrific atrocities caused by the interventions of the South African army in Angola, also known as the South African Border War or the Angolan Bush War. His documentary *Witness Apartheid Aggression* (1984) shows the South African involvement in the violence against the liberating movements ANC, South West Africa People's Organisation (SWAPO) and *Movimento Popular de Libertação de Angola* (MPLA) in the neighbouring countries.

In his editing he combined images of mass graves in Angola with footage from his unfinished documentary *I've been there* in which his cousin Martha is expressing her worries about her bottle brushes and roses that suffer from the summer drought. 'That is how I experienced the contrast', Maarten explains, admitting that his editing was far from subtle. 'I was there, in the middle of that madness and I thought it was important to show the contradiction between the resistance and the other, White, world. [...] But I never felt I was a waging a war against my family. I helped in the fight against the system of Apartheid...'[62] Within his film narrative he placed White South Africa opposite Black resistance. This opposition, though it may have felt that way, was not that simple, as his own involvement and that of other Whites in the Anti-Apartheid Movements shows. Yet, the broadcasting of Maarten Rens's documentaries on Dutch television during the 1980s shows that the primary concern with South Africa in the postwar Netherlands had shifted away from the identification with the *stamverwante* Afrikaners who had opposed British imperialism, to the Black liberation movements and their struggle against White hegemony in Southern Africa.

The Presence of the Past

The South African policy of Apartheid had changed the character of the Dutch-South African connection. That happened not only on the formal political level, where the Dutch government distanced itself from the South African re-gime, but also on the level of Dutch civil society where identification and

---

62   Conversation Henkes and Rens, 27 July 2008.

connectedness with White *stamverwanten* in South Africa was replaced by de-tachment and even aversion.[63] Inevitably this affected the personal relation-ships within the kinship networks linking the Netherlands with South Africa. Different attitudes towards Apartheid needed to be negotiated, either by ig-noring them or by defending or confronting them. In the case of the Huisman/ Rens-Grotenhuis family, the filmmaker Maarten Rens and his cousin Sylvia Huisman played a crucial role in these confrontations and negotiations. As a trusted outsider, Maarten Rens was able to direct his camera to different ways in which racial discourse penetrated the everyday lives of his relatives in South Africa. The unfinished results of this encounter present us with several narra-tives of Whiteness.

The statements by Aunt Margaret and her son Geert fit into a tradition of the liberal or evolutionary narrative, based on the idea that Blacks and Whites were still unequal, although under White leadership their Black compatriots could evolve and attain some kind of equality. Martha, on the other hand, ar-ticulates an essentialist 'narrative of difference', which presented the segrega-tion between Blackness and Whiteness as a 'natural' and immutable fact. In her narrative she combines 'cultural differentialism' and 'biological racism', showing how 'the cultural' slips into 'the biological', and vice versa.[64] Then there are Uncle Rob and his daughter Loes with her Dutch husband, who pres-ent their life and future in South Africa in terms of material prosperity in a sunny country. That the sun in South Africa was not shining for everyone was not a point for consideration; political tensions caused by Apartheid were lurk-ing behind safe stories about the beauty of the land. We may call this the 'es-capist' narrative of ignorance.

Maarten's cousin Sylvia was aware of the complicated situation the people of South Africa found themselves in. She negotiated her position in relation to the racial order of Apartheid during the recordings in 1981. At one moment she was inclined to stress the essential differences in cultural terms, and the next she emphasized the evolutionary or assimilative perspective. The overflow from one register to the other shows how both narratives, the one stressing the assimilation of Blacks into a White South Africa, and the other emphasizing es-sential differences and segregation, were parts of 'a master narrative of White-ness'.[65] By recording and combining these different narratives, the filmmaker managed to show various positions in dealing with Apartheid – from ignoring to accepting, and from confirming to questioning and criticizing – used by his

---

63   Cf. Schutte, *Nederland en de Afrikaners. Adhesie en aversie.*

64   S. Hall, 'The Multi-Cultural Question', in: B. Hesse (ed.), *Un/Settled Multiculturalism: Dia-sporas, Entanglements, 'Transruptions'* (London: Zed, 2001) 209–241, there 223.

65   Steyn, *Whiteness.* See also the Introduction to this book.

relatives in their daily encounters in South Africa. This helps us to understand how the racial order of Apartheid could be accepted as everyday 'normality'.

While his relatives in South Africa offered the filmmaker access to their daily, racialised routines at the time, he and his camera offered them an opportunity to consider those routines from a critical perspective. Rens succeeded in avoiding explicit condemnation of their lifestyle under Apartheid as 'abnormal' or outright 'wrong'. Instead, his recordings show the normality of 'living' Apartheid for them, as 'implicated subjects'. His rough cut offered several openings to question their involvement in everyday 'petty' Apartheid and its racial discourse. It could have been a first step to a critical assessment of the situation they found themselves in. In some way the filmmaker tried to create a space for that kind of assessment with the pre-view of the rough cut within the intimacy of a family gathering. On that occasion, however, he seemed to have banged too hard on the bulkhead behind which his relatives from South Africa stowed away their knowledge of the exclusion, oppression and violence which the Black majority in their home country had to endure. The heated exchange that resulted is indicative of the tension and confusion involved in this kind of transnational and transcultural dynamics. Acknowledging the structural inequality based on race that underpinned their privileged position in society was too much for his South African relatives. Still, this confrontation did not prevent the filmmaker from using the same kinship network a few years later, by inviting his cousin Sylvia (who was absent from the viewing in 1982) to participate in the recordings during the CASA festival.

As in 1981, Sylvia was once again willing to explore the contact zone of Black and White South Africa and talk about the racial order under Apartheid. On this occasion she took up a vulnerable 'intermediate position', as shown by the footage. Her plea for more interaction between Blacks and Whites was embedded in an a-political discourse of 'good will' and did not connect to the political discourse of the militant opposition who dominated the festival in Amsterdam. The fight against structural exclusion based on race and class was the joint starting point of the Anti-Apartheid Movement in the Netherlands as well as in Southern Africa. Sylvia did already question the racial order as organized under Apartheid, but she did not have the analytical tools and related language used by the ANC and the Netherlands Anti-Apartheid Movement in Amsterdam. That did not stop her from getting to know, in her own words, 'new perspectives on the situation' in her home country, and critically reassess her own privileged position and that of her relatives and friends in South Africa. For her close relatives this moment came much later – only after the collapse of Apartheid and the transition to a multiracial and democratic South Africa made a reorientation necessary. Just like Sylvia in 1987, some twenty

years later her sister Loes and her brother Geert express their surprise and impotence about the limited perspective that in those days allowed them to neglect the structural inequality and repression in South Africa.

In 1987 Barbara Masekela was not satisfied with Sylvia's argument that she
could not know about racial exclusion and repression 'as long as she lived in
South Africa'. Loes, on the other hand, is backed by her relatives in the Netherlands, when she takes up that same argument in 2008. They go along with their
cousin's need to afterwards emphasize ignorance or innocence regarding the
injustices during Apartheid[66] The compliance of those who were once much
more critical shows how the second generation today is focused on avoiding
painful confrontations about the Apartheid past in order not to undermine the
kinship network. In hindsight the filmmaker himself wonders whether he, if
born a White in South Africa at the time, would have accepted the privileges of
Apartheid.[67] That seems a sympathetic statement, because he does not con-
gratulate himself on his involvement in the Anti-Apartheid Movement. Nevertheless, he thereby reduces political and moral positions to 'chance': to the
place or nation people happen to be raised, or to the 'colour' with which they
happen to be born. That these categories influence the positions in relation to
Apartheid is beyond dispute, but the outcomes can vary greatly. More importantly: positions can change. This observation does not answer the question
why a small group of White South Africans were actually able to critically reflect on and act against the violent exclusions on the basis of race, while a
majority – including Black – South Africans accepted Apartheid as an inevitable fact of life. And neither does it explain why in the Netherlands a number of
people and organizations remained supporters of Apartheid until the 1990s,
and sometimes even beyond that time.[68]

These controversial positions in the past need further exploration.[69]
Maarten Rens's footage, particularly the performances of his cousin Sylvia,
shows how difficult, but by no means impossible, it was to approach a given
condition 'with fresh eyes' and no longer take the racial order under Apartheid
for granted, even before the Apartheid regime was broken down and racial discourse had to be replaced by new narratives about the past and present of an

---

66   Bailey, 'White Talk'.
67   Conversation Henkes and Rens, 7 Dec. 2008.
68   Peter Mulder, 'Wij gaan op dezelfde weg Zuid-Afrika! Het Apartheidsstandpunt van het
      Gereformeerd Politiek Verbond (1960-1990)' (MA-thesis University of Groningen, 2009).
69   I previously explored the way 'shameful' moral and political positions in the past are neu-
      tralized in public history in: B. Henkes, 'De Bezetting revisited'; M. Eickhoff, B. Henkes and
      F. van Vree, 'De verleiding van een grijze geschiedschrijving. Morele waarden in histo-
      rische voorstellingen', Tijdschrift voor Geschiedenis 123: 3 (2010) 322–339.

FIGURE 6.9   Maarten Rens, filming the African Jazz Pioneers during the celebration of the end
of the Netherlands Anti-Apartheid Movement. Amsterdam, October 1994.

ever changing South African society. At the same time the post-apartheid interviews show that these 'new' narratives by which the acceptance of Apartheid in the past is explained, aim to 'pacify' the controversies, without disman-
tling the deep assumption that Whiteness and European culture was and still
is the main indicator of 'civilization' in general.[70] The study of transnational
kinship networks helps to create a critical space for exploring the intersection
of different political discourses, and provide insights into the interactions by
which the 'abnormality' of a fundamentally unjust system called Apartheid
could be sustained as the 'normality' of everyday life for such a long time by so
many inside and outside South Africa.

---

70   Hall, *Civilising Subjects*, 7.

Epilogue

'Do you know there are Jews in our family?' Freek Henkes asked me the day we met for the first time.[1] Like many children whose parents were involved in the Dutch National-Socialist Movement (NSB), he identified with Jewish victims of National Socialism. No, I knew nothing about Jewish relatives. As far as I could tell, no such family connections had affected the stories and sensitivities I grew up with. I was certainly touched by the collective memory of the Shoah, but I did not want to appropriate that painful history through a family tree with unknown great aunts or other distant relatives. Yet, 'family' – as a category, as a dynamic community, and as an access to stories, knowledge and information – does interest me. As such, family offers and acces to explore how repressive regimes and their racial policies were accepted, supported, legitimised as well as criticised and opposed at the time; and how the protagonists evaluate their attitudes in retrospect.

I have investigated this question by concentrating on six 'cases': six transnational family histories that were marked by National Socialism and Apartheid. This approach was not intended to result in a comparative history, exploring the similarities between the racial policies of both repressive regimes, although the various chapters may invite the reader to make comparisons. Instead, my intention was to move from grand narratives of oppression and resistance to more ambiguous and ambivalent histories, with which to enrich the historiography on doing and undoing race in the twentieth century.

Migration and National Identifications

In my investigation I focused on the process of migration and the reorientations that come with it. Migration acts as a lens through which the significance of race in changing conceptions of the nation-state can be observed. However, to make that dynamic process transparent the personal experiences of individual stakeholders must be taken into account. I explored how various responsibilities and loyalties towards family, nation, and other major ethical obligations towards society and humanity were involved in this process. When concentrating on the nation, historians such as Anderson have already stressed that identification with a national community is an emotional drive that cannot be underestimated in modern history. The family histories presented here

---

1   See the Introduction to this book, 2.

© BARBARA HENKES, 2020 | DOI:10.1163/9789004401600_009

indicate that this identification need not be limited to one nation. When crossing national borders, migrants were and still are stimulated to reflect on their commitment to both their country of origin and their country of residence. A continued connection with the country of origin does not necessarily mean that its government policies can count on their approval. On the contrary, it is precisely with migrants that approval or rejection of the politics of the 'home' country is entangled with their new position in the country of residence. After all, that latter is often seen as the country of their future. We saw this in the narratives of those German migrants who had settled in the Netherlands and distanced themselves from the politics of National Socialism, as well as in the narratives of migrants who had exchanged the Netherlands for South Africa and distanced themselves from Dutch criticism of Apartheid.

Because of their histories of relocation, migrants figure pre-eminently as cultural brokers between the countries of departure and residence. Their exchange of personal observations and experiences with the relatives that stayed behind provide insights into changing constructions of national identities at the interface of two different nations. These changes were unproblematic or even inspiring, as long as the political-moral orientations of the authorities and the populations in both countries ran parallel. How quickly that could change became clear as soon as the Nazis in Germany started to forcibly pursue a strong and 'healthy', exclusively 'Germanic' Third Reich. German migrants in the Netherlands got stuck between Germanness and Dutchness, even if they condemned the Nazi regime. It was all the harder if they continued to cherish the bonds with German relatives who supported the pursuit of a racialised Greater Germanic Empire. Thus, a real or imaginary brother from Germany – in the narratives of Irmgard Brester-Gebensleben and Rie Ton-Seyler – could embody the tension between emotional connection with and aversion to the country of origin.

Dutch migrants in South Africa also found themselves in a complicated position after the cordial relationship between the Netherlands and their new country of residence cooled down. The increasing violence against the Black population in South Africa and the growing anti-Apartheid movements in the Netherlands and worldwide drove the two nations apart. The long-held identification of the Dutch with the White Afrikaner settlers, who were still considered Dutch descendants (*stamverwant*), gradually gave way to a more critical stance. In the Netherlands this process of disidentification was accompanied by a new form of identification, or 'solidarity' as it was then called, with South African Blacks and their pursuit of an inclusive, multiracial society. For their part, Dutch migrants in South Africa rarely questioned the racial order in which they had been implicated since their arrival and which had brought them prosperity. In addition to the many privileges that came with the racial divide, their acceptance of racial inequality was promoted by the mobilization of colonial and racist narratives and images with which they were raised in the Netherlands; the 'cultural archive', as it is refered to the Introduction to this book.

This observation is not meant as a licence to indemnify the people involved from political and moral responsibility, nor is it intended to nail the protagonists down to their Dutch Whiteness. It should, however, be seen as an incitement to examine how Dutch immigrants in Apartheid South Africa as well as German immigrants in the Nazi-occupied Netherlands, and their relatives, can be approached as 'implicated subjects'. This notion of Michael Rothberg's, introduced before, allows us to explore 'a new category of historical responsibility' applicable to a 'range of differentially situated subjects', who were part of a violently racialised past – violence that they may or may not have experienced themselves, and which from a contemporary point of view might seem distant.[2] Rather than predetermining Jews and Gentiles, or Blacks, Whites and Coloureds, as victims, perpetrators or so-called 'bystanders', it seems more fruitful to think about their narrations as a result of specific and inherently dynamic subject positions that arose in the context of racial and national policies.[3]

With my choice to concentrate on 'Gentile' and 'White' experiences and perspectives I wanted to show how histories of racial exclusion cannot be written without taking the 'privileged' into account. Yet, at the same time I am aware of the undeniable asymmetry involved in the different subject positions and questions of identifications and national belongings, a situation all the more lopsided because it is precisely the 'privileged' and their relatives who had the space and self-awareness to privately store and save the kind of ego documents needed for this research project. Their kinship networks figured as a repository for the revealing and detailed stories necessary to discern the dynamics of a 'universe of obligation': to follow the changing subject positions that reinforce, mitigate, domesticate, and render acceptable (or not) the extreme oppression and dehumanising of groups of people on the basis of 'race'.

---

2   Rothberg, 'Trauma Theory', 4.

3   Jacob Dlamini, *Askari. A story of collaboration and betrayal in the anti-apartheid struggle* (Johannesburg: Jacana media, 2014), offers an impressive example of these dynamics. The subtitle does not do justice to this complex history of former ANC fighters who started to collaborate with their captors, because it actually challenges the limits of our knowledge and understanding of betrayal – and also because Dlamini poses questions about how memories remain in the shadow of a dominant narrative of South Africa's past.

Implicated in Racial Exclusion

The mobilization of existing fears of the racialised Other was a crucial element of dehumanisation in the acceptance of a racial order, or the run-up to it. After identifying certain people as a fixed group and representing them as a serious threat to the national community and the well-being of society, measures were taken to make them recognisable as such. If they were not immediately identified by their physical features, they were forced to wear visible signs on their clothing, they were provided with specific identity papers, and subjected to forced relocations to separate residential areas. These and many other humiliating measures made sure that exchanges with the rest of the population became more and more restricted to asymmetric 'contact zones', which strengthened negative representations – and therefore fears – of the Other. How smoothly that process could be implemented is shown by the way Jews in Germany, and also in the Netherlands, once made recognizable by a yellow star, were allocated limited space, became isolated from the non-Jewish population, and were then taken prisoner and deported. With the Jewish refugees from Germany, antisemitism resurfaced in the prewar Netherlands, stimulated by the government that portrayed them as a threat to economic prosperity and the national 'character' (*volkskarakter*). Non-Jews began to look at 'the' Jews as a separate group, and a 'strange element' within the nation.[4]

Ensel and Gans concluded earlier that the process of identifying Jews (including those who personally did not identify themselves as such) and singling them out as a target group in pre-war Germany, started to affect Jews in the Netherlands before the German Nazi occupation even began. Under pressure from the Nazi regime in the occupied Netherlands, contacts between Jews and Gentiles disintegrated more and more. With that divide mutual identifications and feelings of responsibility were alleviated – or postponed to much later. Despite the existing 'othering' of Jews in Dutch society, a vast majority of the population rejected the exclusion and deportation of Jews, if only because these measures had been imposed by a hostile power. This nationalist paradox was best expressed in the often-quoted slogan 'Keep *your* dirty hands off *our* dirty Jews'. (*'Blijf met je rotpoten van onze rotjoden af'*), said to have been uttered during the only openly organised protest against the prosecution of the Jews, in February 1941. Substantial resistance against the racist exclusion and persecution of Jewish fellow countrymen and Jews who had fled from Germany only

---

4   Ensel and Gans, 'The Dutch Bystander', 113.

started much later – too late, when most of them had already been put to death and Nazism was on the losing hand.[5]

The history of the Gebensleben family in Germany reflects how the antisemitic rhetoric of National Socialism hooked up with German nationalism. It is also clear that, despite her criticism of anti-Jewish measures and her involvement in hiding a Jewish child, Irmgard Brester-Gebensleben became implicated in antisemitic policies when advising her non-Jewish brother to distance himself from his 'partly'-Jewish fiancée in Nazi Germany. While many Dutch Gentiles could still ignore the antisemitic persecution after Nazi Germany had invaded the Netherlands, this was impossible for the Plaut-Witte family. With their marriage, which probably saved Lukas's life, the fate of the Jews also became an inevitable part of the biography of his non-Jewish wife Stien. She remembers various forms of support, both during and after the war, but these did not alleviate her and Lukas's existential loneliness in the shadow of the Shoah. The 'accommodation' and therefore implication of the majority of the Dutch population, who had not publicly refused to accept the antisemitic measures, remained a festering wound in their lives. Stien Plaut's dismay about this failure was not directed against anybody in particular; it was the inability to act on the part of Dutch society as a whole that troubled her.

This complicity of Dutch society also returns in the narrative of Mrs. Ton-Seyler, when she expresses her contempt for the many Dutch people 'who turned around' and allied themselves with the Nazi regime: 'you don't have to be a hero, but you can still remain decent'. Although she herself was involved in some form of opposition to nazi policies, she blames herself afterwards for being part of the majority who did not stick out its neck for their Jewish fellow citizens. Afterwards Mrs. Ton explains that she, precisely because she was a German immigrant, wanted to contribute to the resistance against Nazi oppression. Her urge to show loyalty to the recipient country, along with her revulsion at the inhumanities of National Socialism, at times led to activities at the expense of her husband's nerves and the family household. Those feelings of responsibility were stronger than Mr. Ton's appeal to her responsibilities as a mother and wife.

The Dutch Mrs. Beusekom had a different assessment of her responsibilities in Apartheid South Africa. At the forefront of her decisions was her concern for the status and good name of the family, which meant she focussed on the 'White world' in her immediate surroundings. Her criticism of the Apartheid regime in South Africa limited itself to the frictions between sections of the

---

5   J.C.H. Blom, 'De vervolging van de joden in Nederland in internationaal perspectief', in Idem, *Crisis, Bezetting en Herstel*, 134–150.

White population; all the more so because the nationalistic politics of the Afrikaner authorities did not favour her husband's career opportunities. The world of the Black population was and remained a 'foreign country' for her, on the other side of the colour line. Her first awkward observations about racial inequality were discarded almost immediately after arriving in Pretoria. Following colonial representations in the Netherlands about the 'dark continent' and in accordance with the prevailing narrative about the uncivilized and unreliable Blacks, the racial divide in the recipient country was internalized and legitimized in her letters. Also, dealing with the Black domestic staff would not bridge that divide – on the contrary, the closeness strengthened the fears she already had: fear of being infected by her Black subordinates, fear of theft by Black passers-by, and especially her gendered fear of sexual violence by the anonymous Black male body.

The White settlers' fear of Africans (the so-called 'black peril') is a constant in colonial history. At the same time, the consistent violence against the Black body exerted by a White settler minority, from the moment they set foot on African land and occupied the continent, was ignored.[6] Structural colonial violence was continued and expanded by the Apartheid regime in the second half of the twentieth century. Fear of violent Blacks is a recurring theme in the narratives of Dutch migrants and their descendants. Only in the exceptional dialogue that took place in Amsterdam between Sylvia Huisman, born and raised in South Africa as a daughter of Dutch migrants, and the ANC-activist Barbara Masakele, did the latter place the White fear of Blacks in a context of the constant, structural violence exerted by Whites against Blacks.

As long as the Dutch stayed in their country at the North Sea, White supremacy was seldom articulated in daily interactions, although it was very much present in history writing, stories of those who returned from the colonies, children's books and songs, literature, the arts, toys and *bric-à-brac*.[7] Dutch migrants' narratives show how all kinds of degrading stereotypes about Blacks, and the idea of an essential racial divide, had been internalized before they had even left for South Africa. Prior to the life-changing event of emigration, the 'cultural archive' with its many colonial representations was opened, and after arrival in South Africa was never closed again. Still, it was not at all certain how the texts and images from that cultural archive would function and could change meaning in the course of time. That depended on the

---

6   Violence against the Black body is also central to the powerful and passionate vision on the history and actuality of another settler society, the United States, presented by Ta-Nehisi Coates, *Between the world and me* (Melbourne: The Test Publishing Compagny, 2015).

7   Neederveen Pieterse, *White on Black*. See also the Introduction to this book, n. 27.

dynamics within the biographical trajectory in relation to the different domains in which race was done and undone. These dynamics ranged from the
acceptance and rejection of political measures enforced by the government, to
the negotiations within social communities (such as the family, work or the
church) with which newcomers identified themselves, as the Val-Dusseljee
history also show.

Touching Tales

In contrast to the Dutch migrants in South Africa, who ran the risk of exclusion and social isolation if they spoke out against Apartheid, their relatives in
the Netherlands were more and more encouraged to express their criticism
from the 1960s onwards. In April 1960, many Dutch were startled by the news
about the extreme police action against unarmed Black protesters at Sharpeville. With the moral indignation that came with it, the Dutch image of South
Africa began to tilt: 'Sunny' South Africa became 'bloody' South Africa. This
shift was not unrelated to the memories of the Second World War in the Netherlands. The postwar nationalist narrative about 'the' resistance of 'the' Dutch
against 'the' German enemy gradually made way for the realization that 'the'
Dutch had failed to protect Jewish nationals and refugees from antisemitic
persecutions.
    In the course of the 1960s people began to realise how little resistance there
had been to the introduction of ever-increasing antisemitic measures, and
how easily those who were classified as Jews had been marginalized, isolated,
prosecuted and ultimately killed. This inability to prevent the dramatic fate of
Jewish neighbours, friends, colleagues and fellow countrymen who had disappeared from the Dutch streets forever, was decisive for the mobilization of the
protests against contemporary racial repression and exclusion. The memory of
the failing response to the persecution of the Jews started to haunt Dutch society. This memory appeared to have been a strong motor for keen protests
against Apartheid policies in South Africa and the support of other independence movements across the world. Because exclusion and repression on the
basis of 'race' were central to the Apartheid regime, the Dutch Anti-Apartheid
Movement (AABN) was able to make rhetorical use of stories and images that
referred to the antisemitic persecution of Jews under National Socialism.
    The Anti-Apartheid Movement thus touched an open nerve in Dutch soci-
ety that had been there since the 1960s. The reporting of international trials of
Nazi war criminals in the media, the representations of the mass deportation
and murder of Jews in film, documentary, literature and historiography all

contributed to this sensitivity in Dutch memory culture. At the same time, the reports of repression, exclusion and murder in South Africa and other parts of the world drew memories of violent persecution by the Nazi regime into the limelight again. In line with Michael Rothberg's 'multidirectional memory' we could say that there were synergies in which awareness of one event increased attentiveness to other, often only remotely related events.[8]

This kind of synergy, however, did not apply to the memory culture in South Africa. Most Dutch who shortly after the Second World War migrated to this country continued to remember 'the War' in terms of hunger and heroic national resistance against the German enemy. They did not feel challenged by postwar discomfort about the inability to act against antisemitic racism during the Nazi occupation. The painful memory of Jews who had been murdered was not part of the South African memory culture around the Second World War. Despite South Africa's participation on the Allied side, the collective memory of this episode moved in a different direction, if only because a substantial part of the Afrikaner Nationalists, including some of the Nationalist authorities in the Apartheid regime, had identified themselves with Nazi Germany and its antisemitism.[9] The synergy that in the Netherlands brought the narratives about the exclusion of Jews in Europe and of Blacks in Southern Africa together, was absent. For most Dutch migrants the racism of the Nazi's and the South African government were worlds apart, as far as they were able and willing to recognize the racism inherent in Apartheid policies. Their Dutch colonial legacy promoted the acceptance of racial inequality as a necessary 'evil' or an obvious 'good', and to deny racism as such.

Bringing together a range of narratives concerning how racial exclusion policies in six transnational family histories were negotiated, helps to clarify how the legacy of Dutch colonialism and the Shoah shaped the perception of Apartheid policies. It also worked the other way round: the exclusion of people of colour by the Apartheid regime prompted painful memories of Dutch inability to oppose racial policies and racist exclusion. The concepts of 'touching tales' and 'multidirectional memory' helped me to ascertain how Dutch memory culture and shared narratives of the violence of racial repression during National Socialism were fed, and in turn nourished a broad-based emotional involvement in the anti-Apartheid movement. In that sense, this book ties in with a 'colonial turn' in Dutch historiography. In this perspective, memories of racial violence in twentieth century Europe can no longer be seen separately

---

8   Rothberg, *Multidirectional Memory*. See also the Introduction of this book.
9   Henkes, 'Shifting Identities'.

from the colonial history and the racial order that European nations installed elsewhere – and which returned to Europe like a boomerang.[10]

In the Netherlands, since the 1960s the nationalist-driven idea of '*stamverwantschap*' with the White Afrikaners gave way to a sense of solidarity with the political opposition to the Afrikaner Apartheid regime. But that solidarity, too, was not entirely unrelated to the notion of '*stamverwantschap*' in its historical (not genealogical) meaning: there was a sense of complicity in racist violence because of the Dutch colonial involvement that led to a desire for '*Wiedergutmachung*' (reparation), as Mrs. Ton-Seyler so aptly expressed with an anachronistic metaphor for her own personal involvement in the resistance movement against National Socialism. Her statement and other observations and evaluations, written down or told within the context of the family histories above, show the importance of understanding the personal roots of investment in and against oppressive ideas and practices of racial exclusion.

---

10   Arendt, *The Origins*. See also the Introduction to this book, n. 4.

Bibliography

Aalders, G., *Prins Bernhard 1911–2014. Niets was wat het leek* (Amsterdam: Boom, 2014).

Abrams, L., *Oral History Theory* (New York: Routledge, 2010).

Adelson, L.A., *The Turkish Turn in German Literature* (New York: Palgrave Macmillan, 2005).

Aerts, M., 'Het persoonlijke is politiek. Een poging tot herdenken' in: *Dilemma's van het feminisme, Te Elfder Ure* 39 (1986) 78–107.

Aerts, M., 'De brieven Tan-Schepers - een unieke collectie, maar waarom precies?': http://brieven-tan-schepers.nl/index.php/artikelen/item/703-de-brieven-tan-sch epers-eenunieke-collectie-maar-waarom-precies.

Anderson, B., *Imagined Communities. Reflections on the Origin and Spread of Nationalism*, Revised Edition (London/New York: Verso, 2006).

Arendt, H., *The Origins of Totalitarianism* (Cleveland: The World Publishing Company, 1958 (2nd enlarged edition).

Bailey, A., 'White Talk' as a Barrier to Understanding the Problem with Whiteness', in: George Yancy (ed.), *What Is It Like To Be a White Problem?* (Lanham, MD: Lexington Books, 2015).

Baldwin, J., 'Stranger in the village', in: James Baldwin, *Notes of a Native Son* (Boston: Beacon Press, 1955).

Baldwin, J., *The Fire Next Time* (New York, Dial Press, 1963).

Bas, W.G. de, *Gedenkboek Oranje-Nassau-Mecklenburg Lippe-Biesterfeld. Uitgegeven ter gelegenheid van het huwelijk van H.K.H. prinses Juliana met Z.D.H. prins Bernhard* (Amsterdam: Van Holkema en Warendorf, 1937).

Berger, S., 'On taboos, Traumas and Other Myths: Why the debate about German Victims of the Second World War is not a Historians Controversy', in: B. Niven (ed.), *Germans as Victims. Remembering the Past in Contemporary Germany* (New York/ Basingstoke: Palgrave Macmillan 2006) 210–224.

Berghuis, C., *Joodse vluchtelingen in Nederland, 1938–1940: documenten betreffende toelating, uitleiding en kampopname* (Kampen: J.H. Kok, 1990).

Berkel, K. van, *Academische Illusies. De Groningse universiteit in een tijd van crisis, bezetting en herstel, 1930–1950* (Amsterdam: Uitgeverij Bert Bakker, 2005).

Bhaba, H.K., 'Foreword: remembering Fanon. Self, Psyche and the Colonial Condition', in: F. Fanon, *Black Skin, White Masks* (Londen: Pluto Press, 1986) vii–xxvi.

Bijl, P.A.L., *Emerging memory: photographs of colonial atrocity in Dutch cultural remembrance* (D.Phil. thesis, University of Utrecht, 2011).

Blaauw, A., 'Leven en werk van Lukas Plaut', in: *Zenit* 11 (Apr. 1985) 152–153.

Bloem, H., *Een Hollandse familie in zonnig Zuid-Afrika* (Amsterdam: J.H. de Bussy, 1949).

Blok, E., *Loonarbeid van vrouwen 1945–1955* (Nijmegen: Uitgeverij SUN, 1978).

Blom, J.C.H., *Crisis, Bezetting en Herstel. Tien studies over Nederland 1930–1950* (Den Haag: University Press Rotterdam, 1989).

Boer, S. de, 'Nederland en de apartheidskwestie, 1948–1990', in: M. Kuitenbrouwer en M. Leenders (red.), *Geschiedenis van de mensenrechten. Bouwstenen voor een interdisciplinaire benadering* (Hilversum: Verloren, 1996) 259–280.

Boer, S. de, *Van Sharpeville tot Soweto. Nederlands regeringsbeleid ten aanzien van apartheid, 1960–1977* (Den Haag: Sdu Publishers, 1999).

Bogaarts, M.D., 'Weg met de Moffen'. De uitwijzing van Duitse ongewenste vreemdelingen uit Nederland na 1945', *Bijdragen en Mededelingen betreffende de Geschiedenis der Nederlanden/Low Countries Historical Review* (hereafter: *BMGN/LCHR*) 96: 2 (1981) 334 – 351.

Boom, B. van der, *Wij weten niets van hun lot. Gewone Nederlanders en de Holocaust* (Amsterdam: Boom, 2012).

Bosma, M., *Minderheid in eigen land - Hoe progressieve strijd ontaardt in genocide en ANC-apartheid* (Amsterdam: Bibliotheca Africana Formicae, 2015).

Bosscher, D., *Om de erfernis van Colijn. De ARP op de grens van twee werelden 1939 – 1952* (Alphen a/d Rijn: Kluwer, 1980).

Bossenbroek, M., *Holland op zijn breedst. Indië en Zuid-Afrika in de Nederlandse cultuur omstreeks 1900* (Amsterdam: Bert Bakker, 1996).

Bossenbroek, M., *De Meelstreep. Terugkeer en opvang na de Tweede Wereldoorlog* (Amsterdam: Bert Bakker, 2001).

Brown, B.B., 'Facing the 'Black Peril': The Politics of Population Control in South Africa', *Journal of Southern African Studies* 13:3 (1987) 256–273.

Brown, M. and A. Stanton, 'Governance of the public health sector during Apartheid: the case of South Africa', in: *Journal of Governance and Regulation* 5: 1 (2016) 23–30.

Bunting, B., *The Rise of the South African Reich* (n.p.: IDAF, 1986).

Buttler, J., *Excutable Speech: a politics of the performative* (New York: Routledge, 1997).

Clingman, S., *Bram Fischer. Afrikaner revolutionary* (Amherst: University of Massachusetts Press, 1998).

Coates, T., *Between the world and me* (Melbourne: The Test Publishing Compagny, 2015).

Cock, J., *Maids and Madams. A study in the Politics of Exploitation.* (Johannesburg: Ravan Press, 2001).

Cock, P. de, *Radio Freedom: de stem van het verzet* (Amsterdam: AABN, 1987).

Conway, J.K., *When memory speaks. Exploring the Arts of Autobiography* (New York: Vintage Books, 1999).

Cornwell, D.G.N., 'George Webb Hardy's The Black Peril and the social meaning of "Black Peril" in early Twentieth-Century South Africa', *Journal of Southern African Studies* 22: 3 (1996) 441–453.

Cottaar, A., *Zusters uit Suriname: naoorlogse belevenissen in de Nederlandse verpleging* (Amsterdam: Meulenhoff, 2003).

Dam, P. van, *Staat van verzuiling: over een Nederlandse mythe* (Amsterdam: Wereldbibliotheek, 2011).

Dankaart, H., J.J. Flinterman, F. Groot en R. Vuurmans, *De oorlog begon in Spanje. Nederlanders in de Spaanse burgeroorlog 1936–1939* (Amsterdam: Uitgeverij van Gennep, 1986).

Dietz, B., H. Gabel and U. Tiedau (Hrs.), *Griff nach dem Westen. Die 'Westforschung' der völkisch-nationalen Wissenschaften zum nordwesteuropäischen Raum (1919–1960)* (Münster: Waxmann, 2003).

Dlamini, J., *Askari. A story of collaboration and betrayal in the anti-apartheid struggle* (Johannesburg: Jacana media, 2014).

Dobson, M., 'Letters', in: Mariam Dobson and Benjamin Ziemann (eds.), *Reading Primary Sources, The interpretation of texts from the nineteenth and twentieth-century history* (London/New York: Routledge, 2009) 57–73.

Dubow, S., *Scientific Racism in modern South Africa* (Cambridge/New York: Cambridge University Press, 1995).

Dubow, S., *A Commonwealth of Knowledge: Science, Sensibility and White South Africa 1820–2000* (Oxford: Oxford University Press, 2006).

Eickhoff, M., B. Henkes and F. van Vree, 'De verleiding van een grijze geschiedschrijving. Morele waarden in historische voorstellingen', *Tijdschrift voor Geschiedenis* 123, 3 (2010), 322–339.

Elich, J.H., *Aan de ene kant, aan de andere kant. De emigratie van Nederlanders naar Australië 1946–1986* (Delft: Eburon, 1987).

Ellermann, A., 'Discrimination in migration and citizenship', *Journal of Ethnic and Migration Studies*, 45 (2019).

Ensel, R. and E. Gans, 'The Dutch Bystander as Non-Jew and Implicated Subject', in: Christina Morina and Krijn Thijs (eds.), *Probing the Limits of Categorization: The Bystander in Holocaust History* (New York/Oxford: Berghahn, 2018) 107–127.

Es, H.J. van, 'Breukelen in oorlogstijd', *Tijdschrift Historische kring Breukelen*, 10: 2 (1995), 67–92.

Faassen, M. van, "Min of meer misbaar. Naoorlogse emigratie vanuit Nederland: achtergronden en organisatie, particuliere motieven en overheidsprikkels, 1946–1967,' in: S. Poldervaart et al., *Van hot naar her. Nederlandse migratie vroeger, nu en morgen.* (Amsterdam: Stichting beheer IISG, 2001) 50–67.

Faassen, M. van, 'Vrouwen in den vreemde: emigratievoorlichting door het Nederlandse Vrouwen Comité', *Spiegel historiael: maandblad voor geschiedenis en archeologie*, 37: 7–8 (2002) 325–329.

Fanon, Franz, *Black Skin, White Masks* (London: Pluto Press, 1986).

Fasseur, C., *Juliana & Bernhard. Het verhaal van een huwelijk. De jaren 1936–1956* (Amsterdam: Balance Sheet, 2008).

Fein, H., *Accounting for Genocide: National Responses and Jewish Victimization during the Holocaust* (Chicago: University of Chicago Press, 1984).

Fontijn, J., 'Over radicale bekeringen en plotselinge inzichten', *Biografie Bulletin* 11: 1 (2001) 97–106.

Fontijn, J., 'Nogmaals keerpunten in een leven. Identificatie of objectivering', *Biografie Bulletin* 11:1 (2001) 224–229.

Fredrickson, G.M., *Racism: A Short History* (Princeton: Princeton University Press, 2015).

Friedman, S.S., *No haven for the oppressed: United States policy toward Jewish refugees, 1938–1945* (Detroit: Wage State University Press, 1973).

Frijtag Drabbe Kunzel, G von, *Hitler's Brudervolk - The Dutch and the Colonization of Occupied Eastern Europe, 1939–1945* (New York: Routledge, 2017).

Fritzsche, P., 'Preface', in: Hedda Kalshoven-Brester (ed.), *Between two Homelands: Letters across the Borders of Nazi Germany* (Chicago: University of Illinois Press, 2014) ix-xix.

Fröhlich, E. (ed.), *Tagebücher von Joseph Goebbels. Sämtliche Fragmente I, Aufzeichnungen 1923–1941* ii (Munich: De Gruyter, 2000).

Fugard, A., 'The Blood Knot'. *Three Port Elizabeth Plays* (London: Oxford UP, 1974).

Gans, E., '"Vandaag hebben ze niets - maar morgen bezitten ze weer tien gulden." Antisemitische stereotypen in bevrijd Nederland', in: Conny Kristel (red.), *Polderschouw. Terugkeer en opvang na de Tweede Wereldoorlog. Regionale verschillen* (Amsterdam: Uitgeverij Bert Bakker, 2002) 313–353.

Gans, E., *Jaap en Ischa Meijer. Een joodse geschiedenis 192–1956*. Amsterdam: Uitgeverij Bert Bakker, 2008).

Gans, E., 'The Jew as dubious victim', in: Remco Ensel and Evelien Gans (eds.), *The Holocaust*, Israel and 'the Jew'. *Histories of Antisemitism in Postwar Dutch Society* (Amsterdam: Amsterdam University Press, 2017) 62–81.

Gelbin, C.S. and S.L. Gilman, *Cosmopolitanisms and the Jews* (Ann Arbor: University of Michigan Press, 2017).

Geljon, P.A., *Een Nederlandse Overzeebank. De Nederlandsche Bank voor Zuid-Afrika, 1888 – 1969* (Amsterdam: Boom uitgevers, 2017).

Gerber, D.A., *Authors of Their lives. The Personal Correspondence of British immigrant to North America in the Nineteenth Century* (New York: New York University Press, 2006).

Gerding, M., 'Fliegerhorst Havelte, het vliegveld dat niet van de grond kwam' in: themanummer 'Landschap in de Tweede Wereldoorlog', *Noorderbreedte* 29:5 (2005) 10–11.

Giliomee, H., *The Afrikaners. Biography of a people* (Cape Town: Tafelberg, 2003).

Gillis, J.R. (ed.), *Commemorations. The Politics of National Identity* (Princeton: Princeton University Press, 1996).

Gillis, J.R., *A World of their Own Making. Myth, Ritual and the Quest for Family Values* (Cambridge: Harvard University Press, 1997).

Graaff, B.J.H. de, *De mythe van de stamverwantschap. Nederland en de Afrikaners, 1902–1930* (PhD Vrije Universiteit Amsterdam: 1993).

Graaff, B. de, 'De Nederlandse publieke opinie over apartheid 1948–1963: van begrip tot verwerping', *International Spectator 39* (november 1985) 679–685.

Graaff, B. de and L. Markus, *Kinderwagens en Korsetten* (Amsterdam: Bert Bakker, 1980).

Groskamp-ten Have, A., *Hoe hoort het eigenlijk?* (4th ed.) (Amsterdam: Publishing House H.J.W. Becht, 1940).

Guelke, A., *Rethinking the Rise and Fall of Apartheid. South Africa and World Politics* (New York: Palgrave, 2005).

Hack, H., "Dutch Group Settlement in Brazil", in: *Research Group For European Migration Problems* 7: 4 (1969) 9.

Hall, C., *Civilising Subjects. Metropole and Colony in the English Imagination 1830–1867* (Chicago /London: University of Chicago Press, 2002).

Hall, S., 'The Multi-Cultural Question', in: B. Hesse (ed.), *Un/Settled Multiculturalism: Diasporas, Entanglements, 'Transruptions'* (London: Zed, 2001), 209–241.

Hareven, T.K., *Families, History, and Social Change. Life-Course and Cross-Cultural Perspectives* (Boulder: Westview Press, 1999).

Hartland, J.A.A., *De geschiedenis van de Nederlandse emigratie tot de Tweede Wereldoorlog* (Den Haag: Departement van Sociale Zaken en Volksgezondheid, 1959).

Hastrup, K., 'Anthropological Visions, some notes on visual and textual authority', in: I. Crawford and D. Turton (eds.), *Film as ethnography* (Manchester/New York: Manchester University Press, 1992).

Henkes, B. and B. Rzoska, 'Volkskunde und "Volkstumpolitik" der SS in den Niederlanden. H.E. Schneider und seine "Grossgermanischen" Ambitions für den Niederländischen Raum' in: H. Dietz, H. Gabel and U. Tiedau (Hrs.), *Griff nach dem West. Die 'Westforschung' der völkisch-nationalen Wissenschaften zum nordwesteuropäischen Raum (1919–1960)* (Munster: Waxmann, 2003) 291–323.

Henkes, B. and H. Oosterhof, *Kaatje ben je boven? Leven en werken van Nederlandse dienstbodes* (Nijmegen: SUN, 1985).

Henkes, B., 'Levensgeschiedenis om het verleden van huis uit te leren kennen', *IPSO cahier 6. Over de geschiedenis van de CPN* (1981) 110–118.

Henkes, B., 'Changing images of German maids during the inter-war period in the Netherlands: from trusted help to traitor in the nest'. In R. Samuel and P. Thompson (eds.), *The Myths We Live By* (London/New York: Routledge: 1990) 225–238.

Henkes, B, *Heimat in Holland. Duitse dienstmeisjes 1920–1950* (Amsterdam: Babylon De Geus, 1995).

Henkes, B., 'De tweede schuld, of over de last familie te zijn. Nationaalsocialisme en de overdracht van historische ervaringen binnen familieverband', in: N.D.J. Barnouw, et al. (red.), *Tiende Jaarboek van het Nederlands Instituut voor Oorlogsdocumentatie* (Amsterdam: NIOD/Walburg Pers, 1999) 89–113.

Henkes, B., 'Gedeeld Duits-zijn aan de Maas. Gevestigd *Deutschtum* en Duitse nieuwkomers in de jaren 1900–1940' in: P. van der Laar et al. (red.), *Vier eeuwen migratie, bestemming Rotterdam* (Rotterdam: MondiTaal Publishing, 1998) 218–139.

Henkes, B., 'Het vuil, de sterren en de dood'. Lucas Plaut en Stien Witte: portret van een 'gemengd' huwelijk, in: C. van Eijl et al. (red.), *Jaarboek voor Vrouwengeschiedenis 18: Parallelle Levens* (Amsterdam: Stichting beheer IISG, 1998) 91–116.

Henkes, B., 'Familiegoed', series of columns, *Historisch Nieuwsblad* (1998–2000).

Henkes, B., 'Maids on the move. Images of femininity and European women's labour migration during the interwar years', in: P. Sharpe (ed.) *Women, Gender and Labour Migration. Historical and global Perspectives* (London/New York: Routledge, 2001) 224–243.

Henkes, B., '"Mag ons daarop'n Toekoms bou?" Transnationale identificaties in en door brieven tussen Nederland en Zuid-Afrika, 1946–1952', *Tijdschrift voor Sociale en Economische Geschiedenis* 7: 3 (2010) 56–86.

Henkes, B., 'De Bezetting revisited. Hoe van De Oorlog een "normale" geschiedenis werd gemaakt die eindigt in vrede', *BMGN/LCHR* 125: 1 (2010) 73–99.

Henkes, B., 'German Maids in the Netherlands in the Interwar Period', in: K.J. Bade, P.C. Emmer, L. Lucassen and J. Oltmer (eds.), *The Encyclopedia of Migration and Minorities in Europe. From the 17th Century to the Present Cambridge* (Cambridge: Cambridge University Press, 2011) 419–420.

Henkes, B., 'Letter-Writing and the Construction of a transnational Family: A Private Correspondence between the Netherlands and Germany, 1920–1949', in: M. Huisman et al. (eds.) *Life Writing Matters in Europe* (Heidelberg Universitätsverlag Winter, 2012) 177–192.

Henkes, B., '"Hausmädchenheimschaffung" aus den Niederlanden. Gender, "Volksgemeinschaft" und Migrationsregime in der Zwischenkriegszeit', in: J. Oltmer (Hrg.), *Nationalsozialistische Migrationsregime und 'Volksgemeinschaft* (Paderborn: Verlag Ferdinand Schöningh, 2012) 205–217.

Henkes, B., 'Negotiating the '(Ab)normality' of (Anti-) Apartheid: Transnational Relations within a Dutch-South African Family', *South African Historical Journal*, 65:4 (2013) 526–554.

Henkes, B., 'Shifting Identifications in Dutch-South African Migration Policies (1910–1961)', *South African Historical Journal*, 68:4 (2016) 641–669.

Henkes, B., 'De Britten, de Zwarten en de Joden in twintigste eeuws Zuid-Afrika', in: R. Ensel (red.), *Sjacheren met stereotypen. Essays over "de Jood" als sjabloon* (Amsterdam: Het Menasseh ben Israel Instituut, Studies No. XII, 2016) 85–89.

Henkes, B., C. Dullemond and J. Kennedy, 'Inleiding', in: C. Dullemond, B. Henkes and J. Kennedy (red.), *'Maar we wisten ons door de Heer geroepen'. Kerk en apartheid in transnationaal perspectief* (Hilversum: Verloren, 2017) 7–22.

Henkes, B., 'Turbulent Kinship: the Dutch and South Africa', in: Martine Gosselink, Maria Holtrop, Robert Ross (eds.), *Good Hope? South Africa and the Netherlands from 1600* (Amsterdam/Nijmegen: Rijksmuseum Amsterdam/Uitgeverij Vantilt, 2017), 279–291.

Henkes, B., '*Stamverwantschap* and the Imagination of a White, Transnational Community'. The 1952 Celebrations of the Jan van Riebeecks Tercentanary in the Netherlands and South Africa', in G. Blok, V. Kuitenbrouwer and C. Weeda (eds.), *Imagining Communities. Historical Reflections on the Process of Community Formation* (Amsterdam: Amsterdam University Press, 2018) 173–195.

Herzberg, A.J., 'Kroniek der jodenvervolging', in: *Onderdrukking en verzet. Nederland in oorlogstijd*, Vol. 3 (Amsterdam: J.M. Meulenhoff, 1949) 44–49.

Heuvel, H. van den en G. Mulder, *Het vrije woord: de illegale pers in Nederland 1940–1945* (Den Haag: SDU, 1990).

Hoek, G.H., *Zuid-Afrika, land van mogelijkheden en contrasten* (Wageningen: Zomer en Keuning, 1948).

Hofstede, B.P., *Twarted Exodus. Post-War Overseas Migration from the Netherlands* (The Hague: Martinus Nijhoff, 1964).

Hogenkamp, B., H. Hosman, H. de Wit (red.), *Direct Cinema, maar soepel en met mate* (Hilversum: Nederlands Instituut voor Beeld en Geluid/VPRO, 2006).

Hondius, D., *Return: Holocaust Survivors and Dutch Anti-semitism* (Westport: Preager/ABC-CLIO, 2003).

Huyse, L., *Alles Gaat Voorbij, Behalve Het Verleden.* (Amsterdam: Van Gennep, 2006).

Jansen, E., *Soos Familie. Stedelike huiswerkers in Suid-Afrikaanse tekste* (Pretoria: Protea Boekhuis, 2015).

Johnson, R., 'Two Ways to Remember. Exploring Memory as Identity', *Nothing bloody stands still. Annual Magazine of the European Network for Cultural and Media Studies* 1 (1991) 26–30.

Jonckheere, W.F., 'Een dilemma van percepties: De tweeling van Tessa de Loo', *Tydskrif vir Nederlands en Afrikaans* 3:1 (1996) 64–73.

Jones, G., *Tussen onderdanen, rijksgenoten en Nederlanders* (Amsterdam: Rozenberg Publishers, 2007).

Jong, L. de, *De Duitse Vijfde Colonne* (Amsterdam: J.M. Meulenhoff, 1953).

Jong, L. de, *Het Koninkrijk der Nederlanden in de Tweede Wereldoorlog*, Vol. 4 ('s Gravenhage: Staatsuitgeverij, 1972).

Jong, L. de, *Het Koninkrijk der Nederlanden in de Tweede Wereldoorlog*, Vol. 6 ('s Gravenhage: Staatsuitgeverij, 1975).

Jong, L. de, *Het Koninkrijk der Nederlanden in de Tweede Wereldoorlog*, Vol. 7 ('s Graven-hage: Staatsuitgeverij, 1976).

Jong, S. de, 'Cultural Brokers in Post-colonial Migration Regimes', Dhawan V,N. et al. (eds.), *Negotiating Normativity* (Cham: Springer International Publishing Switzer-land, 2016).

Joubert, E., *The Long Journey of Poppie Nongena* (Cape Town: Jonathan Ball Publishers, 1980).

Kalshoven-Brester, H. (red.), *Ik denk zoveel aan jullie. Een briefwisseling tussen Neder-land en Duitsland 1920–1949* (Amsterdam: Uitgeverij Contact, 1991).

Kgari-Masondom, C.K., *A Superstitious respect for the soil? Environmental history, social identity and land ownership - a case study of forced removals from Lady Selbourne and their ramifications, c. 1905 to 1977* (PhD Stellenbosch: University of Stellenbosch, 2008).

Klein, M. and H. Klein, *Käthe Kollwitz: Life and Art* (New York: Holt, Rinehart and Win-ston, 1972).

Klemperer, V., *LTI – Lingua Tertii Imperii; Notizbuch eines Philologen* (Berlin: Aufbau, 1946).

Knowles, C., 'Home and Away. Maps of Territorial and Personal Expansion 1860–97', *The European Journal of Women's Studies* 7:3 (2000) 263–280.

Kossmann, E.H., De Tweede Wereldoorlog', in: *Winkler Prins Geschiedenis van de Lage Landen. Volume 3: De Lage Landen van 1780 tot 1970* (Amsterdam/Brussels: Elsevier, 1977) 268–286.

Kuhn, P. and E. Werkman, *Jan van Riebeeck in Zuid-Afrika* (in the series *De avonturen van kapitein Rob*) (Amsterdam: Het Parool, 1952).

Kuitenbrouwer, M., *The Netherlands and the rise of modern imperialism: colonies and foreign policy, 1870–1902* (Oxford: Oxford University Press, 1992).

Lake, M. and H. Reynolds, *Drawing the Global Colour Line. White Men's Countries and the International Challenge of Racial Equality* (Cambridge: Cambridge University Press, 2008).

Leach, M.S. and D.O. Braithwaite, 'A Binding Tie. Supportive communication of family kinkeepers', *Journal of Applied Communication Research* 24:3 (1996), 200–216.

Levine, P. and A. Bashford, 'Introduction: Eugenics and the Modern World' in: A. Bash-ford and P. Levine (eds.), *The Oxford Handbook of the History of Eugenics* (Oxford and New York: Oxford University Press, 2010).

Lijphart, A., in *The Politics of Accommodation. Pluralism and Democracy in the Nether-lands* (Berkeley: University of California Press, 1968).

Locher-Scholten, E., *Ethiek in fragmenten: vijf studies over koloniaal denken en doen van Nederlanders in de Indonesische archipel, 1877–1942* (Utrecht: Hes, 1981).

Locher–Scholten, E., *Women and the Colonial State: Essays on Gender and Modernity in the Netherlands Indies 1900–1942* (Amsterdam: Amsterdam University Press, 2000).

Loedolff, J.K., *Nederlandse immigrante. 'n sociologiese ondersoek van hul inskakeling in die gemeenskapslewe van Pretoria* (Kaapstad/Pretoria: Haum, 1960).

Loo, T. de, *De Tweeling* (Amsterdam: De Arbeiderspers, 1993).

Malik, K., *The Meaning of Race. Race, History and Culture in Western Society* (London: Macmillan, 1996).

Manten, D.A. and H.J. van Es, ' 'Het protestants-christelijk onderwijs in Breukelen en de Tweede Wereldoorlog', *Tijdschrift Historische Kring Breukelen*, 10: 2, (1995), 93–101.

Markus, H.R. and P.M.L. Moya (eds.), *Doing Race: 21 Essays for the 21st Century* (New York: W.W. Norton & Company, 2010).

Marx, C., *Oxwagon Sentinel: Radical Afrikaner Nationalism and the History of the 'Ossewabrandwag'* (Münster: LIT Verlag, 2008).

Mazower, M., *Dark Continent. Europe's twentieth century* (London/New York: Penguin books, 1998).

Mazower, M., *No Enchanted Palace, The End of Empire and the Ideological Origins of the United Nations* (Princeton, Princeton University Press, 2009).

Mechanicus, P., *In Dépôt. Dagboek uit Westerbork* (Amsterdam: Polak & Van Gennep, 1985).

Meijers, E., *Blanke broeders – zwarte vreemden. De Nederlandse Hervormde Kerk, de Gereformeerde Kerken in Nederland en de apartheid in Zuid-Afrika 1948–1972* (Hilversum: Verloren, 2008).

Meijers, E., 'Het zelf en de ander. De gereformeerde synode en de apartheid 1972–1978', in: D. Boer a.o (red.), *Freedom! Oh Freedom! Opstellen voor Theo Witvliet* (Zoetermeer: Uitgeverij Meinema, 2000) 97–110.

Meyer, B., *'Jewish Mischlinge'. Rassenpolitik und Verfolgungserfahrung 1933–1945* (Hamburg: Dölling and Galitz Verlag, 2002).

Morton, F., 'Slavery in the South African Interior During the 19th Century', In: T. Spear (ed.), *Oxford Research Encyclopedia of African History* (Oxford: Oxford University Press, April 2017).

Mulder, P., *'Wij gaan op dezelfde weg Zuid-Afrika!' Het Apartheidsstandpunt van het Gereformeerd Politiek Verbond (1960–1990)* (MA-thesis University of Groningen, 2009).

National Museum of World Cultures (ed.), *Words matter: An Unfinished Guide to Word Choices in the Cultural Sector. Work in progress* (Amsterdam: Troper museum 2018).

Neame, L.E., *White man's Africa: the problem of a white nation in a black continent* (Cape Town: Stewart, 1952).

Neederveen-Pieterse, J., *White on Black. Images of Africa and Blacks in Western Popular Culture* (Yale: Yale University Press, 1995).

Niven, B., 'Introduction: German Victimhood at the Turn of the Millennium', in: B. Niven (ed.), *Germans as Victims. Remembering the Past in Contemporary Germany* (New York: Palgrave/Macmillan, 2006).

Noer, T.J., *Cold War and Black Liberation: The United States and White Rule In Africa 1948–1968* (Colombia: Univ. of Missouri Press, 1985).

Nys, L., H. de Das, J. Tollebeek & K. Wils (red.), *De zieke natie. Over de medicalisering van de samenleving 1860–1914* (Groningen: Historische Uitgeverij, 2002).

Paton, A., *Cry, the Beloved Country* (New York/London: Charles Scribner's Sons and Jonathan Cape 1948).

Peberdy, S., *Selecting immigrants. National Identity and South Africa's Immigration Policies, 1910–2008* (Johannesburg: Wits University Press, 2009).

Pennings, L., *Voortrekkersbloed. De geschiedenis van de Grote Trek der Zuid-Afrikaanse Boeren en van de val van Koning Dingaan van Zoeloeland* (Zwolle: La Rivière & Voorhoeve, 1926).

Perrot, M., 'Het familieleven', in M. Perrot, (ed.) *Geschiedenis van het persoonlijk leven, deel 4. Van de Franse Revolutie tot de Eerste Wereldoorlog* (Amsterdam: Agon, 1989), 163–167.

Pine, L., *Hitler's 'National Community'. Society and Culture in Nazi Germany* (London: Hodder Arnold, 2007).

Plaut, L., *Photografische photometrie der veranderlijke sterren CV Carinae en WW Draconis* (Leiden: Luctor & Emergo, 1939).

Plessis, A.P. du, *Die Nederlandse emigrasie na Suid-Afrika: sekere aspekte rakende voorbereiding tot aanpassing* (PhD University of Utrecht, 1956).

Poel, S. van der, *Joodse stadjers: de joodse gemeenschap in de stad Groningen, 1796–1945* (Assen: Gorkum BV, 2004).

Portelli, A., 'Living Voices: The Oral History Interview as Dialogue and Experience', *The Oral History Review* 45: 2 (Summer/Fall 2018), 239–248.

Pratt, M.L., *Imperial Eyes: Travel Writing and Transculturation* (London /New York: Routledge, 2008).

Preez, M. du, 'ANC could learn from Afrikaners', *The Mercury*, 3 July 2012.

Presser, J., *Ashes in the Wind* (London: Souvenir Press, 2010).

Presser, J., 'Clio kijkt door het sleutelgat', in: J. Presser, *Uit het werk van J. Presser* (Amsterdam: Athenaeum-Polak & Van Gennep, 1969) 283–295.

Pretorius, F., *Kommandolewe tydens die Anglo-Boere Oorlog 1899–1902* (Kaapstad/Johannesburg: Human & Rousseau, 1991).

Regt, A. de, *Arbeidersgezinnen en beschavingsarbeid: ontwikkelingen in Nederland 18701940; een historisch-sociologische studie* (Meppel: Boom, 1984).

Richter, S., *Einblick in ein kunstpädagogisches Skizzenbuch. Leben und Werk von Eva Eyquem* (Erlangen: FAU University Press, 2017).

Ross, J.R., *Escape to Shanghai: A Jewish Community in China.* (New York: The Free Press, 1994).

Rothberg, M., *Multidirectional Memory: Remembering the Holocaust in the Age of Decolonization* (Stanford: Stanford University Press, 2009).

Rothberg, M., 'Trauma Theory, Implicated Subjects, and the Question of Israel/Palestine', on: https://profession.mla.org/trauma-theory-implicated-subjects-and-thequestion-of-israel-palestine/.

Rothberg, M., *The Implicated Subject. Beyond Victims and Perpetrators* (Stanford: Stanford University Press, 2019).

Ruberg, W.G., *Conventional Correspondence. Epistolary Culture of the Dutch elite, 1770–1850* (Leiden: Brill, 2011).

Said, E., *Culture and Imperialism* (London: Vintage, 1993).

Said, E., 'Always on Top', *London Review of Books* 25: 6 (20 Mar. 2003) 3–6.

Schegman, M., *Het stille verzet: vrouwen in illegale organisaties in Nederland 1940–1945* (Amsterdam: SUA, 1980).

Schoot, A. van der, 'Waarom klonk het Horst Wessellied? Op de gala-avond van Juliana en Bernhard, *Historisch Nieuwsblad* 5 (2019).

Schumacher, P., *Voor het vaderland weg. Nederlandse dienstweigeraars in de Tweede Wereldoorlog* (Amsterdam: Van Gennep, 2007).

Schutte, G.J., *Nederland en de Afrikaners. Adhesie en aversie. Over stamverwantschap, Boerenvrienden, Hollanderhaat, Calvinisme en apartheid* (Franeker: T. Wever, 1986).

Schutte, G.J., *Stamverwantschap onder druk. De betrekkingen tussen Nederland en Zuid-Afrika, 1940–1947* (Amsterdam: Zuid-Afrika Instituut, 2011).

Schwartz, B., *The White Men's World. Memories of Empire* (Oxford: Oxford University Press, 2011).

Sintemaartensdijk, J. and Y. Nijland, *Operation Black Tulip. De uitzetting van Duitse burgers na de oorlog* (Amsterdam: Boom, 2009).

Smit, H., *Gezag is gezag... Kanttekeningen bij de houding van de gereformeerden in de Indonesische kwestie* (Hilversum: Verloren, 2006).

Smits, M., *Holambra: geschiedenis van een Nederlandse toekomstdroom in de Braziliaanse werkelijkheid, 1948–1988* (Nijmegen: Katholiek Documentatie Centrum, 1990).

Speerstra, H., *Het wrede paradijs. Het levensverhaal van de emigrant* (Amsterdam/Antwerpen: Atlas/Contact, 2008).

Steyn, M., *Whiteness Just Isn't What it Used to be. White Identity in a changing South Africa* (New York: State University of New York, 2001).

Steyn, M., '"White Talk": White South Africans and the Management of Diasporic Whiteness' in: A.J. Lopez (ed.), *Postcolonial Whiteness: A Critical Reader on Race and Empire* (New York: State University of New York Press, 2005).

Stoler, A.L., 'Colonial Aphasia: Race and Disabled Histories in France', in: *Public Culture* 23: 1 (2011) 121–156.

Stoltzfus, N., *Resistance of the Heart. Intermarriage and the Rosenstrasse Protest in Nazi Germany* (New York/London: Norton & Compagny, 1996).

Stuhldreher, C., *De legale rest. Gemengd gehuwde Joden onder de Duitse bezetting* (Amsterdam: Boom, 2007).

Swaan, A. de, 'Widening Circles of Identification: Emotional Concerns in Sociogenetic Perspective', *Theory, Culture & Society* 12: 2 (1995) 25–39.

Swaisland, C., *Servants and Gentlewomen to the Golden land. The Emigration of Single Women from Britain to Southern Africa, 1820–1993* (Pietermaritsburg: University of Natal Press, 1993).

Thompsell, A., 'Why Was Africa Called the Dark Continent?', updated till 2 July 2019, on: www.thoughtco.com/why-africa-called-the-dark-continent-43310.

Thörn, H., *Anti-Apartheid and the Emergence of a Global Civil Society* (New York/Oxford: Palgrave Macmillan, 2006).

Trapido, S., 'Imperialism, Settler Identities, and Colonial Capitalism: The Hundred Year Origins of the 1899 South African War', in: R. Ross, A. Mager, & B. Nasson (eds.), *The Cambridge History of South Africa* (Cambridge: Cambridge University Press, 2011) 66–101.

Velde, H. te, *Gemeenschapszin en plichtsbesef. Liberalisme en Nationalisme in Nederland, 1870–1918* (Den Haag: SdU, 1992).

Velmans-van Hessen, E., *Edith's story* (New York: Soho Press, 1999).

Verhoef, G., 'Nedbank: The Continental Approach to Banking in South Africa', in: F.S. Jones ed., *Financial Enterprise in South Africa* (London: Macmillan, 1992).

Vestdijk, S., *Else Böhler, Duitsch diensmeisje* (Rotterdam: Nijgh & Van Ditmar, 1935).

Visser, J.B., 'Inleiding', in: *Officieel programma voor de festiviteiten ter gelegenheid van het huwelijk van Hare Koninklijke Hoogheid prinses Juliana en Zijne Doorluchtige Hoogheid Prins Bernhard op 7 januari 1937, gedurende de feestweek 4–9 januari 1937 te Groningen* (n.p., n.d. [Groningen, 1937]).

Visser, J. (red.), *Witte jassen en bruinhemden: Nederlandse artsen in de Tweede Wereldoorlog* (Breda: Reality Bites Publishing 2010).

Vries, Ph. de, *Geschiedenis van het verzet der artsen in Nederland* (Haarlem: Tjeenk Willink, 1949).

Vries, T. de, *Het meisje met het rode haar. Roman uit het verzet 1942–1945.* (Amsterdam: Querido, 1956).

Vroman, L., 'Vrede', *De Gids* 117: 1 (1954) 5–6.

Wekker, G., *White Innocence. Paradoxes of Colonialism and Race* (Durham /London, Duke University Press, 2016).

Wicomb, Z., *Playing in the Light. A Novel* (New York: The New Press, 2008).

Winter, J., 'The performance of the past: memory, history, identity, in: K. Tilmans, F. van Vree en J. Winter (eds.), *Performing the Past. Memory, History and Identity in modern Europe* (Amsterdam: Amsterdam University Press, 2010) 11–23.

Witz, L., *Apartheid's festival: Contesting South Africa's National Pasts* (Bloomington: Indiana University Press, 2003).

Yuval-Davis, N., *Politics of Belonging: Intersectional Contestations* (London: Sage, 2011).

Zerubavel, E., *The Elephant in the Room. Silence and Denial in Everyday Life* (Oxford: Oxford Press, 2006).

Zijl, A. van der, *Bernhard. Een verborgen geschiedenis* (Amsterdam: Querido, 2010).

Websites

https://anderetijden.nl/aflevering/278/Artsen-in-de-oorlog

https://holambra.nl/?page_id=567

https://jinh.lima-city.de/gene/chris/Descendants_of_Abraham_Plaut_from_Willingshausen

https://www.joodsmonument.nl/nl/page/548003/jacob-mozes-van-gelderen

http://www.meertens.knaw.nl/nvb/english

https://www.parlement.com/id/vjw7l4l9u2mt/troonrede_1950_volledige_tekst

https://www.pasteur.fr/infosci/archives/f-bio.html

https://www.spanjestrijders.nl

http://www.sahistory.org.za/topic/segregationist-legislation-timeline-1950-1959

https://www.tracesofwar.nl/articles/3945/Fliegerhorst-Havelte.htm

https://www.tweedewereldoorlog.nl/nieuwsvantoen/razzia-rondom-bedum/

Index